food network kitchens

FAVRITE
RECIPES

MEREDITH BOOKS® • DES MOINES, IA

Meredith®
B O O K S

Meredith Books
1716 Locust Street
Des Moines, Iowa 50309–3023
meredithbooks.com

Printed in the United States of America.

First Edition.
Library of Congress Control Number: 2008924200
ISBN: 978-0-696-24197-0

When Food Network first went on the air in 1993, we could not have imagined the profound influence we would have on the way Americans cook, what they eat, and how they look at food.

Fifteen years later, we're still cooking up new ideas and serving them to an astounding 28 million homes. We're introducing new ingredients and cuisines and taking viewers on food-themed tours all over the world.

Working alongside the amazing on-air chefs you've been watching all of these years is Food Network Kitchens. This group of incredibly talented shoppers, chefs and cooks, testers and tasters, food stylists, bakers, and recipe developers keeps things moving, looking gorgeous, and tasting great on all of our shows.

In 2003—in celebration of Food Network's 10th anniversary—Food Network Kitchens published its first cookbook, *Food Network Kitchens Cookbook*. Four more cookbooks and thousands of cooking shows followed. With every day that's passed, we've become smarter and even more passionate about helping people live better, simpler, and more joyful lives.

Now, after 15 years on the air, we present *Food Network Kitchens Favorite Recipes*. The recipes in the book are our absolute favorites—handpicked for their fabulousness, their ease, or both.

We felt it was a fitting tribute to the world-class chefs with whom we've had the privilege to work, the behind-the-scenes food professionals who have searched every corner of Manhattan looking for obscure ingredients or walked miles in their clogs over the floors of out kitchens and studios—and especially to every viewer who had been inspired to pick up a whisk or a wooden spoon after watching a Food Network show.

Our first book was created out of the sincere belief that great food is one of life's greatest pleasures. Of all the things that may have changed over the years, that hasn't.

Happy Cooking!

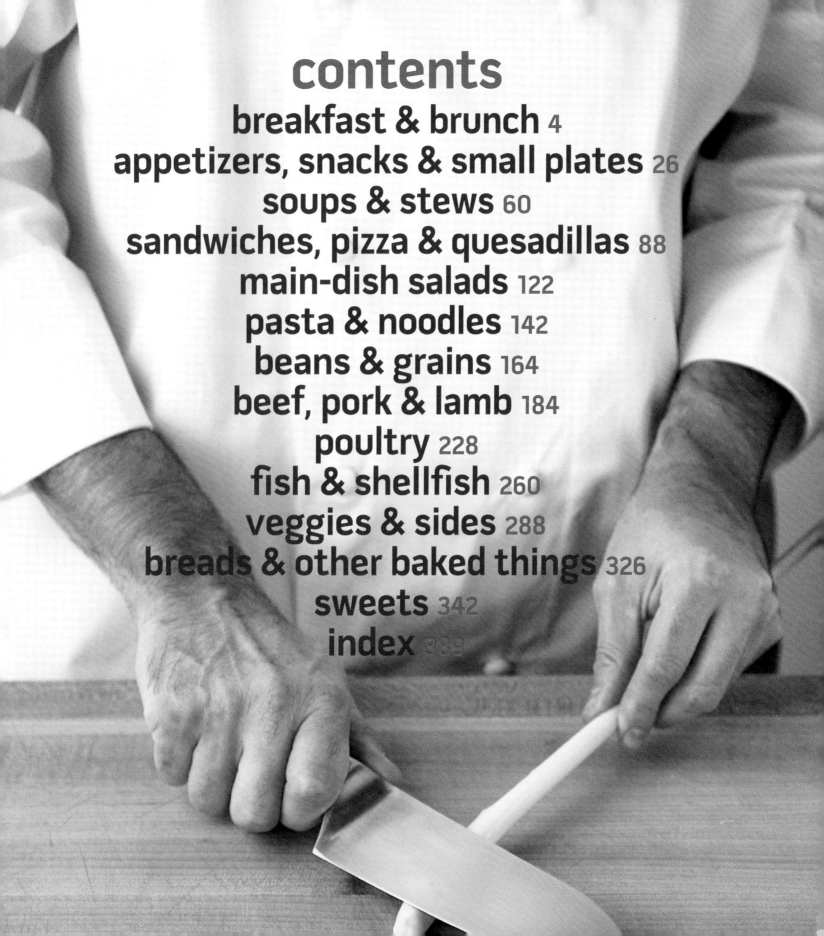

contents

breakfast & brunch

Whether it's a slow-cooked Sunday morning strata or a fresh-fruit smoothie on the fly, always wake up to something good.

No matter how experienced a cook you are, you eventually come to believe that simple is best. Good ingredients make good food.

baked eggs
with farmhouse cheddar & potatoes | 4 servings

3 tablespoons unsalted butter
1½ pounds red-skinned potatoes, diced
¼ cup chopped fresh flat-leaf
    parsley
2 large cloves garlic, minced
1 teaspoon kosher salt
    Freshly ground black pepper
8 large eggs
1 cup shredded extra-sharp
    farmhouse Cheddar
    (about 4 ounces)
    (See tip, right)

1. Preheat the oven to 400°F. Melt the butter in a large, well-seasoned cast-iron skillet over medium heat. Add the potatoes and cook, stirring occasionally, until tender and brown, about 15 minutes. Stir in the parsley, garlic, salt, and pepper to taste and remove from the heat.

2. Push the potatoes aside to make 4 evenly spaced shallow nests and break 2 eggs into each. Bake until the egg whites are cooked and the yolks are still runny, about 10 minutes. Sprinkle the cheese over the eggs and continue baking until it just melts, about 1 minute more. Serve immediately.

FROM THE KITCHENS
Farmhouse Cheddar is not your childhood Cheddar. This creamy and sharp artisanal cheese once produced farm-by-farm in England is experiencing a renaissance. Though the best ones still come from England, we also love some of those coming out of Vermont and Wisconsin.

breakfast burritos | 4 servings

BURRITOS

8	large eggs
½	teaspoon kosher salt
4	10-inch flour tortillas
1	tablespoon extra-virgin olive oil
½	cup shredded Monterey Jack cheese (about 2 ounces)
½	Hass avocado, sliced
	Salsa Verde Asada (see recipe, below)
¼	cup sour cream (optional)

SALSA

Makes about 1½ cups

1½	pounds tomatillos (about 20), husked and well washed
1	small onion, sliced and separated into rings
4	cloves garlic, unpeeled
1	to 2 chipotle chiles in adobo sauce, chopped
2	tablespoons chopped fresh cilantro
2	teaspoons kosher salt
⅛	teaspoon sugar

1. Whisk the eggs and salt together in a large bowl. Spread out a large piece of foil on a work surface. Heat a large skillet on high until very hot. Lay a tortilla in the skillet and cook, turning once, until slightly charred and puffy, about 15 seconds per side. Transfer to the foil and repeat with the remaining tortillas. Wrap the tortillas in the foil and set aside in a warm spot.

2. Heat the oil in the skillet until it just begins to smoke. Add the eggs and stir with a wooden spoon until large, firm curds form, about 2 minutes. Remove from the heat and stir in the cheese.

3. Unwrap the tortillas. Place ¼ of the eggs, ¼ of the avocado, and 1 tablespoon of the salsa in the center of a tortilla. Fold the edge of the tortilla closest to you over the filling, fold in the sides, and then roll the tortilla away from you to form a package. Repeat with the remaining tortillas. Serve with extra salsa and a dollop of sour cream, if desired.

SALSA VERDE ASADA (ROASTED TOMATILLO SALSA)

1. Position a rack in the upper part of the oven and preheat the broiler. Line a broiler pan with foil. Arrange the tomatillos, onion, and garlic on the prepared pan. Broil the vegetables until charred and soft, turning so they cook evenly, about 12 minutes. Cool.

2. Squeeze the garlic cloves out of their skins. Puree the garlic pulp, onion, and chiles in a blender until smooth. Add the tomatillos and their juices and pulse to make a chunky sauce. Add the cilantro, salt, and sugar and pulse just to combine. Transfer the salsa to a bowl and set aside at room temperature for 30 minutes so the flavors come together. If not serving immediately, refrigerate in a sealed container for up to 3 days.

migas | 4 servings

8   large eggs
1   teaspoon kosher salt, plus more for
        seasoning
3   tablespoons olive oil
4   6-inch stale corn tortillas, broken
        into bite-size pieces
1   small link Spanish chorizo
        sausage (about 2 ounces),
        chopped
1   ripe plum tomato, halved, seeded,
        and chopped
1   small onion, chopped
1   clove garlic, chopped
½   cup shredded Monterey Jack cheese
        (about 2 ounces)
      Handful fresh cilantro sprigs,
        chopped
      Freshly ground black pepper

FOR SERVING
      Chipotle hot sauce

1. Crack eggs into a medium bowl, add the 1 teaspoon salt, and lightly beat.

2. Heat oil in a large nonstick skillet over medium heat. Add the broken tortillas to the skillet. Cook, turning until golden and a little crisp, about 3 minutes.

3. Add the chorizo, tomato, onion, and garlic, and cook until the onion is soft, about 4 minutes. Pour the egg over all the vegetables and tortillas. Pause to let the eggs heat slightly, then stir very slowly so the eggs cook evenly into large, fluffy curds. Cook, continuing to stir for 2 to 6 minutes, depending on how set you like your eggs. When eggs are still just soft, remove the pan from the heat and fold in the cheese and cilantro and season with salt and black pepper to taste. Serve with hot sauce.

FROM THE KITCHENS
Migas, from the Spanish for "crumbs," are a classic Texan breakfast, originally eaten during Lent. Because of their connection to Lent, they're often vegetarian, so don't worry if you can't find chorizo.

smoked salmon
& cream cheese frittata | 4 servings

6 large eggs
2 tablespoons milk
2 tablespoons thinly sliced fresh chives
1 tablespoon chopped fresh dill
1 teaspoon kosher salt, plus more for
   greens
   Freshly ground black pepper
2 ounces cream cheese, softened
2 ounces smoked salmon, roughly
   chopped
3 tablespoons extra-virgin
   olive oil
4 cups mesclun salad greens
   (about 3 ounces)
1 teaspoon white wine vinegar

1. Position a rack in the center of the oven and preheat to 375°F. Whisk the eggs, milk, chives, dill, the 1 teaspoon salt, and pepper to taste in a bowl. Using 2 spoons or your fingers, break the cream cheese into bits. Fold the cream cheese and salmon into the egg mixture.

2. Heat 1 tablespoon of the olive oil in an ovenproof 10-inch nonstick skillet over medium-low heat. Pour the egg mixture into the skillet and stir gently to distribute the filling in the pan. Cook until the bottom is set but not brown, about 2 minutes. Transfer the skillet to the oven and bake until the top is almost set but still moist, about 9 minutes. Remove from the oven, cover, and set aside for 5 minutes.

3. Season the greens with salt and pepper and toss with the remaining 2 tablespoons oil and the vinegar. Slip the frittata out of the pan onto a cutting board and cut into 4 wedges. Divide the salad and frittata among 4 plates.

FROM THE KITCHENS
If a recipe calls for chopped smoked salmon, look for packages of smoked salmon trimmings at the deli counter. They're just as delicious as the paper-thin slices and often better priced.

cheese strata
with ham & tomatoes | 6 to 8 servings

STRATA

12	large eggs
1½	cups milk
½	cup heavy cream
1	teaspoon kosher salt
¼	teaspoon freshly ground black pepper
	Pinch freshly grated nutmeg
	Pinch cayenne pepper
1	cup diced baked ham
1	cup Oven-Dried Tomatoes (see recipe, below), chopped
1	tablespoon minced fresh flat-leaf parsley
2	teaspoons thinly sliced fresh chives
2	cups shredded extra-sharp Cheddar cheese (about 8 ounces)
1	pound sourdough bread, crust trimmed, cut into 1-inch cubes
1	tablespoon unsalted butter, melted

TOMATOES

2	pounds ripe plum tomatoes, cored and halved lengthwise
1	teaspoon kosher salt
	Fresh herb sprigs, such as thyme, rosemary, or sage (optional)
	Extra-virgin olive oil

1. Generously butter a 3-quart gratin dish or casserole. Whisk the eggs, milk, cream, salt, black pepper, nutmeg, and cayenne pepper in a large bowl. Toss the ham, tomatoes, parsley, and chives in a small bowl.

2. Scatter ½ cup of the cheese over the bottom of the prepared dish, followed by a third of the bread, and then half of the ham mixture. Repeat and top with a final layer of bread and the remaining 1 cup cheese.

3. Pour the egg mixture over the top and gently press down to make sure the top layer is evenly moistened. Drizzle the melted butter over the top. Cover the strata with plastic wrap and refrigerate for at least 1 hour or overnight.

4. Position a rack in the middle of the oven and preheat to 350°F. Bake the strata, uncovered, until it is golden brown and slightly puffed, about 45 minutes. Let the strata rest 10 minutes before serving.

OVEN-DRIED TOMATOES

1. Preheat the oven to 250°F. Arrange the tomatoes, cut side up, in a single layer on a parchment or foil-lined baking sheet. Sprinkle with the salt. Bake until slightly shriveled but still plump, about 5 hours.

2. If not using immediately, refrigerate the dried tomatoes in a sealed container for up to 4 days. Or layer them with the herb sprigs, if desired. Add olive oil to cover, seal tightly, and refrigerate for up to 2 weeks.

FROM THE KITCHENS
What's not to love about a strata? It's a cheesy, savory bread pudding that fits right into a laid-back cooking scheme. Stratas are a terrific brunch dish—they welcome improvisation and can be assembled in advance or on the spur of the moment.

pancakes | 8 large or 12 small pancakes

1½ cups all-purpose flour
3 tablespoons sugar
1 tablespoon baking powder
½ teaspoon fine salt
 Pinch freshly grated nutmeg
  (optional)
2 large eggs, at room
  temperature
1¼ cups milk
 Dash pure vanilla extract
  (about ¼ teaspoon)
4 tablespoons (½ stick)
  unsalted butter
 Canola oil or other neutral tasting
  oil, for cooking the pancakes

1. Preheat the oven to 200°F. Whisk together the flour, sugar, baking powder, salt, and nutmeg, if using, in a large bowl.

2. Beat the eggs in another bowl. Whisk in about half the milk and the vanilla.

3. In a small saucepan over low heat, melt the butter with the remaining milk, stirring occasionally. Remove from heat. Stir or whisk into the egg mixture.

4. Pour the wet ingredients into the dry ingredients and whisk just until a thick batter forms (a few lumps are OK).

5. Heat a cast-iron skillet, nonstick skillet, or griddle over medium to medium-low heat (or 350°F, if the griddle temperature can be controlled). If using a cast-iron skillet or an older griddle, brush with canola oil. Keeping the skillet at medium to medium-low heat, ladle about ¼ cup (for small pancakes) to ⅓ cup (for large pancakes) of the batter onto the skillet. Make 1 or 2 more pancakes, spacing them evenly apart. Cook until bubbles break the surface of the pancakes, the batter loses its shine, and the undersides are golden brown, about 2 minutes. Slip the spatula under the pancakes and flip. Cook about 1 minute more. Serve immediately or transfer to a platter and keep warm in the oven. Repeat with the remaining batter.

FROM THE KITCHENS
• When a pancake is brown on the first side and the top is bubbly, sprinkle on 2 teaspoons mini chocolate chips or toasted nuts, or 1 tablespoon diced bananas, whole blueberries, or grated apple. Flip gently and continue cooking until the pancake is cooked through, about 2 minutes more.
• This batter is best slightly lumpy; perfectly smooth batter gets you hockey-puck pancakes.
• The first pancake's never quite right. The pan needs to even out its temperature first.
• Don't smash or push down on the pancakes while they're cooking; they'll get dense.
• Straight-to-plate is the best way to serve pancakes. If you've gotta wait, lay the pancakes out in a warm oven. Stacking them steams and toughens the middle ones.
• Top pancakes with berries, preserves, real maple syrup, honey, butter, yogurt, or a little whipped cream.

cornmeal pancakes
with blueberry-maple syrup | 16 pancakes

PANCAKES
- ¾ cup all-purpose flour
- ½ cup cornmeal
- 3 tablespoons light brown sugar
- 1 teaspoon baking powder
- ¼ teaspoon fine salt
- ⅛ teaspoon baking soda
- ⅛ teaspoon freshly grated nutmeg
- 2 large eggs, separated and at room temperature
- 1 cup buttermilk, at room temperature
- ½ cup milk, at room temperature
- 3 tablespoons unsalted butter, melted
- ½ teaspoon pure vanilla extract
  Blueberry-Maple Syrup
  (see recipe, below)

SYRUP
Makes 1 cup
- 1 cup blueberries
- ¼ cup maple syrup
- 1 cinnamon stick
- 1 tablespoon unsalted butter
- 1 teaspoon lemon juice

1. Preheat the oven to 200°F. Set a wire rack on a baking sheet and place in the oven.

2. Whisk the flour, cornmeal, brown sugar, baking powder, salt, baking soda, and nutmeg in a large bowl. Whisk the egg yolks with the buttermilk, milk, melted butter, and vanilla extract in a large glass measuring cup. Whisk the buttermilk mixture into the flour mixture to make a thick batter—take care not to overmix or the pancakes will be dense. In another bowl whip the egg whites until they hold soft peaks. Use a rubber spatula to fold the whites into the batter.

3. Heat a large cast-iron or nonstick skillet over medium heat and coat the surface lightly with butter. Using about ¼ cup per pancake, pour the batter into the skillet, leaving space between pancakes. Cook until bubbles break the surface of the pancakes and the undersides are golden brown, about 2 minutes. Flip with a spatula and cook about 1 minute more. Keep the cooked pancakes warm in the oven while you cook the remaining batter. Serve the pancakes hot with warm Blueberry-Maple Syrup.

BLUEBERRY-MAPLE SYRUP
Toss blueberries with the maple syrup in a small saucepan. Add the cinnamon stick and cook over high heat, stirring occasionally, until the mixture boils and the blueberries just start to pop, about 5 minutes. Remove from the heat, discard the cinnamon stick, and stir in the butter and lemon juice. Serve warm.

FROM THE KITCHENS
When folding whipped whites into a batter—be it for pancakes, soufflés, or cakes—don't add them all at once. Lighten the batter with about a third of the whites before delicately folding in the rest.

potato pancakes with pink applesauce | 4 to 6 servings

PANCAKES

1	medium yellow onion
2	pounds waxy potatoes, such as red-skinned or Yukon gold (about 4 medium), peeled (see tip, page 309)
2	tablespoons all-purpose flour
1	tablespoon chopped fresh thyme, plus sprigs for garnish
2	teaspoons kosher salt
1/8	teaspoon freshly grated nutmeg
	Freshly ground black pepper
1	large egg, lightly beaten
	Vegetable oil
	Pink Applesauce (see recipe, below)
	Crème fraîche or sour cream

APPLESAUCE
Makes 3 to 4 cups

2 1/2	pounds tart red apples, such as McIntosh
3	tablespoons sugar
3	tablespoons water
1	tablespoon freshly squeezed lemon juice

1. Preheat oven to 200°F. Set a wire rack on a baking sheet and place in oven. Grate onion on a box grater into a large bowl. Shred potatoes into the same bowl, shredding down the length of potato to form long strands. Toss potatoes with the onion as you work to keep them from discoloring. Put potato mixture in a clean dish towel and wring out excess liquid. Return mixture to bowl and toss it with flour, chopped thyme, salt, nutmeg, and pepper to taste. Stir in the egg.

2. Heat 1/4 inch oil in a large cast-iron or other heavy skillet over medium heat. Using 2 heaping tablespoons per pancake, spread the batter in the skillet, pressing lightly to form thin 3-inch pancakes. To keep the pancakes crisp, don't overcrowd the pan. Cook until golden, 3 to 4 minutes per side, turning once. Keep the cooked pancakes warm in the oven while you cook the remaining batter. Serve the pancakes with Pink Applesauce and crème fraîche.

PINK APPLESAUCE

1. Cut the apples into chunks with their skins and seeds. (If you don't have a food mill, peel and seed the fruit; your applesauce just won't be pink.) Put the apples, sugar, water, and lemon juice in a large saucepan and bring to a boil over high heat. Lower the heat, cover, and simmer gently until the apples are very soft, about 15 minutes. Uncover the pan and cook, stirring frequently to prevent scorching, until the apppesauce thickens, about 5 minutes.

2. Puree the mixture in a food mill or blender. Serve warm or refrigerate in a tightly sealed container for up to 1 week.

carrot-bran muffins

12 muffins

1	cup whole wheat flour
¾	cup all-purpose flour
¾	cup wheat bran
1½	teaspoons baking soda
1	teaspoon ground cinnamon
¼	teaspoon fine salt
½	cup crushed canned pineapple (with its juice)
½	cup honey
⅓	cup walnut oil
2	large eggs, lightly beaten
2	cups peeled and grated carrots (about 2 medium)
¾	cup golden raisins
⅔	cup chopped walnuts
1	heaping tablespoon unsalted sunflower seeds

1. Position a rack in the center of the oven and preheat to 375°F. Line twelve ½-cup muffin cups with paper liners. Whisk whole wheat and all-purpose flours with the wheat bran, baking soda, cinnamon, and salt in a medium bowl.

2. Stir the pineapple, honey, oil, and eggs into the carrots in a medium bowl. Stir the carrot mixture into the flour mixture just until evenly moist; the batter will be very thick. Fold in the raisins and walnuts. Divide the batter evenly among the muffin cups and sprinkle the sunflower seeds over the tops. Bake until firm when pressed gently, about 20 minutes. Turn the muffins out of the cups and cool on a rack; serve warm.

FROM THE KITCHENS
Nut oils such as walnut, hazelnut, and almond add moistness and a lovely flavor to quick breads. Once opened, store nut oils in the refrigerator to preserve their peak flavor.

This is the primal coffeecake. A moment after this shot was taken, all we were left with were a couple of crumbs.

sour cream–pecan coffee cake

one 8-inch cake (8 servings)

CRUMBS

½ cup granulated sugar
6 tablespoons packed dark brown sugar
1 cup pecans, toasted and chopped
2 tablespoons all-purpose flour
1 tablespoon pure vanilla extract
1 teaspoon ground cinnamon
2 tablespoons unsalted butter, melted

CAKE

2 cups all-purpose flour
1 teaspoon baking soda
1 teaspoon ground cinnamon
½ teaspoon fine salt
Generous pinch freshly grated nutmeg
1 cup sour cream
1½ teaspoons pure vanilla extract
8 tablespoons unsalted butter, softened (1 stick)
1 cup granulated sugar
2 large eggs, at room temperature

1. Preheat the oven to 350°F. Line the bottom of an 8-inch square cake pan with parchment paper; butter the paper and the sides of the pan. For the crumbs: Combine the granulated and brown sugars, the pecans, flour, vanilla, and cinnamon in a small bowl. Add the butter and stir to make moist, coarse crumbs. Set aside.

2. For the cake: Sift the flour, baking soda, cinnamon, salt, and nutmeg into a medium bowl. Mix the sour cream with the vanilla in a small bowl. Beat the butter and sugar in a large bowl with an electric mixer on medium speed until light and fluffy, about 5 minutes. Add the eggs 1 at a time, beating well after each addition. Add the flour mixture in 3 parts, alternating with the sour cream mixture in 2 parts, beginning and ending with the flour.

3. Spread ⅔ of the batter in the prepared pan and sprinkle half the crumbs over the top. Spoon the remaining batter in mounds on top, and then spread it out evenly. Sprinkle the rest of the crumbs over the cake and bake until the top is brown and a toothpick inserted in the center comes out clean, about 1 hour and 10 minutes. Cool the cake in the pan on a rack for 20 minutes, and then turn it out of the pan, invert, and cool.

FROM THE KITCHENS

A familiar route to light-as-a-feather cakes is to carefully alternate the wet and dry ingredients into the batter's base. This gradual incorporation prevents overmixing the flour. Keeping a light touch when adding flour—be it a cake, muffin, or quick bread—always pays off with a tender crumb.

maple & bacon monkey bread

1 large loaf (10 to 12 servings)

6	tablespoons unsalted butter
2	cups milk
¼	cup granulated sugar
1	package active dry yeast (¼ ounce)
2	large egg yolks, beaten
	Vegetable oil
5½	cups all-purpose flour, plus additional for kneading
1	tablespoon fine salt
12	slices bacon or 10 ounces slab bacon, diced
1	cup maple sugar (see tip, below)

1. Melt 4 tablespoons of the butter in a medium saucepan over medium-low heat. Add milk and granulated sugar and heat, stirring, until lukewarm (about 110°F). Sprinkle yeast over surface; set aside until foamy, about 10 minutes. Whisk egg yolks into the yeast mixture.

2. Lightly oil a large bowl. Whisk flour and salt in another large bowl. Stir yeast mixture into flour mixture to make a soft dough. Turn dough onto a floured work surface and knead until soft and elastic, about 8 minutes. Shape dough into a ball and put in the oiled bowl. Cover bowl with a clean kitchen towel and let rise at room temperature until double in size, about 2 hours.

3. While dough rises, cook bacon in a large skillet over medium-high heat until barely crisp. Drain on paper towels; toss with maple sugar. Butter a 12-cup Bundt pan and sprinkle a bit less than half the sugar-bacon mixture in bottom.

4. Turn dough onto a clean, unfloured surface and press into a rectangle. Cut the dough into 36 equal pieces and shape each piece into a ball. Arrange half the balls of dough in 2 layers in the Bundt pan and sprinkle remaining sugar-bacon mixture over them. Arrange remaining balls of dough on top, setting as many as possible in the hollows of the first layer.

5. Cover with a kitchen towel. Set aside at room temperature until doubled, about 2 hours; or cover with plastic wrap and refrigerate overnight. (If refrigerated, bring to room temperature 1 hour before baking.)

6. Position a rack in the center of the oven and preheat to 400°F. Melt the remaining 2 tablespoons butter and pour over the bread. Bake 15 minutes, tent with aluminum foil, and continue baking until golden brown and an instant-read thermometer inserted in the dough registers 190°F, about 25 minutes. Cool in the pan on a wire rack for 10 minutes; unmold and cool on the rack for 1 hour before serving.

FROM THE KITCHENS
Twice as sweet as granulated white sugar, maple sugar is a New England specialty made by continuing to boil maple syrup until all of the liquid evaporates. Look for it in the baking section of your supermarket.

cream scones
with blueberries | 8 scones

1¾ cups all-purpose flour
3 tablespoons sugar, plus additional
    for sprinkling
2½ teaspoons baking powder
½ teaspoon fine salt
6 tablespoons cold unsalted butter,
    cut into ½-inch cubes
¼ cup dried blueberries
2 teaspoons finely grated orange zest
1 large egg
¼ cup heavy cream, plus additional
    for brushing

1. Preheat the oven to 425°F. Line a baking sheet with parchment paper. Whisk flour with the 3 tablespoons sugar, baking powder, and salt in a medium bowl. Toss the butter with the flour mixture to coat and, using your fingers, rub in the butter until the mixture resembles coarse meal. Add the blueberries and orange zest and toss.

2. Beat the egg with the ¼ cup cream and stir into flour mixture to make a shaggy, loose dough. Turn dough onto a lightly floured surface and pat into a 6-inch round. Cut into 8 wedges and put on the baking sheet, leaving a few inches between each. Brush tops with heavy cream and sprinkle with sugar. Bake until golden brown, 12 to 15 minutes. Serve warm.

maple granola-to-go | 12 servings

1½   cups rolled oats
1   cup mixed dried fruit, such as diced
     apricots, dates, and pears, or
     blueberries, cranberries, currants,
     and raisins
¼   cup toasted wheat germ
¼   cup green pumpkin seeds (pepitas)
¼   cup pecans, coarsely chopped
¼   cup whole unskinned almonds,
     coarsely chopped
2   tablespoons sesame seeds
2   tablespoons unsalted butter
½   cup maple syrup
2   teaspoons pure vanilla extract
2   large egg whites, lightly beaten

1. Preheat the oven to 225°F. Toss the oats, dried fruit, wheat germ, pumpkin seeds, pecans, almonds, and sesame seeds in a large bowl.

2. Melt the butter with 2 tablespoons of the maple syrup in a small saucepan over medium-low heat. Remove from the heat and stir in the vanilla extract. Pour the syrup mixture over the oat mixture and stir to coat evenly.

3. Spread the mixture on a baking sheet. Bake until golden brown, stirring occasionally, about 1½ hours. Remove the mixture from the oven, but leave the oven on.

4. Transfer the granola to a large bowl. Stir in the remaining 6 tablespoons maple syrup and the egg whites. Spray twelve ½-cup nonstick muffin cups with nonstick cooking spray and firmly press about ⅓ cup of the mixture into each. Bake until set, about 45 minutes. Transfer the muffin tin to a rack and cool 15 minutes before unmolding. Store cooled granola up to 1 month at room temperature in a tightly sealed container.

FROM THE KITCHENS
If you can't find green pumpkin seeds—also called pepitas—at your supermarket, look in a Latino market, or use sunflower or other peeled seeds.

the flexible smoothie | 2 servings

1 very ripe banana—frozen is great
1 cup frozen berries, such as
   strawberries, raspberries,
   or blackberries (about 6 ounces)
½ cup or one 6-ounce container plain,
   vanilla, or lemon low fat yogurt
½ cup orange juice, juice blend,
   or chilled green tea
2 ounces soft tofu (optional)
1 to 2 tablespoons honey,
   or to taste

We're giving you a smoothie recipe, but you don't really need one.
Add whatever you've got. You'll need:
   • Something for body (yogurt, tofu, soy or regular milk).
   • Something for flavor (fruit, orange juice, honey, or maple syrup).
   • Something to chill (frozen fruit, ice).
   • And if you want, something for health (like wheat germ or protein powder).

1. Put everything in a blender and puree until smooth.

2. Pour into 2 tall glasses and serve.

2-by-4 fruit salad

serves 4 to 6

2 navel oranges or small
    grapefruits or 1 of each, peeled and
    pith removed
2 cups berries, such as
    strawberries, raspberries,
    blackberries, blueberries,
    or a combination
2 pieces seasonal fruit (see
    tip, below)
2 bananas, peeled and sliced
¼ cup honey
¼ cup water or white wine
1 cinnamon stick
    Pinch kosher salt
½ vanilla bean
1 1-inch piece fresh ginger, thinly sliced
    into coins (optional)

1. Halve or quarter the oranges and/or grapefruits top to bottom, and slice crosswise into thin pieces. Rinse the berries and pat dry on a paper towel. Halve or quarter the strawberries if large. Prepare the seasonal fruit as needed. Toss the citrus, berries, bananas, and seasonal fruit in a large bowl.

2. Stir the honey, water, cinnamon stick, and salt together in a small saucepan. Split the vanilla bean lengthwise and use a paring knife to scrape the seeds out of the pod; add the seeds and pod to the pan. Add ginger, if using, to the pan. Bring to a boil and pour over the fruit. Set aside for 30 minutes to 1 hour for the flavors to come together. Remove ginger and vanilla bean (or tell people not to eat it) and serve.

FROM THE KITCHENS
- Two-by-four is a great rule for fruit salads in general: Think 2 each of 4 fruits. Try chunks of peaches, plums, or nectarines in summer; sliced apples or pears or a handful of grapes in fall; pomegranate seeds in winter; or quartered fresh figs in spring.
- Add some flavor with a splash (2 tablespoons) of alcohol: Stir plain or flavored rum, brandy, or orange liqueur into the honey mixture after it comes off the heat and before you pour it over the fruit.

appetizers, snacks & small plates

When you're hungry for something to stimulate appetites and conversation, here's a big batch of our very best little bites.

Glossy, plump, and gorgeous, our Citrus-Spiced Mixed Olives are primo party starters. Toss 'em together, then leave them out while you mingle with your guests.

citrus-spiced mixed olives | 2 cups

3 tablespoons olive oil
2 cloves garlic, smashed
1½ teaspoons crushed red pepper
1 large sprig fresh rosemary,
    2 bay leaves, or both
    Zest of 1 orange, peeled in long strips
      with a vegetable peeler
    Zest of 1 lemon, peeled in long strips
      with a vegetable peeler
12 ounces mixed olives, such as
    kalamata, niçoise, or cerignola,
    drained
½ teaspoon kosher salt
    Freshly ground black pepper

Put the olive oil, garlic, red pepper, herbs, and citrus zests in a medium skillet. Heat over medium-high heat, swirling the pan until the mixture is fragrant, 3 to 4 minutes. Add the olives, salt, and pepper and cook, stirring occasionally, until the garlic is golden and the zest begins to curl, about 5 minutes more. Discard and remove bay leaves, if using. Serve warm or at room temperature.

tuscan bean dip | 4 servings

1 small baguette, thinly sliced
4 cloves garlic
1½ teaspoons kosher salt, plus
    additional for seasoning
¼ cup extra-virgin olive oil
2 sprigs fresh rosemary, leaves
    stripped (about 1½ tablespoons)
    Pinch crushed red pepper
1 15-ounce can cannellini beans, rinsed
    and drained
    Crisp vegetables, for dipping
    (optional)

1. Preheat the oven to 400°F. Lay bread on a baking sheet. Rub each slice with a clove of garlic and sprinkle with a pinch of salt; reserve garlic clove. Toast in oven until golden, about 8 minutes.

2. Chop all garlic cloves. Cook garlic in the olive oil in a small skillet over medium-high heat, stirring, until it is golden, about 3 minutes. Pull skillet from heat; stir in rosemary and red pepper and cool slightly.

3. Put beans, the 1½ teaspoons salt, and all but 1 teaspoon of the rosemary oil in a food processor and process until smooth. Scrape puree into a serving bowl and drizzle with reserved rosemary oil. Serve with toasted baguette and, if desired, raw vegetables.

sweet & spicy mixed nuts | 2 cups

1   large egg white
3   tablespoons dark brown sugar
1   tablespoon kosher salt
2   teaspoons dried oregano
¾   teaspoon ground coriander
½   teaspoon ground cumin
¼   heaping teaspoon cayenne pepper
     Pinch ground cloves
2   cups unsalted mixed nuts

1. Preheat the oven to 250° F. Line a baking sheet with aluminum foil or parchment paper.

2. Whisk the egg white, brown sugar, salt, oregano, coriander, cumin, cayenne, and cloves in a medium bowl until thoroughly blended and slightly foamy. Add nuts and toss to coat evenly. Spread nuts on the prepared baking sheet and roast, stirring every 15 minutes, for 45 minutes. Nuts will be fragrant and slightly darker but still a bit moist (they crisp as they cool). Cool completely in pan and serve at room temperature. Store in an airtight container for up to 5 days.

spiced edamame | serves 4 to 6 as an appetizer, 10 as party food

1   1-pound bag frozen edamame,
     in the pod (green soybeans)
2   teaspoons kosher salt, plus
     more for seasoning
1   teaspoon chili powder
¼   teaspoon crushed red pepper
     flakes
½   teaspoon dried oregano

1. Bring a medium pot of water to a boil. Season with some salt. Add the edamame pods and cook, uncovered, until heated through and crisp-tender, 5 to 6 minutes. Drain in a colander and pat dry.

2. While the edamame boil, heat the 2 teaspoons kosher salt, chili powder, and pepper flakes in a small dry skillet over medium heat, stirring until hot and fragrant, about 2 minutes. Remove from the heat and crumble in the oregano. Toss the drained edamame pods with the chili salt. Serve warm with a side bowl on the table for the empty pods.

FROM THE KITCHENS
Edamame are green soybean pods. They're low-fat, high-protein, and tasty. You'll see them steamed and salted wherever sushi is sold or precooked in the frozen food section of your supermarket. To eat them, pick them up with your fingers, put the pod in your mouth, and squeeze the inner seeds out with your teeth. Discard the outer pod once you've gotten all the seeds out.

In the Food Network Kitchens, timing is everything. So, put any or all of these yummy nibbles on your party production schedule. Then sit back, relax, and enjoy your own show.

spinach & artichoke dip

6 servings

1   large egg yolk
¼   cup heavy cream
½   teaspoon kosher salt
     Pinch freshly grated nutmeg
     Dash hot sauce
2   tablespoons extra-virgin olive oil
4   scallions (white and green parts),
        thinly sliced
2   cloves garlic, peeled and minced
1   10-ounce bag fresh baby spinach,
        roughly chopped
2   6-ounce jars marinated artichokes,
        drained and chopped
6   ounces cream cheese, cut into small
        pieces
4   ounces feta cheese, crumbled
        (about ½ cup)
     Tortilla chips, toasted bread, and/or
        red and yellow bell pepper strips,
        for dipping

1. Preheat the oven to 350°F. Lightly oil a 4-cup gratin dish. Whisk the egg yolk, cream, salt, nutmeg, and hot sauce in a small bowl. Set aside.

2. Heat the olive oil in a large skillet over medium heat. Add the scallions and garlic. Cook until the garlic is fragrant and the scallions begin to soften, about 2 minutes. Add the spinach and artichokes and cook, stirring, until the spinach wilts, about 3 minutes. Add the cream cheese and stir until melted, about 1 minute.

3. Remove the pan from the heat and stir in the cream mixture. Fold about three-fourths of the feta cheese into the dip and transfer it to the prepared gratin dish. Scatter the remaining cheese on top. Bake until the center of the dip is just set and the edges are golden brown, about 30 minutes. Serve warm or at room temperature with the tortilla chips, toasted bread, or pepper strips.

FROM THE KITCHENS
- On your trip down the spice aisle, opt for whole nutmeg over ground. Grate it just before using for maximum freshness.
- Before serving, wrap the hot gratin dish in a pretty napkin or cloth to add a splash of color and to protect your guests' fingers from getting burned.

really onion dip

makes 4 cups

3 medium onions, 2 unpeeled,
   1 peeled
1 cup extra-virgin olive oil
2 cups mayonnaise
½ cup sour cream
1 tablespoon white wine vinegar
2 teaspoons kosher salt
2 scallions (white and green parts),
   minced
  Freshly ground black pepper
  Hot pepper sauce
  Potato chips, for serving

1. Preheat the oven to 425°F. Rub unpeeled onions with a bit of the olive oil; roast until soft, about 45 minutes. Cool and peel.

2. Finely dice the peeled raw onion. Heat a large skillet over medium-high heat; add remaining oil and heat until quite hot. Add diced onion and cook, stirring occasionally, until edges begin to brown, about 5 minutes. Turn to medium-low and cook until onion is golden brown, about 18 minutes. Scrape onion, oil, and juices into a sieve over a bowl. Drain onions and spread on a paper towel-lined plate. Cool the strained oil.

3. Puree roasted onions in a food processor. Add mayonnaise, sour cream, vinegar, and salt; pulse until smooth. With the motor running, drizzle in ¼ cup of the flavored reserved oil. Transfer to a serving bowl. Stir in scallions, pepper, and hot sauce to taste. Refrigerate at least 3 hours. Scatter the fried onions over the top just before serving with potato chips.

crab cakes | 12 small cakes

CRAB CAKES

1	pound lump crabmeat
4	tablespoons unsalted butter
¼	cup finely chopped onion
1	rib celery, minced
1	clove garlic, minced
1½	teaspoons kosher salt
1	large egg
¼	cup heavy cream
¼	teaspoon grated lemon zest
2	tablespoons freshly squeezed lemon juice
1	tablespoon whole-grain mustard
2	teaspoons finely chopped fresh flat-leaf parsley
2	teaspoons finely chopped fresh dill
¾	teaspoon hot pepper sauce
	Freshly ground black pepper
⅓	cup cracker meal, plus additional for coating
1	tablespoon vegetable oil
	Spicy Red Pepper Sauce (see recipe, below) or Remoulade (see page 277)

PEPPER SAUCE
Makes about 1 cup

½	cup piquillo peppers (see tip, right)
¼	cup fresh flat-leaf parsley leaves
3	tablespoons mayonnaise
3	tablespoons extra-virgin olive oil
1½	hot pepper sauce, or to taste
1	teaspoon Dijon mustard
1	clove garlic, peeled
½	teaspoon kosher salt

1. Spread the crabmeat on a pan and carefully pick out and discard any bits of shell. Transfer the meat to a bowl. Line a baking sheet with waxed or parchment paper.

2. Melt 1 tablespoon of the butter in a small skillet over medium heat. Add the onion, celery, garlic, and ½ teaspoon of the salt and cook until soft, about 5 minutes; cool. Stir the mixture gently into the crab, keeping the crabmeat in lumps.

3. Lightly beat the egg with the cream, lemon zest, lemon juice, mustard, parsley, dill, hot sauce, the remaining 1 teaspoon salt, and pepper to taste. Again working with a light hand, toss the egg mixture with the crab. Stir in the ⅓ cup cracker meal. Shape the mixture into 1½-inch patties. Place them on the prepared baking sheet, cover, and refrigerate for 1 hour.

4. Preheat the oven to 200°F and place another baking sheet inside. Cover the bottom of a pie tin or rimmed plate with cracker meal and lightly pat the crab cakes in the meal to coat both sides. Heat a large skillet over medium heat and add the remaining 3 tablespoons butter and the oil. Cook the crab cakes in batches, turning once, until golden, about 2 minutes per side. Keep cooked cakes warm in the oven. Serve with Spicy Red Pepper Sauce or Remoulade.

SPICY RED PEPPER SAUCE
Puree peppers, parsley, mayonnaise, olive oil, hot pepper sauce, mustard, garlic, and salt in a blender until smooth. Pour sauce into a bowl and set aside. Cover and refrigerate if storing, up to 2 days. Bring sauce to room temperature before serving.

FROM THE KITCHENS
Piquillo peppers are fire-engine red peppers from Spain that are slowly roasted over a wood fire, then peeled and packed in their own juices. One of our favorite finds, they add sweetness and a little heat to sauces and salad dressings.

Crab cakes are enjoyed with enthusiasm up and down the Eastern Shore at beachside crab shacks and white-linen establishments alike.

We wanted a new spin on shrimp cocktail. We tried many dips and loved these three so much we couldn't choose one. Make one or try all three.

grilled shrimp cocktail | 6 servings

SHRIMP

1	pound medium shrimp with tails, peeled and deveined
	Oil or melted butter for grilling
	Kosher salt
	Freshly ground black pepper
½	lime
	Tunisian Pesto (see recipe, below) or Fresh Green Chutney (see recipe, page 38) or Wasabi Guacamole (see recipe, page 39)

PESTO

Makes 1 cup

2	cups packed fresh cilantro (leaves and some stems)
1	cup packed fresh parsley (leaves and some stems)
¼	cup almonds
1	or 2 cloves garlic
½	cup extra-virgin olive oil
½	teaspoon kosher salt
	Pinch cayenne pepper (optional)

Preheat a grill pan or outdoor grill to medium-high. Toss shrimp with just enough oil or butter to coat lightly, then season with salt and pepper to taste. If cooking on an open grill grate, thread the shrimp on skewers or place in a grill basket. Grill shrimp until they just curl and are translucent, about 1½ minutes on each side. Squeeze lime over the shrimp and serve warm or at room temperature with dip.

TUNISIAN PESTO

1. Combine the cilantro, parsley, almonds, and garlic in a food processor and pulse until coarsely chopped. Add about ⅓ cup of the oil and process until fully incorporated and smooth. Add the salt and a pinch of cayenne pepper, if desired. Serve immediately with Grilled Shrimp (see recipe, above) or freeze.

2. If using immediately, add the remaining oil and pulse until smooth. If freezing, transfer to an airtight container and pour the remaining oil on top. Freeze up to 3 months.

FROM THE KITCHENS

When you add raw garlic to a pesto or dip, it starts out mellow. But after garlic sits for a bit, it ends up strong. If you like your pesto intense or are adding it to a cooked dish, use both cloves—but for a tempered taste add just a single clove.

fresh green chutney | makes ¾ cup

1   1-inch piece peeled fresh ginger
3   scallions (white and green parts),
      cut into large pieces
1   cup fresh mint
      (leaves and some stems)
1   cup fresh cilantro
      (leaves and some stems)
¼   cup plain yogurt
1   jalapeño, stemmed
      (with seeds for more heat,
      without seeds for less)
1   tablespoon freshly squeezed
      lime juice
½   teaspoon kosher salt
1   to 2 tablespoons water (optional)

With the machine running, drop ginger into the bowl of a food processor and process until coarsely chopped. Scrape down the sides of the bowl, then add scallions, mint, cilantro, yogurt, jalapeño, lime juice, and salt. Process to a textured paste similar in consistency to pesto, adding water to adjust the consistency, if desired. Serve with Grilled Shrimp (see recipe, page 37).

FROM THE KITCHENS
This chutney is also great with grilled lamb and chicken, and super as a spread for sandwiches, rice crackers, or crispy Indian pappadam.

Speed-strip bunches of leafy herbs such as cilantro and parsley by holding them inverted at their stem end. Using a downward motion and a very sharp chef's knife, shave off the leafy greens in short, quick strokes.

wasabi guacamole | makes 1¼ cups

1 slightly heaping tablespoon
  wasabi powder
1 tablespoon water
1 ripe Hass avocado
1 scallion (white and green parts),
  finely chopped
1 tablespoon freshly squeezed
  lime juice
1 teaspoon finely grated peeled fresh
  ginger
½ teaspoon mirin (a sweet Japanese
  rice wine) (optional)
½ teaspoon kosher salt
2 tablespoons chopped fresh cilantro

Whisk wasabi and water in a small bowl to make a thick paste; turn bowl over and set aside. Halve the avocado; press a knife into the pit, then twist and lift it out. Score the flesh with the tip of a knife, then use a spoon to scoop flesh out of skins into a medium serving bowl. Mix in the wasabi, scallion, lime juice, ginger, mirin (if desired), and salt with a fork to make a textured dip. Stir in the cilantro. Serve with Grilled Shrimp (see recipe, page 37).

FROM THE KITCHENS

Turning the wasabi bowl upside down accomplishes two goals: The wasabi won't be quite as harsh as when it is first mixed, and its flavor will concentrate and bloom (in a good way!). This dip is great for sliced cucumbers, snow peas, or rice crackers.

oysters on the half shell
with two sauces

4 to 6 servings

1 to 2 dozen medium oysters such as Bluepoint, Chesapeake, Hood Island, or Wellfleet, shucked

MIGNONETTE
- 1 tablespoon coarsely ground white pepper
- 1 medium shallot, very finely minced
- ¼ cup white wine vinegar

SOY-LIME SAUCE
- ¼ cup soy sauce
  Juice of 1 lime (about 2 tablespoons)
- 2 tablespoons finely sliced scallions (white and green parts)
- 1 teaspoon finely grated fresh ginger
- 1 clove garlic, peeled and finely minced
- ¼ teaspoon chile paste, such as sambal oelek

WHITE MIGNONETTE
Whisk the sauce ingredients in a small bowl. Serve with chilled oysters.

SPICY SOY-LIME SAUCE
Whisk the sauce ingredients in a small bowl. Serve with chilled oysters.

FROM THE KITCHENS
- Oysters are always sold by place name, since the waters in which they grow contribute to their unique taste. East Coast oysters tend to be brinier than their Pacific cousins, but both are equally tasty. Serve different kinds together for a fun tasting experience.
- Rinse the oysters before you open them, but never wash them once they're opened—you'll wash off all the flavor. There may be a little grit in the shell once they're opened, but just scoop it out with the tip of your oyster knife.
- Freshly ground pepper is the essential ingredient in a classic mignonette sauce. It's best to grind your own so the flavor is fresh and bright. Adjust your pepper mill to a coarse grind or use a spice mill to get just the right consistency.

1. Lay an oyster rounded side down on a towel on the counter; angle the shell hinge toward you. 2. Pry an oyster knife or church key bottle opener into the hinge. Rock the knife gently up and down to pop open the shell. 3. Slip the knife along the shell to free the oyster, taking care not to lose the delicious liquor. 4. Serve immediately or refrigerate up to 4 hours.

herb-stuffed deviled eggs

makes 12 halves

6 large eggs
3 tablespoons mayonnaise
2 teaspoons Dijon mustard
1 tablespoon extra-virgin olive oil
1½ teaspoons finely chopped cornichons (see tip, right)
1½ teaspoons finely chopped fresh chives
1½ teaspoons minced fresh flat-leaf parsley, plus small whole leaves for garnish
1½ teaspoons minced fresh tarragon
⅛ teaspoon kosher salt

1. Put the eggs in a saucepan with enough cold water to cover. Bring to a boil, cover, and remove from the heat. Set aside for 10 minutes. Drain the eggs and roll them between your palm and the counter to crack the shell, then peel under cool running water. Halve eggs lengthwise and carefully remove the yolks from the whites. Slice a thin sliver from the rounded bottom of each half so they sit without wobbling on a serving platter. Mash the yolks in a bowl with a fork.

2. Whisk the mayonnaise and mustard into the yolks. Gradually whisk in the olive oil, starting with a few drops and then adding the rest in a steady stream. Stir in cornichons, chives, parsley, tarragon, and salt.

3. Spoon the yolk mixture back into the whites. Garnish with parsley leaves. The eggs can be stuffed several hours in advance, covered, and refrigerated until ready to serve.

FROM THE KITCHENS

Cornichons are French gherkins—small, tart pickles that often accompany pâtés and smoked fish. They add just the right crunch to our deviled eggs.

bacon-wrapped dates with manchego

4 servings

12 whole dates
3 ounces Manchego cheese
12 slices lean bacon
Kosher salt
Freshly ground black pepper

1. Prepare an outdoor grill with an indirect medium fire.

2. Slice into the dates lengthwise, just deep enough so that you can pull out the pits with your fingers. Discard the pits. Cut cheese into sticks to fit into the dates. Tuck some cheese inside each date, pressing to enclose the cheese. Wrap a slice of bacon around each date, trim all but an inch of overlap, and secure with a toothpick. Season with salt and black pepper to taste.

3. Grill, turning as needed, until the bacon is cooked through and crisp, about 10 minutes. Transfer to a platter. Serve warm or at room temperature.

warm goat cheese wrapped in grape leaves | 6 to 8 servings

2 or 3 large jarred, brined grape leaves, stems trimmed
8 ounces Bûcheron cheese, rind on (see tip, below)
   Slightly heaping ½ teaspoon anise seeds or fennel seeds
   Slightly heaping ¼ teaspoon crushed red pepper
2 tablespoons sambuca or ouzo (optional)
2 tablespoons extra-virgin olive oil
   Baguette slices, for serving

1. Soak the grape leaves in water for 5 minutes, then drain. Sprinkle the cheese with the anise and crushed red pepper. Wrap a grape leaf around the bottom of the cheese. If using the sambuca, place the cheese on a rimmed plate and sprinkle with sambuca. Wrap the top of the cheese with another grape leaf or two, using just enough leaves to form a single layer, then refrigerate for at least 1 hour.

2. Prepare an outdoor grill with a medium-low fire. Brush cheese bundle with the olive oil and grill, turning, until the cheese is a little oozy and leaves are slightly charred, about 4 minutes. Transfer to a plate and serve with baguette slices.

FROM THE KITCHENS
• Bûcheron is a mild goat cheese sold in rounds. The rind is edible and can be left on for this recipe. If you can't find it, substitute any disk of soft, mild goat cheese.
• Brined grape leaves range in size, and you don't know what yours will be until you open the jar. If the leaves are really huge, you may need to trim the thick stem from the middle of the leaf—it's too tough to eat.

1. Place seasoned cheese on top of a grape leaf. 2. Bring points of grape leaf up around the cheese and press gently to get leaf to stick to cheese. 3. Wrap top of cheese with another grape leaf or two, using just enough leaves to form a single layer. 4. Don't worry if leaves don't hold fast; they'll stick once cheese is grilled.

SAY CHEESE We are in awe of gorgeous cheese. A crumbly blue, a grating Parm, a chunky Cheddar, and a runny Camembert are all you need for a well-rounded sampling.

Cheese is the original quick-and-easy. It's great as last-minute finger food or as a light meal with bread and wine. Follow our 5 cheese tips and make the most of this simplest of starters:

SERVE cheese at room temperature (20 minutes on your counter is fine).

GO with the odds for eye appeal—three, five, or even just one cheese on a plate works.

MIX IT UP with different
- textures—soft, firm, hard
- milks—cow, goat, sheep
- places—a tour of England-France-Spain or a sampling from Vermont

PRESENT IT WITH PANACHE
- Do nothing. Keep the cheese whole and let people slice their own.

- Chunk it. Serve hard cheese such as pecorino Romano or Parmesan in craggy nuggets.
- Spoon it. Lop off the top of a ripe Brie or Camembert and let guests scoop their own.

PAIR CHEESE WITH WHAT YOU HAVE
- herb-cured olives
- marinated or pickled mushrooms or peppers
- salami, country ham, or prosciutto
- roasted nuts
- fruit chutneys
- dried apricots or figs
- fresh apples, grapes, or pears
- honey
- crusty bread

blasted balsamic chicken wings

4 to 6 servings

½ cup red currant jelly
⅓ cup balsamic vinegar
1 teaspoon soy sauce
2 teaspoons kosher salt, plus
   additional for seasoning
1 teaspoon cayenne pepper
1 teaspoon garlic powder
1 teaspoon onion powder
3 pounds chicken wings
   (no wing tips)

1. Preheat the oven to 450°F. Line a baking sheet with aluminum foil.

2. Bring the currant jelly, vinegar, and soy sauce to a boil in a small saucepan over medium-high heat and simmer until thick and glossy, 5 to 7 minutes. While the mixture cooks, stir together the 2 teaspoons salt, cayenne, and garlic and onion powders to break up any lumps. Whisk the spices into the jelly mixture. Toss the wings with the jelly mixture in a large bowl, making sure all of the wings are coated evenly.

3. Place the chicken meaty side down on the baking sheet and reserve the excess sauce. Roast the chicken, turning halfway through cooking, until dark or almost lacquered looking, 17 to 18 minutes for small wings and up to 25 minutes for bigger, meatier wings. Then turn on the broiler and broil the chicken for 3 to 4 minutes, until wings are richly colored and glossy.

4. Toward the end of cooking the chicken, return sauce to small saucepan and bring to a boil, reduce the heat, and simmer for 1 to 2 minutes. When the wings are done, sprinkle them with salt to taste, pour the hot sauce over, toss, and serve immediately.

FROM THE KITCHENS

Grocery store balsamic vinegar is an everyday condiment—it's inexpensive and great in salad dressings and sauces. The expensive stuff that comes in small bottles and vials is worth having too. Use it sparingly, drizzled over Parmesan cheese or savored with strawberries.

grilled pork pinchos | 4 to 6 servings

PORK

6	cloves garlic, peeled
1	tablespoon kosher salt
1	tablespoon hot Spanish smoked paprika
2	teaspoons ground coriander
2	teaspoons ground cumin
2	teaspoons ras al hanout (see recipe, below)
2	tablespoons extra-virgin olive oil, plus additional for brushing
1½	tablespoons sherry vinegar
	Freshly ground black pepper
1	pound boneless pork shoulder (see tip, right)

SPICE MIXTURE

Makes about 3/4 cup

3	slightly heaping tablespoons five-spice powder
2	tablespoons ground cardamom
2	tablespoons ground ginger
1	tablespoon ground nutmeg
1	tablespoon ground turmeric
1	tablespoons cayenne pepper

1. In the morning or a day before grilling, smash the garlic cloves, sprinkle with the salt, and, with the flat side of a large knife, mash and smear the mixture to a coarse paste. Mix the garlic paste and the paprika, coriander, cumin, and ras al hanout in a medium bowl. Whisk in the 2 tablespoons olive oil, vinegar, and black pepper to taste.

2. Trim excess fat from the pork and cut into 1-inch cubes. Add the pork to the bowl, tossing until all the pieces are evenly coated with the spice paste. Cover and refrigerate for at least 6 hours or overnight.

3. If using wooden skewers, soak them in water for 30 minutes before Step 4. Prepare an outdoor grill with a hot fire.

4. Thread 3 to 4 pieces of pork onto each skewer. Lightly brush the pork with oil. Grill the skewers, turning once, until the meat chars but is still moist, about 5 minutes per side.

RAS AL HANOUT

Mix five-spice powder, cardamom, ginger, nutmeg, turmeric, and cayenne in a small bowl. Store in a sealed container for up to 2 months.

FROM THE KITCHENS

▪ When making kebabs from pork shoulder, ask your butcher for "Boston butt." We love this economical yet rich cut for kebabs. It has more meat and less sinew and cartilage than the "picnic" cut from the shoulder, so you'll be able to get bigger, meatier chunks.

▪ Ras al hanout, which means "head of the shop," is an idiosyncratic blend of spices from North Africa. The mix can be very exotic and is reputed to include aphrodisiacs as well as aromatics. This is a streamlined version that we love on meat and chicken.

pork satay | 4 servings

⅓ cup water
⅓ cup freshly squeezed lime juice
    (2 to 3 limes)
3 tablespoons sugar
2 tablespoons fish sauce (see tip,
    page 160)
1 teaspoon sambal oelek (sweet-hot
    Southeast Asian chile paste)
1 clove garlic, minced
1 pork tenderloin (about 1 pound)
2 tablespoons vegetable oil, plus
    additional for brushing
  Kosher salt
  Freshly ground black pepper
1 small whole carrot, finely grated
  Boston or Bibb lettuce and coarsely
    chopped fresh mint and cilantro,
    for serving

1. Whisk water, lime juice, sugar, and fish sauce in a small bowl until sugar dissolves. Stir in sambal oelek and garlic.

2. Slice pork crosswise into ½-inch-thick slices. Toss slices with about ¼ cup of the marinade and the 2 tablespoons vegetable oil. Set aside for 15 minutes. Reserve the rest of the marinade to use as a dipping sauce.

3. Heat a grill pan or outdoor grill to medium-high heat. If you're using bamboo skewers on an outdoor grill, soak the skewers in water for 30 minutes before using. Thread one piece of pork on each skewer and lay skewers on a baking sheet or large plate. Brush the meat lightly with some oil and season with salt and pepper to taste. Working in batches, grill the skewers, without moving them, until browned on the first side, about 1 minute. Turn the skewers and grill until the second side is browned and the meat is opaque at the edges, about 1 minute more. Transfer the satays to a clean platter.

4. Stir a heaping tablespoon of grated carrot into reserved marinade to make dipping sauce. Serve satays with the sauce, remaining grated carrot, lettuce leaves, mint, and cilantro. Have guests slip pork from the skewer and wrap each piece in a lettuce leaf with some mint and cilantro.

FROM THE KITCHENS
Served on a pretty platter alongside ruffled lettuce and strewn sprigs of mint and cilantro, pork satay is an easy way to bring a touch of exotica to the table. It's also a fun icebreaker that encourages everyone to get involved at the table.

summer rolls | makes 12 rolls

DIPPING SAUCE

- ¼ cup water
- 3 tablespoons rice vinegar
- 1 tablespoon sugar
- 2 teaspoons kosher salt
- 2 tablespoons finely grated carrot
- 1 clove garlic, minced
- 1 scallion (white and green parts), minced
- ½ to 1 serrano chile (with seeds), stemmed, halved, and thinly sliced crosswise

ROLLS

- 2 ounces Vietnamese-style rice vermicelli (glass noodles)
- 1 medium carrot, peeled
- 3 medium radishes
- 1 Kirby cucumber, quartered lengthwise and seeded
- 2 scallions (white and green parts), very thinly sliced
- ⅓ cup fresh cilantro
- 1 tablespoon peanut oil
- Juice of ½ a lime
- 1½ teaspoons kosher salt
- 12 to 16 6-inch round Vietnamese-style rice spring roll skins
- 12 medium cooked and peeled shrimp, halved lengthwise (about 4 ounces)
- 24 fresh mint leaves (about ¼ cup)

1. Whisk all sauce ingredients in a small bowl. Set sauce aside.

2. Bring a pot of water to a boil over high heat and salt it generously. Add the noodles, cover, and turn off the heat. When noodles are soft but not mushy (after about 3 minutes), stir with a fork to separate the strands. Drain in a colander and rinse with cool water. Shake the colander to remove excess water. Put noodles in a large bowl.

3. Cut the carrot, radishes, and cucumber into long, thin, matchstick-size strips with a knife or hand-held mandoline. Toss the vegetables with the noodles along with the scallions, cilantro, peanut oil, lime juice, and salt.

4. Fill a large bowl with cold water. Dip a spring roll skin in the water, soaking just until pliable. Place the skin on a work surface and pat very dry with paper towels. (See photos, below, for remaining instructions.) Place roll seam side down on a serving platter and repeat with remaining ingredients to make 12 rolls. Serve with sauce.

FROM THE KITCHENS

Vietnamese rice spring roll skins are also called galettes de riz and banh trang. They're available in Asian markets, specialty food stores, and online. The rice spring roll skins are very fragile, so having a few extra on hand helps if some tear or soak for too long.

1. Mound ¼ cup of the vegetable mixture across the bottom center of the spring roll skin and top with 2 shrimp halves and 2 mint leaves for a pretty finish. 2. Fold the edge of the skin closest to you over filling and fold in the sides. 3. Roll tightly to seal.

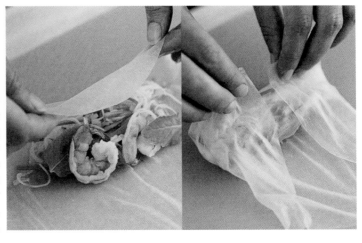

Just when we think we've seen it all, something surprising shows up in our kitchen, like Greek-style stuffed grape leaves going Asian.

vietnamese-style beef in grape leaves

16 pieces

STUFFED GRAPE LEAVES

1	tablespoon peanut or vegetable oil, plus additional for grilling
½	small onion, chopped
1	clove garlic, minced
8	ounces ground beef
2	tablespoons salted cashews, chopped
2	tablespoons finely minced fresh lemongrass
1½	teaspoons sugar
1½	teaspoons fish sauce (see tip, page 160)
½	teaspoon chile paste, such as sambal oelek
½	teaspoon kosher salt
16	jarred, brined grape leaves, rinsed, drained, and patted dry
8	short skewers
	Vietnamese Dipping Sauce (see recipe, below)

SAUCE   Makes 1 cup

⅓	cup water
⅓	cup freshly squeezed lime juice
2	tablespoons fish sauce
3	tablespoons sugar
1	tablespoon finely grated carrot
1	teaspoon chile paste, such as sambal oelek
1	clove garlic, minced

1. Heat the oil in a small skillet over medium heat. Add the onion and garlic and cook until soft, about 2 minutes. Cool slightly. Put the ground beef in a large bowl and stir in the onion mixture, cashews, lemongrass, sugar, fish sauce, chile paste, and salt.

2. Lay a grape leaf, stem side up, on your work surface with the tip of the leaf pointing away from you; snip off the little stem piece. Place a heaping tablespoon of the beef mixture in the center of the leaf. Fold the bottom of the leaf over the filling, fold in the sides, and then roll the leaf up to make a tight package. Repeat with the remaining leaves and filling.

3. Thread 2 rolls lengthwise onto each skewer. Preheat a grill pan or outdoor grill to medium. Lightly brush the grill pan with oil and grill the packages for 2 minutes on each side; the grill marks should be quite distinct, and if the leaves char and even fray a bit, that's fine. Serve warm or at room temperature with Vietnamese Dipping Sauce.

VIETNAMESE DIPPING SAUCE
Whisk the water with the lime juice, fish sauce, and sugar in a small bowl until the sugar is dissolved. Stir in the carrot, chile paste, and garlic. If not using immediately, refrigerate the sauce in a sealed container for up to 2 days. Serve at room temperature. Stir right before using.

FROM THE KITCHENS
If you're using bamboo skewers, be sure to soak them in water for about an hour before threading them so they don't burn on the grill.

summer salsa
with a shot

4 to 6 servings

1   clove garlic
2   teaspoons kosher salt, plus
     additional for seasoning
4   medium ripe tomatoes, cored
     and diced
¼   medium red onion, finely diced
1   jalapeño, stemmed and minced
     (with seeds for more heat)
¼   cup chopped fresh cilantro
1   to 2 tablespoons silver tequila
     (optional)
     White corn tortilla chips, for dipping

1. Smash the garlic clove, sprinkle with 1 teaspoon of the salt, and, with the flat side of a large knife, mash and smear the mixture to a coarse paste. Mix the garlic, tomatoes, onion, jalapeño, and cilantro in a serving bowl. Add the tequila, if desired, and season with the remaining salt, adding more to taste if necessary.

2. Serve immediately or cover with plastic wrap and set aside for 1 hour at room temperature. Serve with the tortilla chips.

FROM THE KITCHENS
• Why mash instead of mince garlic? For raw dips and sauces, when the garlic is reduced to a smooth paste, it flavors a dish more evenly and less harshly than if added in pieces. Another reason to love this "smushing": It's quicker than mincing.
• The best tomatoes—juicy with a bright, summer-sweet taste—are vine-ripened. A cue for great taste is a deep, rich color all the way up to the stem, but a full tomato aroma counts too. Don't be shy: It's OK to sniff a tomato. Store your tomatoes at room temperature, not in the refrigerator; chilling deadens their taste and mars their texture.

guacamole | 4 to 6 servings

2 cloves garlic, peeled
2 teaspoons kosher salt
¼ medium red onion, minced
3 ripe Hass avocados
½ cup grape or cherry tomatoes, diced
¼ cup roughly chopped fresh cilantro
1 to 2 jalapeño or serrano chiles (with seeds for more heat, without seeds for less), stemmed and minced
Juice of 1 lime (about 2 tablespoons)
White corn tortilla chips, for dipping

1. Smash the garlic cloves, sprinkle with 1 teaspoon of the salt, and, with the side of a large knife, mash and smear the mixture to a coarse paste. Put in a bowl with onion.

2. Halve the avocados lengthwise; carefully tap your knife into the pits, twist, and lift them out. Knock the knife on the edge of the counter and the pit will drop off. Score the flesh with the tip of a knife and use a spoon to scoop the avocado from the peel into the onion mixture.

3. Mix the tomatoes, cilantro, chiles, lime juice, and the remaining 1 teaspoon salt with the avocados with a rubber spatula or large fork just until combined, keeping the guacamole chunky. Serve immediately with tortilla chips. (Guacamole's more than just a dip. Use it as a spread for sandwiches and wraps or as a topping for grilled fish or vegetables.)

FROM THE KITCHENS
• A ripe avocado will yield to gentle pressure. Skin should be black, with almost no traces of green. Tuck hard avocados in a brown paper bag at room temp with an apple or banana and they will ripen faster.
• The heat level of jalapeños can vary widely. Some are fiery, others tame, so it's a good idea to add them according to your taste. A chile's seeds harbor a lot of the heat, so if the chile is a scorcher, hold them back—and if you want to raise the heat level, add more of them.

bruschetta | 4 to 6 servings

1 loaf French bread or coarse country bread, cut crosswise on a sharp angle into ½-inch-thick slices
  Extra-virgin olive oil
  Kosher salt
1 large clove garlic, smashed and peeled

1. Preheat the broiler or a stovetop grill pan to high.

2. Drizzle both sides of the bread slices very lightly with olive oil and season with salt to taste. If using a broiler, lay the bread on a baking sheet.

3. Toast the bread under the broiler or on the grill pan until the edges char a bit and the surface is golden. Turn and toast the other side. Rub the garlic all over the surface of the toasted bread to flavor it. Serve warm or at room temperature.

UPGRADES
In Italian, bruschetta means roasted over coals—but grilling or broiling is fine. Garlic and olive oil is the classic topping, but no one's going to look at you funny for experimenting. Try a dollop of good-quality fresh ricotta, store-bought pesto or tapenade, sautéed mushrooms, our Tuscan Bean Dip (page 29) or the Little Tomato Salad with Fresh Herbs (page 314), or a smear of soft cheese, like Brie, goat cheese, or soft herb cheese. We also like it topped with lightly dressed arugula and thin slices of good ham or prosciutto or a piece of smoked fish.

FROM THE KITCHENS
Good bread is key here. What do we mean by good bread? Something with character, crust, and color. Something that smells yeasty and inviting. If you've got a bakery nearby, check out its bread, or try those "freshly baked" breads at the grocery store.

soups & stews

Whether it's a starter or a whole meal, nothing warms the soul and satisfies the body like a bowl of soup.

minute minestrone | 4 to 6 servings

SOUP
- ¼ cup extra-virgin olive oil
- 1 medium onion, halved and sliced
- 3 garlic cloves, chopped
- 2 teaspoons kosher salt, plus more for seasoning
  Freshly ground black pepper
- 2 medium zucchini (about 1 pound), halved lengthwise and sliced into half-moons
- 1 14.5 ounce can diced tomatoes
- 1 14.5-ounce can Great Northern, cannellini, or navy beans, rinsed and drained
- 3 to 4 cups low-sodium chicken broth (about 2 small cans or 1 quart box)
- 2 to 4 tablespoons prepared pesto or tapenade, such as olive, tomato, or artichoke

FOR SERVING
  freshly grated Parmesan cheese
  Bruschetta (see recipe, page 58) (optional)

1. Heat the olive oil in a large saucepan over medium heat. Add the onion and garlic; season with the 2 teaspoons salt and some black pepper; cook, stirring occasionally, until the onion wilts, about 5 minutes. Add the zucchini and tomatoes and cook until the tomatoes look dry, about 10 minutes. Add the beans and broth and adjust the heat so the soup simmers. Cook, uncovered, until the vegetables are tender, about 10 minutes more.

2. Just before serving, stir in the pesto and season with salt and black pepper to taste. Pour into warmed soup bowls and serve with grated cheese and Bruschetta, if desired.

FROM THE KITCHENS
Soup recipes are incredibly forgiving of improvisation (they tend to reward it), and minestrone's a great place to practice—use any vegetables you've got in the house to make this soup your own. Add other vegetables: Sliced mushrooms, carrots, or yellow squash are all good. Little noodles (like stars, tubes, broken spaghetti, whatever) also work. The noodles absorb the broth, so add about a cup more broth to keep it soupy.

creamless creamy vegetable soup

4 servings

2 tablespoons unsalted butter

2 sprigs fresh thyme or pinch dried thyme

½ small onion or 2 shallots, thinly sliced

1½ teaspoons kosher salt, plus more for seasoning

3 russet potatoes, peeled and cut into small bite-size chunks or 1 butternut squash (about 2 pounds), peeled, seeded, and cut into small bite-size pieces (or 2 10-ounce packages frozen squash)

5 cups water or low-sodium chicken broth (3 small cans or 1-quart box plus 1 cup)

Freshly ground black pepper

FOR SERVING

¼ cup plain yogurt or sour cream (optional)

chives, chopped, for garnish (optional)

1. Melt the butter in a large saucepan over low heat. Strip the thyme leaves from the stems and discard the stems. Add the onion or shallot, thyme, and 1½ teaspoons salt. Increase the heat to medium and cook, stirring occasionally, until the onion is tender, about 5 minutes. Add the potato or squash and water or broth. Bring to a boil, reduce the heat and simmer, uncovered, until the vegetables are totally tender, about 20 minutes.

2. Puree the soup in the pot with an immersion blender or in small batches in a blender (keep the lid cracked to allow steam to escape), until smooth. Return to the pot and reheat. If using yogurt or sour cream, stir it in, but don't let the soup boil or it will curdle. Season with salt and black pepper to taste. Sprinkle with chives, if using, and serve warm.

FROM THE KITCHENS

- If you don't have an immersion blender, be safe. Cool the soup for at least 5 minutes and transfer to a regular blender, filling no more than halfway. Don't seal the top. Lift one corner up a little to let the steam escape, put a kitchen towel on top, pulse a few times, then blend on high till smooth.
- Upgrade the potato soup by adding a handful (about 2 ounces) of shredded Cheddar cheese to the warm potato soup. Whisk until melted, then stir in about a cup of defrosted broccoli pieces.
- Upgrade the squash soup by adding 1½ teaspoons curry powder to the onions while they are cooking. Scatter chopped cilantro over the finished soup.
- Upgrade either soup by stirring in crumbled, cooked bacon and chopped chives right before serving. Or, instead of stirring the yogurt or sour cream into the soup, whisk it in a bowl to thin it out, then use a spoon to drizzle a free-form design on each serving of soup.

We always try to cook what's in season: strawberries in spring, corn in summer, pumpkins in fall. Try this delectable corn chowder on a summer night and you'll taste why.

corn chowder
with summer herb salad | 6 servings

CHOWDER

8	ears fresh corn, preferably white, shucked
6	tablespoons unsalted butter
8	scallions, white parts chopped, green reserved for Herb Salad
6	cloves garlic
1	tablespoon kosher salt
2	teaspoons sugar
	Freshly ground black pepper
3	sprigs fresh parsley
3	sprigs fresh thyme
1	bay leaf
6	cups water
	Summer Herb Salad (see recipe, below)

SALAD
Makes about 2 cups

½	cup torn fresh basil
½	cup roughly chopped fresh dill fronds (stems and leaves)
⅓	cup chopped scallion greens
3	tablespoons torn tarragon
1	tablespoon extra-virgin olive oil
1	teaspoon kosher salt
	Freshly ground black pepper
1	large ripe tomato, cored and roughly chopped

1. Shear the corn kernels from the cobs with a knife. Put about ⅔ of the kernels in a large bowl. Set aside the remaining kernels for adding to the soup before serving. Working over the large bowl, run a knife along the cobs to press out the milky liquid. Snap or cut 3 of the cobs in half; discard the remaining cobs.

2. Melt the butter in a soup pot over medium-low heat. Add the scallion whites, garlic, salt, sugar, and pepper to taste. Cook, covered, stirring occasionally, until the vegetables are soft and fragrant, about 12 minutes. Add the larger amount of corn kernels, with their milk, and cook, covered, stirring occasionally, until the corn is tender, about 10 minutes. Tie the parsley, thyme, and bay leaf together with kitchen twine and add to the soup along with the reserved cobs and water. Bring mixture to a boil, reduce the heat, and simmer, uncovered, until slightly thickened, about 30 minutes. Remove the herb bundle and cobs and discard.

3. Puree the soup in batches in a blender (or in the pot with an immersion blender) until creamy. Return the puree to the pot, add the reserved corn kernels, and simmer over medium heat, uncovered, until the whole corn kernels are just tender, about 5 minutes. Taste and adjust the salt and pepper. Divide the chowder among soup bowls and mound a generous portion of the salad in the center of each bowl. Pass any remaining herb salad at the table.

SUMMER HERB SALAD
In a large bowl combine the basil, dill, scallion greens, tarragon, oil, salt, and pepper to taste. Add the tomato and toss to combine. Serve immediately.

slow-cooker bean & barley soup | 4 to 6 servings

1 cup dried multibean mix or
   Great Northern beans,
   picked over and rinsed
6 cups water
1 14-ounce can whole tomatoes,
   with juice
3 cloves garlic, smashed
2 ribs celery, chopped
2 medium carrots, chopped
½ medium onion, chopped
½ cup pearl barley
1 bay leaf
1½ tablespoons kosher salt, plus
   additional for seasoning
2 teaspoons dried Italian herb blend
   Freshly ground black pepper
½ ounce dried porcini mushrooms
   (optional)
3 cups cleaned baby spinach leaves
   (about 3 ounces)
1 cup freshly grated Parmesan cheese
1 tablespoon balsamic vinegar
   Extra-virgin olive oil

1. Put beans, water, tomatoes and their juices, garlic, celery, carrots, onion, barley, bay leaf, 1½ tablespoons salt, herb blend, pepper, and porcini mushrooms (if desired) in a slow cooker; cover and cook on LOW until the beans are quite tender and the soup is thick, about 8 hours.

2. Stir in the spinach, cheese, and vinegar, cover, and let the soup be until the spinach wilts, about 5 minutes. Remove and discard bay leaf. Taste and season with salt and black pepper to taste.

3. Ladle the soup into warmed bowls and drizzle each serving with olive oil.

FROM THE KITCHENS
We like to stir in spinach just at the end of cooking and drizzle in extra-virgin olive oil right before serving. The warm soup gently wilts the greens and coaxes out nuances in the olive oil that add a whole new dimension of flavor.

white bean & escarole soup

4 to 6 servings

2   tablespoons extra-virgin olive oil,
      plus additional for drizzling
2   ounces pancetta, chopped (about
      ⅓ cup)(see tip, page 305)
1   small onion, chopped
4   cloves garlic, minced
1   small sprig fresh rosemary
¼   teaspoon crushed red pepper flakes
1   head escarole (about 1 pound),
      coarsely chopped
5   cups low-sodium chicken broth
2   15-ounce cans Great Northern or
      cannellini beans, rinsed and
      drained
1   cup chopped canned plum tomatoes
    Kosher salt and freshly ground black
      pepper
    Chunk of Parmesan cheese

1. Heat 2 tablespoons of the olive oil in a soup pot over medium heat. Add the pancetta and cook until brown, about 5 minutes. Transfer pancetta to a plate with a slotted spoon. Add the onion to the pot and cook, stirring occasionally, until soft and golden, about 10 minutes. Add the garlic, rosemary, and red pepper and cook until onion is translucent, about 3 minutes.

2. Stir in the escarole and cook until just wilted, about 2 minutes. Add the chicken broth, beans, and tomatoes and bring to a gentle simmer. Cover and cook for 10 to 15 minutes, stirring once or twice, until the broth has been slightly thickened by the starch from the beans and the escarole is deep green. Stir in the reserved pancetta and season with salt and pepper to taste. Ladle the soup into warm bowls. Drizzle some olive oil and grate a good soup spoon or so of Parmesan cheese over each serving.

FROM THE KITCHENS
We love to ladle hot soup into very warm bowls (just heat them a little in your oven). So little effort for such a big difference.

watermelon curry with grilled shrimp

4 to 6 servings

CURRY

5	pounds watermelon
1	3-inch-long piece peeled fresh ginger
4	cloves garlic
3	tablespoons water
2	tablespoons Madras-style curry powder (see tip, below)
2	teaspoons kosher salt
	Pinch cayenne pepper
3	tablespoons vegetable oil
1	3-inch-long cinnamon stick
1	teaspoon sugar
½	cup chopped fresh mint
2	teaspoons freshly squeezed lime juice

SHRIMP

1	pound medium-large shrimp, shelled and deveined
2	tablespoons unsalted butter, melted
	Kosher salt and freshly ground black pepper
½	of a lime
	Grilled Indian flat bread or pappadam (Indian lentil crackers), for serving (optional)

1. For the curry: Remove the rind from the watermelon; cut the flesh into 1-inch chunks and remove the seeds. Puree 2 cups of the chunks. Set aside the remaining chunks and the puree separately.

2. If you have a mini-food processor, blend the ginger, garlic, water, curry powder, salt, and cayenne pepper to a paste. To make the spice paste by hand: Finely grate ginger into a small bowl. Smash the garlic cloves, sprinkle with the salt, and, with the side of a large knife, mash and smear the mixture to a coarse paste. Stir the paste and the water, curry powder, and cayenne into the ginger.

3. Heat the oil in a large skillet over medium-high heat. Add the cinnamon stick and cook until it unfurls, about 30 seconds. Add the ginger-garlic paste and cook, stirring constantly, until it is quite fragrant and lightly browned, about 3 minutes. Add the reserved watermelon puree and the sugar, reduce the heat, and simmer until thick, about 5 minutes. Stir in the reserved watermelon chunks and simmer for 2 minutes more. Transfer the curry to a bowl and cool. Stir in the mint and lime juice and refrigerate, covered, until thoroughly chilled. (You can prepare the curried watermelon a day ahead and refrigerate. If you do, add the chopped mint and lime juice right before serving.)

4. For the shrimp: Heat a grill to medium-hot or a grill pan over medium heat. Toss the shrimp with the butter in a large bowl; season with salt and pepper to taste. Grill the shrimp, turning once, until just cooked through, about 4 minutes. Transfer the shrimp to a plate or bowl and squeeze the lime over them.

5. To serve, ladle the curried watermelon into serving bowls and arrange the shrimp in the centers. Serve with grilled Indian flat bread or crispy pappadam, if desired.

FROM THE KITCHENS
The city of Madras on the southeastern coast of India spawned two classics: its famous namesake fabric and a moderately hot curry powder. At its most basic, Madras-style curry includes ground coriander, turmeric, chiles, cumin, and fennel.

wild mushroom soup | 4 to 6 servings

7   cups water
½   ounce dried porcini mushrooms
      (about ⅔ cup)
6   slices bacon
2   tablespoons unsalted butter
3   leeks (white and light green part
      only), sliced and well rinsed
3   teaspoons kosher salt
1   pound mixed wild mushrooms, such
      as shiitake, cremini, or portobello,
      cleaned, trimmed, and sliced
    Freshly ground black pepper
¼   cup Madeira or cognac
3   sprigs fresh flat-leaf parsley
3   sprigs fresh thyme
1   bay leaf
½   cup crème fraîche, plus additional
      for garnish

1. Bring 1 cup of the water to a boil in a small saucepan and add the dried porcini. Set aside to soften, about 20 minutes. Scoop the mushrooms from the liquid and chop coarsely. Reserve the mushrooms in a small bowl. Ladle ⅔ cup of the soaking liquid into a measuring cup, taking care to leave any grit at the bottom of the saucepan.

2. Line a plate with paper towels. Cook the bacon in a soup pot over medium heat until crisp, about 5 minutes. Transfer the bacon to the plate. Add the butter, leeks, and 1½ teaspoons of the salt to the drippings in the pot and cook, stirring occasionally, until the leeks are soft, about 10 minutes. Add the fresh and reserved soaked mushrooms, pepper to taste, and the remaining 1½ teaspoons salt. Increase the heat to high and cook, stirring occasionally, until the mushrooms are wilted, about 5 minutes. Add the Madeira or cognac and cook, uncovered, until the mixture is almost dry. Add the remaining 6 cups of water and the reserved mushroom soaking liquid and bring to a simmer. Tie the parsley, thyme sprigs, and bay leaf together with a piece of clean kitchen string and toss in the pot. Cover, reduce heat if necessary, and simmer until the mushrooms are tender, about 30 minutes.

3. Scoop out about 2 cups of the mushrooms with a slotted spoon and puree in a blender with 1 cup of the broth and the ½ cup crème fraîche until very smooth. Stir puree into soup. Taste and add salt and pepper, if desired. Remove herb bundle. Ladle soup into warm bowls. Spoon a bit of crème fraîche and crumble some bacon over each serving.

FROM THE KITCHENS
Strain the soaking liquid for dried mushrooms through a clean paper towel or cheesecloth placed in a fine sieve to remove any grit. Use the liquid to flavor soups, sauces, or broth for risotto.

pistou

6 servings

SOUP

¾	cup dried cannellini beans
1	whole clove
½	medium onion
1	medium carrot, peeled
1	bay leaf
2	teaspoons kosher salt
2	tablespoons extra-virgin olive oil
1	medium onion, chopped
1	medium carrot, peeled and sliced
½	fennel bulb, cored and chopped
4	cloves garlic, smashed
1	tablespoon kosher salt
1	15-ounce can whole tomatoes
6	red-skinned potatoes, quartered
1	tablespoon chopped fresh thyme
1	cup diced butternut squash
¼	cup small pasta, such as ditalini
1	strip lemon zest

PESTO

Makes about ⅔ cup

2	cups loosely packed basil leaves
2	tablespoons toasted pine nuts
2	tablespoons freshly grated Parmigiana-Reggiano cheese
¼	teaspoon minced garlic
½	teaspoon kosher salt
¼	cup plus 1 tablespoon extra-virgin olive oil

1. Put the beans in a medium pot of cold water, bring to a boil, and boil for 5 minutes. Remove from the heat, cover, and soak for 1 hour. Drain. Stick the clove in the onion half and add it to the bean pot with the whole carrot, the bay leaf, 2 teaspoons salt, and 8 cups of cold water. Bring to a boil, reduce the heat, and simmer, covered, until tender, about 1 hour. Set the beans and their liquid aside. Remove the onion and bay leaf.

2. Heat the olive oil in a large soup pot over medium heat. Add the chopped onion, sliced carrot, fennel, garlic, and 1 tablespoon salt. Cook, stirring occasionally, until the vegetables are tender, about 10 minutes. Add the beans and their liquid, the tomatoes and their juice, the potatoes, thyme, and 2 cups water, and cook until the potatoes are crisp-tender. Add squash, pasta, and lemon zest and cook until the squash is tender, about 20 minutes. Ladle the soup into warm bowls and garnish each with a healthy spoonful of Basil Pesto.

BASIL PESTO

In a food processor, combine the basil, pine nuts, cheese, garlic, and salt and puree. With the motor running, drizzle in the olive oil until incorporated. If not using right away, refrigerate with a piece of plastic wrap pressed to the surface of the pesto to prevent discoloration for up to 3 days.

FROM THE KITCHENS

Pistou is a Provençal vegetable soup finished with a flourish of basil pesto. If you can't find cannellini beans, dried Great Northern work just fine.

Add a swirl of chile and homey tortillas to comforting chicken soup and you have a bold hug of a meal.

tortilla soup | 4 servings

2   tablespoons vegetable oil
1   medium onion, chopped
2   cloves garlic, sliced
1   chipotle chile en adobo, minced
1   tablespoon chili powder
2   teaspoons kosher salt
6   cups chicken broth, low-sodium
    canned
1   cup corn kernels, fresh or frozen
    and thawed
1   ripe tomato, chopped
1   cup shredded cooked chicken
½   cup cilantro leaves
¼   cup freshly squeezed lime juice
    (about 2 limes)
    About a dozen corn tortilla chips,
    broken a bit
    Lime wedges (optional)

1. Heat the oil in a medium saucepan over medium heat. Add the onion, garlic, chipotle, chili powder, and salt and cook until the onion softens, about 5 minutes. Add the chicken broth, bring to a boil, reduce the heat slightly, and simmer, uncovered, for 10 minutes. Add the corn and cook for 5 minutes more.

2. Pull the saucepan from the heat and stir in the tomato, chicken, cilantro, and lime juice. Divide the tortilla chips among 4 warmed bowls, ladle the soup on top, and serve with lime wedges, if desired.

FROM THE KITCHENS
Get every last drop of juice from those little limes. Before halving, microwave them for a few seconds and roll them under the palm of your hand to release the juice from the pulp.

Classic and
cool, fresh
and fast
never go
out of style.

gazpacho | 4 servings

2 cloves garlic
1 tablespoon kosher salt, plus additional for seasoning
2 pounds ripe tomatoes, cored and quartered
2 Kirby cucumbers (or ½ of a peeled regular cucumber or 4 inches of an English cucumber) (about ½ pound), quartered and cut into 2-inch pieces
3 scallions (white and green parts), quartered
1 small poblano pepper, seeded and roughly chopped
2 cups chilled tomato juice
2 to 3 tablespoons sherry or red wine vinegar
¼ teaspoon hot sauce
2 or 3 ice cubes
¼ cup extra-virgin olive oil, plus additional for garnish
⅓ cup fresh flat-leaf parsley
⅓ cup fresh mint
Freshly ground black pepper

1. Smash the garlic cloves, sprinkle with the 1 tablespoon salt, and, with the flat side of a large knife, mash and smear the mixture to a coarse paste. Put the paste in a large bowl and toss with the tomatoes, cucumbers, scallions, poblano, tomato juice, vinegar, hot sauce, and ice.

2. Working in batches, ladle the mixture into a blender and process to make a slightly coarse puree, then transfer to a serving bowl. With the last batch, while the motor is running, drizzle in the ¼ cup olive oil until incorporated. Chop the parsley and mint by hand or in a minichopper and stir most of the herbs into the soup. Season the soup with salt and black pepper to taste.

3. Ladle the soup into chilled bowls, scatter the reserved herbs over the soup, and drizzle with olive oil.

FROM THE KITCHENS
Why buy regular cukes when you can buy Kirbys? Also called pickling cucumbers, these small, 3- to 6-inch-long cucumbers are always unwaxed, a time-saver because they never need to be peeled. They're also sweeter than your standard cucumber.

miso soup | 4 servings

4   cups chicken or mushroom broth or
       water (2 small cans or 1 quart box)
1   2-inch piece fresh ginger, unpeeled,
       thinly sliced into coins
4   shiitake mushrooms, stems
       discarded and caps thinly sliced
2   cups baby spinach leaves, washed,
       or large spinach leaves, washed
       and torn (optional)
¼   cup to ⅓ cup yellow or red miso paste
8   ounces soft or silken tofu,
       cut into ½-inch cubes
2   scallions, thinly sliced (white
       and green parts)
1   to 2 teaspoons soy sauce
1   to 2 teaspoons toasted sesame
       seeds or gomasio (see tip,
       page 162) (optional)

1. Put the broth, ginger, and shiitake mushrooms in a medium saucepan and simmer until the mushrooms are soft, about 3 minutes. Add the spinach, if using, and cook until it wilts, about 1 minute.

2. Remove the broth from the heat and whisk in ¼ cup miso until smooth; taste, and add remaining miso, if necessary. Add the tofu and scallions. Season with soy sauce and sesame seeds, if using. Ladle soup into warmed bowls and serve.

FROM THE KITCHENS

• Miso (fermented soy paste) comes in a few different colors, depending on the grain it's made from, which can be rice, barley, or soybean. Yellow miso is mellower and sweeter, and red miso is bolder and fuller flavored. Keep all miso in the fridge. Once you add the miso, don't let the soup boil. Intense heat changes the flavor of the miso.
• If you're having trouble finding these ingredients, check out an Asian market or a health food store. Either should have everything you need.
• Shiitake mushrooms have broad, flat caps and tough, woody stems. The stems are too chewy to eat, though they add lots of flavor when simmered in broth. If you can't find fresh, buy dried and soak them in hot water for half an hour before using.
• Upgrade this soup by adding grated carrots with the mushrooms, or use a variety of mixed mushrooms.

hot & sour soup | 4 servings

5 cups low-sodium chicken
   broth (about 3 small cans
   or 1¼ 1-quart boxes)
1 4-inch piece fresh ginger, unpeeled,
   thinly sliced into coins
½ package soft or firm tofu
   (about 7 ounces), cut into small
   cubes (see tip, page 182)
3 scallions, thinly sliced
   (white and green parts)
2 cups baby spinach leaves,
   washed, or large leaves,
   washed and torn (optional)
1 tablespoon soy sauce
   Generous pinch sugar
1 tablespoon plus 1 teaspoon
   rice or cider vinegar
   Lots of freshly ground black pepper
   Dark sesame oil (optional)

1. Bring the broth and the ginger to a boil in a large saucepan over high heat. Adjust the heat so the broth simmers and cook to lightly flavor with the ginger, about 5 minutes.

2. Stir in the tofu, scallions, spinach, if using, and soy sauce. Cook until tofu is heated through and the spinach wilts, about 2 minutes more. Season with a pinch of sugar, the vinegar, and lots of black pepper. Serve drizzled with sesame oil, if desired.

FROM THE KITCHENS
• Lots of different ingredients can contribute heat to food (fresh hot pepper, hot sauce, chile oils, crushed red pepper flakes). Here, it's freshly ground black pepper. Use a pepper grinder. Always. It doesn't need to be expensive—look for whole peppercorns packaged for a grinder in the spice aisle.
• Upgrade this soup by adding sliced mushrooms, grated carrots, or leftover chicken or pork with the scallions.

thai shrimp & rice soup | 4 servings

4   cups chicken broth, low-sodium
       canned
1   to 2 teaspoons chile-garlic sauce
       (also called Sriracha)
1   rib celery, thinly sliced on an angle
1   medium carrot, peeled, quartered
       lengthwise, and thinly sliced
1   4-inch piece lemongrass, thinly sliced
       (see how-to, below)
2   tablespoons fish sauce
2   teaspoons sugar
1   pound medium shrimp without tails,
       peeled and deveined
2   cups cooked rice, preferably jasmine
       Freshly squeezed juice of 1 lemon
       (3 to 4 tablespoons)
½   cup coarsely chopped fresh cilantro
       (leaves only)

1. Put the chicken broth, chile-garlic sauce, celery, and carrot in a medium saucepan and bring to a simmer. Add the lemongrass, fish sauce, and sugar and simmer another 5 minutes.

2. Stir in the shrimp and rice and simmer just until the shrimp are pink and opaque, 2 to 3 minutes more.

3. Pull the saucepan from the heat and stir in the lemon juice and cilantro. Ladle the soup into warmed bowls.

FROM THE KITCHENS
Keep peeled and deveined shrimp on hand in the freezer. They defrost quickly in a bowl with cool running water flowing over it. If your shrimp aren't already deveined, use a paring knife to make a cut down the outside of the curve of the shrimp, then pull out the thin gray vein you find.

1. Remove the tough outer layers of the lemongrass stalk (usually two or three pieces). 2. Cut off the root end of the lemongrass.

3. Place your knife flat against the cut end and trim stalk. 4. Slice the stalk starting at the bottom and moving up until it becomes too tough and woody.

Twice is nice when it comes to rice, so next time make a double batch. Use the leftovers in this soup, a salad, or stuffing.

manhattan whole clam chowder

4 to 6 servings

1½ tablespoons olive oil
3 ounces diced pancetta (about ½ cup) (see tip, page 305)
1½ celery ribs with leaves, thinly sliced
1 medium onion, chopped
¼ teaspoon crushed red pepper flakes
¼ cup minced garlic
¼ cup tomato paste
2 cups bottled clam juice
2 cups low-sodium chicken broth
6 small red-skinned potatoes, quartered
1 tablespoon fresh thyme
1 bay leaf
1 28-ounce can whole peeled tomatoes (with liquid), roughly chopped
¼ teaspoon Worcestershire sauce
Freshly ground black pepper
36 littleneck clams, scrubbed
2 tablespoons chopped fresh flat-leaf parsley
Crusty bread, for serving (optional)

1. Heat the oil in a large soup pot over medium heat. Add the pancetta and cook until just brown. Add the celery, onion, and red pepper flakes and cook, stirring occasionally, until soft, about 10 minutes. Add the garlic and cook, stirring frequently, until fragrant, about 2 minutes. Stir in the tomato paste and cook for 2 minutes more.

2. Increase the heat and add the clam juice, chicken broth, potatoes, thyme, and bay leaf. Bring the soup to a boil, lower the heat, and simmer, uncovered, until the potatoes are tender, about 15 minutes.

3. Stir in the tomatoes and their juices, the Worcestershire sauce, and black pepper to taste and simmer for 5 minutes. Add the clams, cover, and simmer until the clams open, about 8 minutes. (Discard any unopened clams.) Remove the bay leaf. Divide the soup among warm bowls and sprinkle each serving with some of the parsley. Serve immediately with crusty bread, if desired.

FROM THE KITCHENS

Littlenecks are small, hard clams that run about 1½ inches across. As for all clams and mussels, buy those that are firmly closed (or that shut when tapped) and are free of any strong aromas. When you come home from the market, take the clams out of their bag and put them in a colander. Cover the clams with a damp towel and set the colander in a bowl of ice in the refrigerator. If storing for a day or more, pour off the melted ice and add fresh as needed.

quick beef chili | 4 servings

3   tablespoons extra-virgin olive oil
1   medium yellow onion, chopped
5   cloves garlic, chopped
1   tablespoon kosher salt
2   teaspoons chili powder
1   teaspoon dried oregano
1   tablespoon tomato paste
1   chipotle chile en adobo, finely
      chopped, with 1 tablespoon of
      sauce (see tip, page 157)
1   pound ground beef chuck
1   cup Mexican lager-style beer
      (about ¾ of a bottle or can)
1   14½-ounce can whole peeled
      tomatoes, with their juices
1   cup chicken broth
      (about ½ small can)
1   15-ounce can kidney beans, rinsed
      and drained

FOR SERVING
    Grated Monterey Jack cheese or
      other Mexican cheeses such as
      queso blanco, queso fresco, or
      cotija añejo; sour cream; tortilla
      chips; cilantro sprigs and/or sliced
      scallions, for garnish (optional)

1. Heat the olive oil in a large, heavy skillet over medium-high heat. Add the onion, garlic, salt, chili powder, and oregano and cook, stirring, until fragrant, about 3 minutes. Stir in the tomato paste and the chipotle chile and its sauce; cook 1 minute more. Add the beef, breaking it up with a wooden spoon, and cook until the meat loses its raw color, about 3 minutes. Add the beer and simmer until reduced by about half, about 5 minutes.

2. Add the tomatoes to the chili by crushing them through your fingers into the skillet and add the juices from the can. Add the broth and beans and bring to a boil. Cook, uncovered, stirring occasionally, until thickened, 8 to 10 minutes.

3. Ladle the chili into bowls and serve with the garnishes of your choice.

FROM THE KITCHENS
• A skillet's larger surface area reduces sauces faster than simmering them in a saucepan.
• Chili's the kind of food that everyone has an opinion on. There are all kinds of regional chili traditions, from Cincinnati's cinnamon-and-noodles to Texan cubed-meat-and-spices (with nothing else)—and there are countless books on the subject. If you're looking to become a chilihead (which is what the International Chili Society calls its members), check out our website (foodnetwork.com) for several hundred recipes.

chicken, spinach & gnocchi soup

4 servings

Kosher salt
2 cups prepared gnocchi
4 cups low-sodium chicken broth
4 cloves garlic, thinly sliced
2 tablespoons unsalted butter
Pinch sugar
3 cups cleaned baby spinach leaves
2 cups shredded cooked chicken
Freshly ground black pepper
Hunk of good Parmesan or other grana-style (hard grating) cheese

1. Bring a medium saucepan of cold water to a boil over high heat, then salt it generously. Add the gnocchi and cook, stirring occasionally, until al dente, about 3 minutes. Drain and set aside.

2. Meanwhile, put ¼ cup of the chicken broth, garlic, butter, and sugar in a large saucepan over medium-low heat, bring it to a simmer, and cook, uncovered, until the garlic is tender, about 1 minute. Add the spinach and let it wilt for about 30 seconds. Add the remaining 3¾ cups chicken broth and the chicken and bring just to a simmer. Stir in the gnocchi and bring to a full boil. Taste and season with salt and a generous amount of pepper to taste—use a light hand with the salt because the cheese is salty.

3. Ladle the soup into warmed shallow bowls and shower each with some freshly grated cheese.

FROM THE KITCHENS
Save your leftover rinds of Parmesan and add to soups, braises, and sauces. It beefs up flavor and also makes use of every ounce of your pricey Parmesan.

thai-style chicken noodle soup

6 servings

Vegetable oil
6 cloves garlic, thinly sliced crosswise
5 ounces rice stick noodles
7 cups low-sodium chicken broth
¼ cup fish sauce (see tip, page 160)
3 scallions (white and green parts),
   thinly sliced on an angle
1 small carrot, peeled and thinly sliced
   One-inch piece ginger, unpeeled and
   thinly sliced into coins
1 teaspoon sugar
2 cups shredded roasted chicken
⅓ cup roughly chopped fresh dill fronds
   (stems and leaves)
⅓ cup roughly chopped fresh cilantro
⅓ cup torn fresh basil
⅓ cup roughly chopped fresh mint
   Lime wedges

1. Heat about ½ inch of oil in a small, heavy-bottomed skillet over medium-low heat until just warm. Add the garlic and fry, stirring occasionally, until fragrant and golden, about 15 minutes. Scoop the garlic from the oil with a slotted spoon, drain, and cool on a piece of paper towel. (Reserve the fragrant oil for use in salad dressings or marinades or for drizzling over grilled meat, fish, or bread.) While the garlic cooks, soak the noodles in a large bowl of warm water to soften, about 10 minutes. Drain.

2. Put the chicken broth, fish sauce, scallions, carrot, ginger, and sugar in a soup pot and bring to a simmer, uncovered, over medium-high heat. Add the noodles and chicken and simmer until noodles are the desired doneness. Stir in the dill, cilantro, basil, and mint. Ladle the soup into warm bowls and sprinkle with some of the reserved crisped garlic. Serve with lime wedges to squeeze over soup.

roasted chicken stock

makes about 3 quarts

5 pounds mixed chicken bones and
   wings, backs, and/or necks
2 tablespoons vegetable oil or
   chicken fat
3 medium carrots, quartered
2 ribs celery, quartered
1 to 2 dark green leek tops (optional)
3 cloves garlic, unpeeled
1 large tomato, chopped
3 generous sprigs flat-leaf parsley
2 sprigs fresh thyme or 1 teaspoon
   dried
2 bay leaves
¼ teaspoons black peppercorns
2 cloves

1. Preheat the oven to 450°F. Spread the bones out in a large roasting pan. Roast until golden brown, about 1 ½ hours. Drain and discard any liquid the bones give off as they roast.

2. While the bones roast, heat the oil in a stockpot over medium-high heat. Add the vegetables and cook, stirring occasionally, until brown, about 30 minutes.

3. When bones are cooked, transfer them to the stockpot; add a splash of water to the roasting pan, stir to scrape up any brown bits, and pour the liquid into the stockpot. Add parsley, thyme, bay leaves, peppercorns, and cloves and enough cold water to cover the bones. Bring to a boil over high heat, then reduce heat to keep stock at a gentle simmer for 4 to 5 hours. Skim any fat or foamy scum that rises to the surface.

4. Strain stock through a fine-meshed strainer into 1 large or several smaller containers. Cool stock by placing container(s) in an ice-water bath or in very cold water in the sink. Stir stock occasionally to cool it as quickly as possible. Cover containers tightly and refrigerate up to 5 days or freeze up to 3 months.

chicken & andouille gumbo | 6 to 8 servings

8   cups Roasted Chicken Stock
       (see recipe, page 84)
1   head garlic, unpeeled, halved
       horizontally
1   heaping tablespoon pickling spice
1   teaspoon crushed red pepper flakes
1   teaspoon anise seeds (optional)
1   bay leaf
1   large strip lemon zest
6   tablespoons vegetable oil or
       rendered chicken fat
2   medium onions, sliced
2   green or red bell peppers, stemmed,
       seeded, and cut into thin strips
1   rib celery, chopped
4   cloves garlic, chopped
6   ounces fresh okra, tops trimmed and
       halved lengthwise
1   15-ounce can peeled whole plum
       tomatoes, with their juice
4   teaspoons kosher salt, plus
       additional for seasoning
    Freshly ground black pepper
½   cup all-purpose flour, plus additional
       for dredging
6   whole chicken legs, split into
       drumsticks and thighs
       (about 6 pounds)
12 ounces raw andouille sausage, in
       one piece
3   scallions (white and green parts),
       thinly sliced on the diagonal
4   cups cooked white rice

1. Put the stock in a medium saucepan along with the garlic head, pickling spice, pepper flakes, anise seeds, if desired, bay leaf, and lemon zest. Bring to a boil over high heat, turn the heat as low as it will go, cover, and let the stock steep.

2. Heat 2 tablespoons of the chicken fat or vegetable oil in a large Dutch oven or heavy pot over medium heat, add onions, and cook until soft, brown, and aromatic, about 20 minutes. Stir in bell peppers, celery, and chopped garlic and cook 10 minutes. Add okra and cook until soft, about 5 minutes. Add tomatoes, crushing them through your fingers into the pot, their juices, the 4 teaspoons salt, and a generous amount of pepper.

3. Meanwhile, pour a good amount of flour into a shallow baking dish. Heat a large heavy skillet over medium-high heat and add 2 tablespoons of the chicken fat. Season the chicken with salt and black pepper to taste and dredge in flour. Cook chicken in batches until brown on both sides but not cooked through, about 15 minutes total, transferring the pieces to a platter as they cook. Then cook the sausage until brown, about 10 minutes. Set the skillet aside with the drippings. Slice the sausage and add it to the vegetables along with the chicken. Strain the chicken stock into the pot and simmer while you make the roux.

4. Add the remaining 2 tablespoons of chicken fat to the skillet and heat on medium until shimmering. Whisk in the ½ cup flour and cook, stirring with a wooden spoon in a figure-eight pattern, until the roux is a dark mahogany brown, about 10 minutes. Pull the pan from the heat and cool slightly. Discard any excess fat that comes to the surface and then whisk the roux into the gumbo. Bring the gumbo to a full boil, then reduce the heat so that it simmers gently for 15 minutes more. Stir in the scallions. Remove bay leaf. Serve the gumbo with rice.

Cocktails with paper umbrellas are for tourists. Those in the know go for this devilishly spicy Caribbean Pepper Pot instead.

caribbean chicken pepper pot

6 servings

¼ cup vegetable oil

1 medium onion, halved and sliced

2 bay leaves

1½ tablespoons kosher salt, plus
    additional for seasoning

2 teaspoons ground allspice

1 heaping teaspoon dried thyme

⅓ cup tomato paste
  Freshly ground black pepper

8 skinless, bone-in chicken thighs
  (about 2⅔ pounds)

3½ cups water

1 Scotch bonnet chile, pierced
  (if you like it really hot, mince it)

8 ounces fresh okra, trimmed,
  halved crosswise

3 thick sweet potatoes (about
  2 pounds), each cut into
  4 rounds with skin on

1 bunch collard greens (about 1 pound),
  stems removed, chopped

1. Heat a 7-liter pressure cooker over medium heat. Stir in the oil, onion, bay leaves, 1½ tablespoons salt, the allspice, and thyme; cook, uncovered, until soft, about 8 minutes. Increase the heat to high, stir in the tomato paste, and cook, stirring and scraping, until it turns brick red, about 2 minutes.

2. Season the chicken with some salt and black pepper to taste and add it to the pot, turning to coat with the tomato and onion. Stir in the water, then add the chile, okra, potatoes, and collard greens in that order. You don't need to stir—the collards will cook down and keep everything moist as the cooker comes up to pressure. Close the pressure cooker lid and bring the pressure up to high (which can take up to 10 minutes), then reduce the heat, if necessary, to maintain an even pressure for 7 minutes. Remove from the heat and gently press the pressure indicator stem until no more steam comes out. Carefully open the pot. Remove and discard bay leaves. Ladle the stew into bowls and serve.

FROM THE KITCHENS
Not for the faint of heart, Scotch bonnets are about as fiery as a chile gets. If you can't find one, substitute a habañero.

sandwiches, pizza & quesadillas

Who says you need a knife and fork to eat good food properly? Here's to handheld fare of every kind—and to good manners, too.

Everyone knows Thanksgiving leftovers are tastier than the meal itself. This sandwich, which uses both cranberry sauce and roast turkey, is no exception.

monte cristos

4 servings

¼ cup Dijon mustard
¼ cup mayonnaise
8 slices challah bread
   (about 1 inch thick)
6 ounces sliced Muenster cheese
12 ounces thinly sliced cooked
   turkey breast
   Kosher salt
   Freshly ground black pepper
⅔ cup whole-berry cranberry sauce
   or relish
3 large eggs
¼ cup milk
4 tablespoons unsalted butter

1. Mix the mustard and mayonnaise together in a small bowl. Lay the bread on a work surface and spread about 1 tablespoon of the mustard mixture on one side of each piece.

2. Lay the cheese on half of the bread slices, top with the turkey, and season with salt and pepper to taste. Spread the cranberry sauce on the remaining 4 bread slices and close the sandwiches, pressing each one together slightly.

3. In a pie plate or other shallow dish, whisk the eggs with the milk and salt and pepper to taste. Heat 2 large skillets over medium-low heat and divide the butter between them. Dip each sandwich in the egg mixture to coat completely—including the sides. Lay 2 sandwiches in each skillet and cook until bread is golden brown and cheese has melted, turning once, about 5 minutes per side. Halve and serve immediately.

FROM THE KITCHENS

We like our Monte Cristos with other meats, too, such as leftover roast pork or chicken.

muffuletta | 4 servings

OLIVE SALAD
- ½ cup extra-virgin olive oil
- 3 tablespoons water
- 1 small carrot, peeled and thinly sliced
- 1 small rib celery, thinly sliced
- ½ cup small cauliflower florets
- ½ teaspoon dried thyme
- ½ teaspoon dried oregano
- ¾ cup pitted large green olives, such as Manzanilla, finely chopped
- ¼ cup pitted black olives, such as kalamata, finely chopped
- 2 tablespoons chopped jarred pimiento
- ½ teaspoon kosher salt
- 1 tablespoon chopped fresh flat-leaf parsley

SANDWICHES
- 1 6-inch round Italian bread with sesame seeds
- 2 tablespoons extra-virgin olive oil
- 6 ounces sliced provolone cheese
- 6 ounces sliced mortadella
- 4 ounces sliced soppressata (see tip, page 315), sweet or hot

1. To make the olive salad: Put the oil, water, carrot, celery, cauliflower, thyme, and oregano in a medium saucepan. Bring to a boil over medium heat, cover, reduce the heat to medium-low, and then simmer until the vegetables are crisp-tender, about 6 minutes. Transfer the mixture to a bowl and stir in the olives, pimiento, and salt. Cool, then add the parsley.

2. To assemble the sandwich: Slice the bread in half horizontally, then pull out some of the inside from each half to make a pocket. Brush the inside of the top half with olive oil. Pack the bottom half with the olive salad. Layer the cheese and meats over the salad and top with the remaining bread. Wrap the muffuletta very tightly with plastic wrap. Place the sandwich in a broad, shallow container and weight it with something heavy (we use a cast-iron skillet) for at least 1 hour at room temperature. Cut muffuletta into quarters and serve with plenty of napkins.

FROM THE KITCHENS
Olive salad is what separates a muffuletta from any other hero, but don't confine its use to this sandwich. It pairs well with grilled fish, chicken, or steak. Make a double batch and keep it on hand to round out a quick dinner.

extra-virgin olive oil

celery

cauliflower

black olives

pimiento

green olives

flat-leaf parsley

dried oregano

carrots

dried thyme

A New Orleans favorite, this incredibly indulgent sandwich can be found almost nowhere else but The Big Easy. Now you can bring it home where it belongs.

southwestern pulled brisket sandwiches

4 servings

3 pounds beef brisket
Kosher salt
Freshly ground black pepper
2 tablespoons vegetable oil
5 cloves garlic, peeled and smashed
1 Spanish onion, halved and
   thinly sliced
1 tablespoon chili powder
2 teaspoons ground coriander
2 teaspoons ground cumin
¼ cup apple cider vinegar
1½ cups water
1 14½-ounce can whole peeled
   tomatoes, with their juices
2 whole canned chipotle chiles
   en adobo
2 bay leaves
3 tablespoons molasses
Soft sandwich buns
Pickled jalapeños

1. Season the beef generously with salt and pepper to taste. Heat a large, heavy skillet over medium-high heat. Add the oil and heat just until beginning to smoke. Add the meat and cook, turning once, until browned on both sides, about 10 minutes total. Transfer the meat to the slow cooker; leave the skillet on the heat.

2. Add garlic, onion, chili powder, coriander, and cumin to drippings in the skillet and stir until fragrant, about 1 minute. Add vinegar and boil until it's almost gone, scraping the bottom of the pan with a wooden spoon. Stir in water and pour the mixture over the brisket. Crush the tomatoes through your fingers into the slow cooker; add the tomato juices, chipotles, bay leaves, and molasses. Cover the cooker, set it on LOW, and cook the brisket until it pulls apart easily with a fork, about 8 hours.

3. To serve, leave the meat in the slow cooker and use 2 forks to pull it apart and stir it evenly into the sauce; season with salt and pepper to taste. Remove and discard bay leaves. Pile the meat on sandwich buns and serve with jalapeños. (This is also great rolled up in tortillas.)

FROM THE KITCHENS
Perfectly suited to long, slow cooking, brisket can be bought in two different cuts. We prefer the "point cut" because it has more fat—which we all know means more flavor.

Slow-cooked homemade barbecue has never been easier. Get all of the sweet, tangy, and smoky attributes of pit cooking without lighting a fire.

miso chicken sandwiches
with ginger mayonnaise

4 servings

CHICKEN

- ¼ cup light miso (see tip, page 76)
- ¼ cup dark sesame oil
- ¼ cup soy sauce
- 1 tablespoon finely grated peeled fresh ginger
- 4 boneless, skinless chicken breast halves, pounded very thin (about 1 pound total)

MAYONNAISE

- ½ cup mayonnaise
- 2 teaspoons rice vinegar
- 2 teaspoons soy sauce
- 2 teaspoons finely grated peeled fresh ginger
- 1 teaspoon Asian chili sauce or hot pepper sauce
- ½ teaspoon dark sesame oil

SANDWICHES

- 8 slices multigrain sliced sandwich bread
- 1 Hass avocado, halved, seeded, peeled, and thinly sliced
- ½ medium cucumber, thinly sliced
- 1 cup sprouts (such as alfalfa), broccoli, or radishes

1. For the chicken: Heat the broiler and line a broiler pan with aluminum foil, or prepare an outdoor grill. Stir the miso, sesame oil, soy sauce, and ginger together in a bowl and brush both sides of the chicken with the mixture. Broil on the prepared pan, 6 inches from the heat, or grill, turning once, until cooked through, about 2 minutes per side.

2. For the flavored mayonnaise: Whisk the mayonnaise with the vinegar, soy sauce, ginger, chili sauce or hot pepper sauce, and sesame oil in a small bowl.

3. To assemble the sandwiches: Halve each chicken breast on an angle. Spread 4 slices of bread with the flavored mayonnaise and top with the chicken, avocado and cucumber slices, sprouts, and remaining bread slices. Cut sandwiches in half and serve.

patty melts | 4 servings

8   ounces ground sirloin
8   ounces ground chuck
½   teaspoon kosher salt, plus additional
        for seasoning
     Freshly ground black pepper
3   tablespoons vegetable oil
2   medium onions, thinly sliced
2   to 3 tablespoons unsalted butter,
        softened
8   slices rye bread
8   slices Swiss or American cheese
        (about 3 ounces)

1. Break both meats by hand into small pieces onto a large piece of waxed or parchment paper. Sprinkle the ½ teaspoon salt and some pepper over the meat. Bring the meat together by hand, avoiding kneading it, and don't worry if it seems loosely knit. (This light touch keeps the meat from getting tough.) Divide into 4 portions, then into balls by gently tossing from hand to hand; finally, press each one into an oval patty somewhat larger than the slices of bread.

2. Heat 1 tablespoon of the oil in a large cast-iron skillet over medium heat. Add the onions, season with some salt and pepper, and cook until golden, about 7 minutes. Put in a bowl. Wipe out the skillet and add another 1 tablespoon of oil. Cook the patties in batches in the remaining oil until well browned, about 1 to 3 minutes per side for medium burgers.

3. Butter each bread slice on one side. Lay the bread, butter side down, on the counter. Divide the onions among 4 bread slices and top with a slice of cheese, a patty, another slice of cheese, and a slice of bread, butter side up. Heat the cast-iron skillet over medium heat. Cook the sandwiches, in batches if needed, turning once, until the bread is lightly browned and the cheese has melted, 1 to 2 minutes per side. Halve the melts and serve.

blue cheese steak sandwiches | 6 servings

SANDWICHES

- 6 crusty rolls, such as Portuguese, split
- ⅓ cup Dijon mustard
- 1½ pounds grilled medium-rare steak, thinly sliced
  Kosher salt and freshly ground black pepper
- 12 ounces Saga blue cheese, cut into 12 slices (see tip, below)
  Roasted Shallots (see recipe, below), roughly chopped
- 4 cups loosely packed watercress, washed and dried

ROASTED SHALLOTS

- 8 shallots, unpeeled
- ¼ cup extra-virgin olive oil
- 1 tablespoon kosher salt, plus additional for seasoning
  Freshly ground black pepper

1. Preheat the broiler. Spread the rolls out on a pan and toast on both sides.

2. Slather the bottom half of each roll with some of the mustard and top with slices of the steak, overlapping the slices slightly. Season to taste with salt and pepper. Cover each portion of meat with 2 slices of cheese. Broil until the cheese is lightly browned and melted, about 1 minute.

3. Transfer the open-faced sandwiches to the work surface. Top each sandwich with some of the roasted shallots and watercress. Slather the tops with the remaining mustard and cover the sandwiches. Slice in half and serve.

ROASTED SHALLOTS

1. Preheat the oven to 400°F. In a large bowl, toss the shallots with olive oil, 1 tablespoon salt, and pepper to taste in a large bowl. Spread out on an aluminum foil-lined baking sheet. Bake until the shallots are very tender, about 40 minutes. Set aside to cool.

2. Slice off the tips of the shallots and discard. Gently squeeze the shallots from their skins and season with additional salt and pepper to taste.

FROM THE KITCHENS

- Saga blue, a delicately veined blue cheese from Denmark, has the texture of a firm cream cheese and a mellower flavor than many other blue cheeses.
- Don't hide your wooden cutting boards in the kitchen. A well-worn board or a pizza paddle can be the perfect backdrop for a spread of sandwiches, tarts, or cheeses.

lamb burgers with feta

BURGERS

2	pounds ground lamb
½	cup plain whole-milk yogurt
1	tablespoon dried savory
3	cloves garlic, minced
	Finely grated zest of 1 lemon
¼	to ½ teaspoon crushed red pepper
1½	teaspoons kosher salt, plus additional for seasoning
	Freshly ground black pepper
7	ounces feta cheese, crumbled into chunky pieces
	Extra-virgin olive oil, for brushing
6	small plain pita pocket breads (see tip, below)
	Sliced onions, tomatoes, and cucumbers, for garnish
	Arugula and fresh mint leaves, for garnish
	Tzatziki (see recipe, below) (optional)

TZATZIKI

Makes about 1 cup

2	cups plain whole-milk yogurt or 1 cup Middle Eastern-style plain yogurt
1	cucumber, peeled and seeded
2	teaspoons kosher salt, plus additional for seasoning
½	garlic clove, peeled
1	tablespoon extra-virgin olive oil
1	teaspoon freshly squeezed lemon juice
½	teaspoon dried mint, finely crumbled

1. Prepare an outdoor grill with a medium-high fire.

2. Using your hands, mix the ground lamb, yogurt, savory, garlic, zest, red pepper, 1½ teaspoons salt, and black pepper to taste in a large bowl. Gently mix in the crumbled feta. Divide meat mixture into 6 equal portions, then into balls by gently tossing them from hand to hand. Shape into 1-inch-thick loosely packed oval patties. Press the center of each patty so it is slightly thinner than the edges.

3. Brush the burgers with olive oil and season with salt and black pepper to taste. Grill the burgers, turning once, until firm to the touch with a little bit of give, 8 to 10 minutes. Set aside while grilling pitas. Slit a burger-size opening in the pitas, brush with olive oil, and season with salt and black pepper to taste. Grill until lightly toasted. Serve the burgers in the pitas with the garnishes of your choice and Tzatziki, if desired.

TZATZIKI

1. Stir yogurt and put in a coffee filter-lined strainer over a bowl. Let drain in refrigerator for at least 12 hours or overnight. (If using thick Greek or Middle-Eastern yogurt, skip this step). Discard watery liquid in bottom of bowl and put drained yogurt in a medium bowl.

2. Grate cucumber on wide-holed side of box grater into another bowl. Sprinkle grated cucumber with 2 teaspoons salt and toss gently. Set aside 20 minutes, then squeeze cucumbers to express as much liquid as possible. Add the cucumber to the bowl of yogurt.

3. Smash garlic, sprinkle with a generous pinch of salt, and, with the flat side of a large knife, mash and smear to a coarse paste. Add garlic, oil, lemon juice, and mint to cucumber-yogurt mixture and stir to combine. Refrigerate for about an hour so flavors come together.

FROM THE KITCHENS

▪ We found the "mini" pitas to be perfectly sized. The burgers fit snugly in the pocket without excess bread.
▪ We love savory and know you'll be wild about it too. This familiar Mediterranean flavoring tastes like a blend of thyme, oregano, and a bit of rosemary. There are two varieties of this underutilized herb—summer and winter. Both are fantastic—very food-friendly with meat, fish, poultry, potatoes, eggs, or tomatoes.

grilled latin pork burgers

6 servings

⅓ cup lard or corn oil

6 cloves garlic, chopped

2 tablespoons dried oregano, preferably Mexican

2 tablespoons ground ancho chile powder

2 tablespoons sugar

1½ teaspoons ground coriander

1 teaspoon ground cumin

½ teaspoon ground allspice

¼ teaspoon ground cloves

1¾ pounds coarsely ground pork

2 teaspoons kosher salt, plus additional for seasoning

Freshly ground black pepper

1 large red onion, sliced into ½-inch-thick rounds

Olive oil, for brushing

6 thick slices Jack or Cheddar cheese (about 8 ounces)

3 hero rolls, halved crosswise to make 6 buns

1. Heat the lard in a skillet over medium-low heat and add the garlic, oregano, ancho chile powder, sugar, coriander, cumin, allspice, and cloves. Cook and stir until fragrant and garlic is golden, about 3 minutes. Transfer to a small bowl to cool completely.

2. Prepare an outdoor grill with a medium-hot fire.

3. Using your hands, gently mix the spice mixture into the ground pork in a large bowl. Season with 2 teaspoons of the salt and black pepper to taste. Divide meat mixture into 6 equal portions, then into balls by gently tossing from hand to hand. Gently shape into ½-inch-thick loosely packed oval patties. Press the center of each patty so it is slightly thinner than the edges. Thread a long skewer through the sides of the onion slices (if you're using a wooden skewer, soak it in water 30 minutes before grilling).

4. Brush the burgers and onions with oil and season with salt and black pepper to taste. Grill the burgers on the first side until lightly charred, about 5 minutes. Flip and continue to cook just until cooked through, about 5 more minutes. Lay a slice of cheese on top of each burger, cover with a disposable aluminum pan, and cook until melted, about 2 minutes more. Grill the onions until charred and tender, about 12 minutes, turning once. Cool slightly and break apart. Let burgers rest off the heat while toasting the buns.

5. Brush the buns with oil and grill until lightly toasted. Serve the burgers on the buns with the grilled onions.

salmon burgers | 4 servings

1¼ pounds skinless salmon
     fillets, very cold
1 large egg
1 shallot, minced
2 tablespoons chopped fresh flat-leaf
     parsley
1 tablespoon chopped fresh dill
2 teaspoons whole-grain mustard
2 teaspoons kosher salt, plus
     additional for grilling
1 teaspoon finely grated lemon zest
  Olive oil, for grilling
  Freshly ground black pepper
4 hamburger buns or English muffins
  Tomato slices (optional)
  Tartar sauce, mustard, or other
     condiments of your choice

1. Cut the salmon into 1-inch cubes and put in the freezer for 5 minutes. Process the egg, shallot, parsley, dill, mustard, salt, and lemon zest in a food processor until fairly smooth. Add half of the chilled salmon and pulse to make a chunky paste. Add the remaining salmon and pulse 10 times to make a rough-textured mixture. Wet your hands with cool water and shape the mixture into 4 patties, each about ¾ inch thick. Place each patty on a square of waxed or parchment paper and refrigerate, lightly covered, for 30 minutes.

2. Heat a stovetop grill pan or outdoor grill to medium-high heat. Brush the tops of the patties with olive oil and season with salt and pepper. Pick each patty up by its paper and turn it oil-side down onto the pan or grill; the paper should peel right off. Cook the patties without pressing, and don't move them until you see distinct grill marks, about 3 minutes. Brush the tops lightly with olive oil and season to taste with salt and pepper. Flip the patties and cook until they give just a bit when you press them with your fingertip, about 1½ minutes. Transfer the burgers to a platter, cover loosely with foil, and let rest for 2 minutes. Toast the buns or English muffins until golden. Serve the burgers on the toasted buns with tomato, if desired, tartar sauce, mustard, or your favorite condiment.

An East Coast specialty, one bite of these luxurious lobster rolls and you can almost smell the salt air.

lobster rolls | 4 servings

¼ cup mayonnaise
1 tablespoon freshly squeezed lemon
   juice
2 teaspoons Dijon mustard
1 small rib celery, peeled and minced
1 tablespoon minced fresh chives
2 teaspoons minced fresh flat-leaf
   parsley
½ teaspoon kosher salt
   Freshly ground black pepper
2 teaspoons minced fresh tarragon
   or basil (optional)
2 cups diced cooked lobster meat
   (about 14 ounces) (see note, right)
2 teaspoons unsalted butter
4 hot dog rolls, preferably New
   England-style (top-split, with
   pale sides)

1. Mix the mayonnaise, lemon juice, mustard, celery, chives, parsley, salt, and pepper to taste in a large bowl. Using a rubber spatula, fold in first the tarragon or basil, if desired, and then the lobster until just combined. Refrigerate, covered, for at least 1 and up to 24 hours.

2. When ready to serve, melt the butter in a large skillet over medium-high heat. Toast the sides of the rolls in the hot butter, two at a time, until golden, about 30 seconds per side. Split the rolls open, mound the lobster salad inside, and serve immediately.

FROM THE KITCHENS

• It goes without saying that a great lobster roll should be full of nuggets of fresh lobster. But passionate fans of this enduring New England sandwich—and we count ourselves among that crowd—feel strongly about the bun as well. The plain roll in contrast to the lavish lobster is what makes this summer sandwich so sublime.

• To dispatch a live lobster humanely before it's dropped into boiling water, hold a sharp chef's knife over the lobster's head, right where there's an "x" in the shell. Push the point of the knife rapidly all of the way down to the cutting board, then quickly push the length of the blade forward onto the board. Drop the lobster into a very large pot of boiling water and cook for 6 to 8 minutes, or until the shell is completely red. Remove the lobster from the pot and let cool. To remove the meat, twist off the tail from the body. Remove the claws by twisting them off. Pull off the flippers at the end of the tail and push the meat out through the front end of the shell with your fingers. Bend the lower, smaller pincer on the claw side-to-side and pull it away from the claw. With the back of a chef's knife, crack the top side of the claw. Open the claw and pull out the meat. With kitchen shears, cut open the smaller pincer and arm sections and remove the meat from those also.

grilled halloumi, scallion & mint flatbread | 6 servings

⅓ cup plus 2 tablespoons extra-virgin olive oil, plus additional for brushing
2 teaspoons crumbled dried mint
¾ teaspoon crushed red pepper
1 pound halloumi cheese (see tip, below)
½ clove garlic, peeled
Kosher salt
1 large ripe tomato (about 12 ounces), cored and roughly chopped
1 tablespoon capers
Freshly ground black pepper
2 bunches scallions (white and green parts), trimmed
3 flatbreads or pocketless pita breads

1. Put ⅓ cup of the olive oil, the mint, and red pepper in a shallow dish. Slice the cheese into ½-inch-thick pieces (about 12 slices) and put in a single layer in the oil, turning to coat. Set aside at room temperature for 2 hours or cover and refrigerate for up to 24 hours.

2. Prepare an outdoor grill with a medium fire.

3. Smash the garlic clove, sprinkle with a pinch of salt, and, with the flat side of a large knife, mash and smear the mixture to a coarse paste. Toss tomato, capers, garlic, and remaining 2 tablespoons olive oil in a bowl and season with salt and black pepper to taste.

4. Place the cheese on the grill, reserving the marinade. Dip the scallions in the marinade, then grill them, turning as needed, until wilted and lightly charred, about 3 minutes. Coarsely chop the scallions. Cook the cheese, turning as needed, until browned, about 5 minutes per side. Return the grilled cheese to the marinade, if desired—especially if it marinated for a short amount of time.

5. Brush the flatbreads with olive oil and grill to warm through. Cut the breads in half, tuck 2 pieces cheese and some scallions into each folded flatbread half, top with the tomato mixture, and serve.

FROM THE KITCHENS
Halloumi, a brined sheep's or goat's milk cheese from Cyprus, is finding its way into supermarkets and good cheese stores. It is firm and doesn't melt like other cheeses, but browns superbly. It's the ultimate grilling cheese. In a pinch, use a dry feta as a stand-in.

grilled fajitas | 4 servings

STEAK
- ½   cup lime juice (about 4 limes)
- ½   cup chopped fresh cilantro leaves, roots, and stems
- ½   cup sherry vinegar
- ¼   cup extra-virgin olive oil
- 1   small red onion, chopped
- 1   jalapeño, roughly chopped
- 1   teaspoon freshly ground black pepper
- 1¼   pounds beef skirt steak

PICO DE GALLO
- 1   large ripe tomato, cored and chopped
- 1   to 2 serrano or jalapeño peppers, minced
- ¼   medium red onion, minced
- ½   teaspoon kosher salt, plus pinch for garlic
- 1   clove garlic, peeled
- ¼   cup chopped fresh cilantro
- 2   tablespoons extra-virgin olive oil

PEPPERS AND ONIONS
- 2   poblano peppers, seeded and sliced
- 1   red bell pepper, seeded and sliced
- 1   medium red onion, sliced
- 1   tablespoon extra-virgin olive oil
- 1   tablespoon dried oregano
- 1   teaspoon kosher salt, plus additional for seasoning
-   Freshly ground black pepper
- 1   tablespoon sherry vinegar

FIXIN'S
- 8   large flour tortillas
- 1   Hass avocado, halved, seeded, peeled, and thinly sliced
- 2   cups shredded cheddar cheese (about 8 ounces)
- ½   cup sour cream

1. For steak: Whisk all marinade ingredients except steak in a large shallow dish. Add steak to marinade, turning to coat. Cover and refrigerate several hours.

2. Prepare an outdoor grill with a hot fire.

3. For the pico de gallo: Toss tomatoes, chiles, onion, and the ½ teaspoon salt in a bowl. Smash the garlic, sprinkle with the pinch of salt, and, with flat side of a large knife, mash and smear to a coarse paste. Stir garlic paste into salsa with cilantro and olive oil.

4. For peppers and onions: On a large sheet of heavy aluminum foil, toss peppers and onion with olive oil, oregano, 1 teaspoon salt, and black pepper to taste. Bring edges of foil up and crimp closed. Place package on edge of grill and cook until vegetables are tender, about 10 minutes. Season with vinegar and salt and black pepper to taste.

5. Meanwhile, remove steak from marinade, pat dry, and season with salt to taste. Grill, turning once, until slightly charred and crisp, 4 to 6 minutes total. Rest steak for about 5 minutes. Grill tortillas until lightly charred, 1 to 2 minutes. Cut meat into 4-inch- long segments, then cut against the grain on an angle. Transfer to a platter and serve with vegetables and fixin's.

panini with bresaola, endive & provolone

4 servings

1 tablespoon unsalted butter
1 Belgian endive, separated into leaves
½ teaspoon sugar
1 teaspoon balsamic vinegar
4 ciabatta rolls
4 slices aged provolone cheese
   (about 4 ounces)
8 thin slices bresaola (Italian
   air-dried beef) (about 2 ounces)
   Extra-virgin olive oil

1. Melt the butter in a large skillet over medium heat. Add the endive leaves, rounded side down, and cook until slightly wilted and brown. Turn the leaves, press gently with a spatula, and cook until pliable, about 3 minutes. Sprinkle with sugar, add the vinegar, turn the endive to coat, and cook until lightly glazed, about 1 minute. Cool.

2. Heat a sandwich press to medium-high. Slice the rounded tops off the rolls and halve horizontally. Lay a slice of provolone on the bottom half of each roll, followed by ¼ of the bresaola and endive, and finally the top of the roll. Brush both sides of the panini lightly with olive oil—take care not to soak the bread or the panini will be greasy. Cook each panini in the press until the cheese melts and the bread browns, about 4 minutes. Serve.

FROM THE KITCHENS
Ciabatta, which means "slipper" in Italian, is a broad, chewy bread with a thin, crisp crust. It makes great panini, but if you can't find it, feel free to use another rustic bread. Good bread goes stale in the refrigerator. Store it either in an old-fashioned bread box or well wrapped in the freezer.

Who says a sandwich can't be cool? Versatile, fast, and outfitted with any style of filling, panini deserve their superstar status.

salami & provolone panini

4 servings

- 8 slices (about 3/8 inch thick) country-style white bread
- 1/2 cup prepared onion jam
- 6 ounces sliced provolone cheese
- 4 ounces sliced hard salami, such as soppressata or cappicola
- 4 teaspoons Dijon mustard
- 1 clove garlic, halved
   Extra-virgin olive oil, for brushing the pan

1. Heat a sandwich press or a grill pan over medium heat. (If you don't have either one, use a cast-iron or heavy-bottomed skillet.) Spread 1 side of all the bread with 1 tablespoon onion jam. Top half the bread with a few pieces of provolone and then some salami. Spread 1 teaspoon mustard over the salami and top with the remaining bread, jam side down.

2. Rub both sides of each panini with the garlic clove. If using a sandwich press, cook the sandwiches, 1 or 2 at a time, until the bread is golden brown and the cheese has melted, about 4 minutes. If using a grill pan or skillet, brush it lightly with olive oil, add 1 or 2 panini, and cook, pressing with a spatula, for about 1 1/2 minutes, then turn and cook, pressing, until the bread is golden brown and the cheese has melted, about 1 1/2 minutes more. Halve and serve immediately

FROM THE KITCHENS
Great panini need strong shoulders to lean on, and crusty bread is the natural choice. If you don't use the entire loaf, slice the rest and freeze it for the next time you need a quick sandwich.

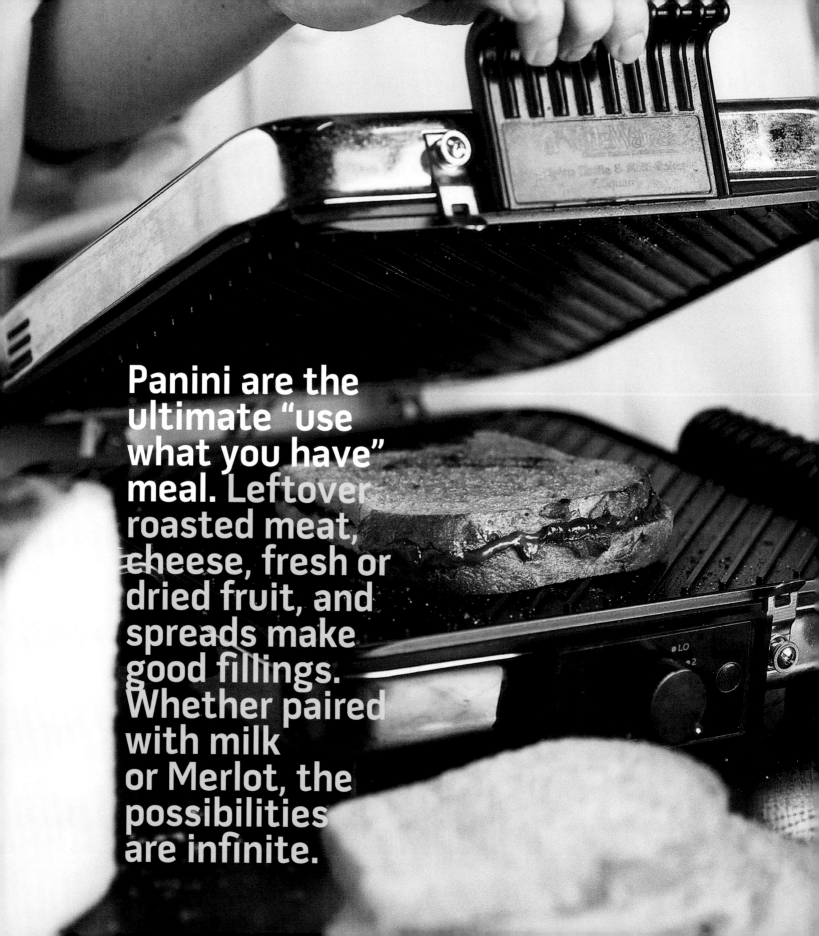

Panini are the ultimate "use what you have" meal. Leftover roasted meat, cheese, fresh or dried fruit, and spreads make good fillings. Whether paired with milk or Merlot, the possibilities are infinite.

PERFECT PANINI

- Use a cast-iron or heavy-bottomed skillet if you don't have a sandwich press (waffle irons don't work!).
- Multigrain bread is a healthy alternative to white bread.
- Leftover roasted or grilled vegetables make great fillings.

LAWS TO PRESS BY

- Limit fillings to four.
- Use dry ingredients so your panini don't get soggy.
- Forgo leafy greens and mayonnaise (neither is tempting when warm).
- Use a light hand when brushing bread with oil.

STAFF FAVORITES

- Roast asparagus with goat cheese and olive spread
- Smoked trout with horseradish cream cheese and apple slices
- Roast turkey with jalapeño Jack cheese and cranberry relish
- Smoked ham with fontina
- Leftover roast lamb with Tunisian Pesto (see page 37)
- Nutella with orange marmalade

antipasta pizza | 4 to 6 servings

TOPPING

- 4   medium ripe tomatoes (about 1½ pounds), diced
- 3   ounces thinly sliced cappicola, torn into bite-size pieces
- ½   cup pepperoncini, stemmed and roughly chopped (about 18)
      Kosher salt
- 2   10-ounce tubes prepared pizza dough or No-Fuss Pizza Dough (see recipe, below)
      Extra-virgin olive oil
- 6   ounces fresh goat or feta cheese
- ½   cup torn fresh basil
- 1   tablespoon chopped fresh oregano

DOUGH

- 1   cup tepid water (about 100°F)
- 3   tablespoons extra-virgin olive oil, plus additional as needed
- 2   teaspoons sugar
- 1½   teaspoons kosher salt
- 3   cups all-purpose flour, plus additional for kneading
- 1½   teaspoons active dry yeast

1. Preheat the oven to 425°F. Mix together the tomatoes, cappicola, and pepperoncini and season with salt to taste.

2. Line the backs of 2 baking sheets with parchment paper. For prepared dough: Unroll one tube of dough on a work surface and gently stretch into an 11x16-inch rectangle. Transfer to a prepared pan. Repeat with the other dough. For homemade dough: Dust work surface lightly with flour. Flatten a ball of dough. Press the edge with your fingers, rotating and stretching it into a disk about 10 inches across. Transfer to a prepared pan. Cover with a kitchen towel. Repeat to make 3 more crusts.

3. Brush a little olive oil over each crust and crumble cheese evenly on top. Scatter tomato mixture over crusts (hold back juice or crust will get soggy). Bake until bottom is brown and crust is crisp, 15 to 18 minutes. Sprinkle basil and oregano over pizza and serve.

NO-FUSS PIZZA DOUGH

Stir water, oil, sugar, and salt in a liquid measuring cup until sugar dissolves. Whisk flour and yeast in a large bowl. Make a well in the center and add liquid. With a wooden spoon or your hand, stir flour into liquid to make a rough dough. Pull dough into a ball. Turn dough onto a work surface dusted with flour. Knead until dough is smooth and elastic, about 5 minutes, using a little flour if necessary to keep from sticking. Divide dough into 4 equal portions, form into balls, and put on a lightly oiled baking sheet. Brush tops with oil, cover with plastic wrap, and set aside to rise until doubled, about 45 minutes.

Homemade pizza faster than delivery? You bet! With our recipe for homemade 'za, you'll be sofa surfing—slice in hand—in less than 30 minutes.

grilled roasted garlic & arugula pizzas

Makes 4 ten-inch pizzas

DOUGH

- 1 cup tepid water
- 3 tablespoons extra-virgin olive oil, plus additional as needed
- 2 teaspoons sugar
- 1½ teaspoons kosher salt
- 3 cups all-purpose flour, plus additional for kneading
- 2½ teaspoons active dry yeast (1 package)

TOPPINGS

- 2 heads garlic, tops trimmed
- 5 tablespoons extra-virgin olive oil, plus additional for drizzling
- ½ teaspoon kosher salt, plus additional for seasoning
- 2 teaspoons aged sherry vinegar Freshly ground black pepper
- 3 cups arugula, stems trimmed
- 4 thin slices prosciutto (about 3½ ounces), cut into ½-inch ribbons
- 4 ounces crumbled fresh goat cheese (about ½ cup)

1. To make dough: Stir water, oil, sugar, and salt in a liquid measuring cup until the sugar dissolves. Whisk flour and yeast in a large bowl, make a well in the center, and add liquid mixture. With a wooden spoon or your hand, gradually stir flour into liquid to make a rough dough. Pull dough together into a ball. Turn onto a work surface dusted with flour. Knead until dough is smooth and elastic, about 10 minutes, using a little flour if necessary to keep it from sticking.

2. Shape dough into a ball. Put in a large, lightly oiled bowl and turn it to coat with oil. Cover the bowl with plastic wrap and let rise until double in size, about 1 hour. Punch dough down, knead briefly, shape into a ball, cover, and let rise until soft and puffy, about 45 minutes.

3. While dough is rising, roast garlic: Preheat the oven to 350°F. Put garlic on a double layer of aluminum foil, drizzle with olive oil, sprinkle with ¼ teaspoon of the salt, seal foil, and roast until soft, 45 minutes to 1 hour. Cool garlic and squish cloves from skins into a small bowl. Whisk in 3 tablespoons of the olive oil.

4. To prepare a charcoal grill: Fill a chimney starter with briquettes and heat until lightly covered with ash. Scatter a layer of cold hardwood charcoal over one-quarter of the grill. Spread hot briquettes on top and heat to medium-high. Set grill grate on top and cover, making sure vents are open, and heat 5 minutes. (Or preheat half of a gas grill for direct and indirect grilling.)

5. Meanwhile, dust your work surface lightly with flour. Divide dough evenly into 4 balls and press into flour, flipping to dust both sides. Hold one piece of dough up like a steering wheel and rotate and stretch it to make an 8-inch disk. Put it on a piece of plastic wrap and cover with a kitchen towel. Repeat with remaining dough.

6. Brush 1 disk of dough with oil. Place oil side down over hot coals. Cook, rotating frequently, until golden, 1 to 2 minutes. Brush top with oil and flip with spatula. Cook 1 to 2 minutes, rotating, then move to cool side of grill. Repeat with another disk. Season with salt and black pepper to taste, spread with a heaping tablespoon of garlic, and cook, covered, until brown and crisp, about 8 minutes, rotating halfway through.

7. While pizzas grill, whisk vinegar, remaining ¼ teaspoon salt, and black pepper to taste in a medium bowl. Whisk in remaining 2 tablespoons olive oil. Add arugula and prosciutto and toss. Remove pizzas from grill, dot with goat cheese, and pile salad on top.

No wonder parties wind up in the kitchen (ours do too). It's where the action is—and you can sample straight from the pan.

chicken & mushroom quesadillas

4 servings

1 large boneless, skinless chicken breast (about 8 ounces)
Kosher salt and freshly ground black pepper
4 tablespoons vegetable oil or lard
3 tablespoons unsalted butter
5 ounces white mushrooms, sliced (about 3 cups)
1 teaspoon kosher salt
½ teaspoon ground cumin
½ medium onion, finely chopped
3 cloves garlic, minced
½ pickled jalapeño, minced, plus 1 tablespoon of the jar juices
1 19-ounce can black beans, rinsed and drained
2 8-inch flour tortillas
2 cups grated white Cheddar cheese (about 8 ounces)
Avocado slices (optional), sour cream, and salsa, for serving

1. Season the chicken breast with salt and pepper to taste. Heat a 10-inch skillet over medium heat; add 1 tablespoon of the oil or lard. Cook the chicken until nicely browned on both sides and firm when you press it gently with your fingertip, about 10 minutes total. Cool the chicken slightly and then tear into bite-size pieces.

2. Melt 1 tablespoon of the butter in the same skillet over medium heat. Add the mushrooms, ½ teaspoon of the salt, the cumin, and some black pepper and cook, stirring occasionally, until the mushrooms are dry, about 4 minutes. Transfer mushrooms to a small bowl.

3. Add the remaining 3 tablespoons oil or lard to the skillet, along with the onion, garlic, jalapeño and the jar juices, and the remaining ½ teaspoon salt. Cook until the onion is translucent, about 5 minutes. Add the beans and mash them into the onion mixture until the mixture is almost smooth but still dotted with bits of bean. Set aside.

4. Now build the quesadillas: Lay the tortillas on your work surface and spread ¼ of the beans on half of each one. Follow the beans with ¼ of the cheese, half of the chicken, half of the mushrooms, and finally the rest of the cheese. (You will have about half the beans left over; you can refrigerate them for up to 2 days.) Fold the tortillas over to encase the filling.

5. In a clean skillet fry each quesadilla in 1 tablespoon of the remaining butter until blistered and golden on both sides, about 4 minutes total. Cut into wedges with a pizza wheel or serrated knife. Serve with the avocado slices, if desired, sour cream, and salsa.

fresh cheese quesadillas
with arugula & radish

4 servings

SALSA

- 1 pound vine-ripe tomatoes (about 2 tomatoes)
- ¼ small red onion
- 1 tablespoon chopped fresh cilantro
- 1 teaspoon chipotle hot sauce
- 1 teaspoon kosher salt

QUESADILLAS

- 4 8-inch flour tortillas
- ⅓ cup soft cheese, such as fresh goat, ricotta, or crumbled feta
- ½ medium bunch arugula
- 3 radishes, sliced
- Kosher salt

1. Make the salsa: Halve the tomatoes and grate them on the largest side of a box grater in to a bowl, discarding the skins. Grate the onion into the tomato and then stir in the cilantro, hot sauce, and salt.

2. Make the quesadillas: Toast a tortilla directly over a gas burner (or in a dry cast-iron skillet if you have electric burners), turning it with tongs occasionally until slightly blistered on both sides. Transfer the tortilla to a work surface. Scatter some cheese on half the tortilla and top with some arugula leaves and radish slices. Season with salt to taste. Fold the tortilla over and press firmly. Repeat with the remaining ingredients. Serve warm or at room temperature with the salsa.

FROM THE KITCHENS
Grating tomatoes and onions on the large-hole side of a box grater is a speedy alternative to chopping.

zucchini, poblano & ricotta quesadillas | 4 servings

1 teaspoon coriander seeds

3 medium zucchini, sliced lengthwise about ⅓ inch thick

3 poblano chiles, stemmed, halved and seeded

Extra-virgin olive oil, for brushing

2 teaspoons kosher salt

Freshly ground black pepper

1 cup fresh ricotta (see tip, below)

⅓ cup chopped fresh cilantro, plus a handful of leaves for garnish

2 scallions (white and green parts), sliced (about 3 tablespoons)

1 jalapeño, seeded and minced (or leave seeds in for more heat) (about 2 teaspoons)

1 teaspoon finely grated lime zest

4 12-inch flour tortillas

4 lime wedges

Summer Salsa with a Shot (see page 56) and Guacamole (see page 57), if desired

1. Prepare an outdoor grill with a medium-hot fire.

2. Toast coriander seeds in a dry skillet over high heat until fragrant, about 30 seconds. Coarsely grind seeds with a mortar and pestle or crush with the bottom of a pan.

3. Lightly brush zucchini and poblanos with olive oil and grill, turning as needed, until tender and lightly charred, about 4 to 6 minutes. Season the zucchini with the crushed coriander, 1½ teaspoons of the salt, and black pepper to taste. Cut into bite-size chunks and set aside to cool slightly. Peel skin from poblanos with a knife and thinly slice.

4. Mix the ricotta, chopped cilantro, scallions, jalapeño, lime zest, ¼ teaspoon of the salt, and black pepper to taste in a medium bowl. Lay out the tortillas and spread one-quarter of the cheese mixture over half of each tortilla, leaving about a ½-inch border around the edge. Divide the grilled vegetables among the tortillas and fold the tortillas in half. Brush the quesadillas lightly with oil, sprinkle with remaining ¼ teaspoon salt, and grill on both sides until the cheese warms and the outside is golden brown, about 2 minutes.

5. Place each quesadilla on a plate, scatter the cilantro leaves over the top, and serve with lime wedges and, if desired, Summer Salsa with a Shot and Guacamole.

FROM THE KITCHENS

▪ Look for fresh ricotta in a good cheese shop or Italian grocery. It will be firmer and less watery than the ricotta sold in plastic tubs in the grocery store. If you can get only the grocery-store ricotta, put it in a cheesecloth- or coffee filter-lined strainer over a bowl and refrigerate at least a couple of hours or overnight to drain off excess moisture.
▪ If you have a mandoline—a handheld tool much like a planer with a finely honed blade—use it to get long, uniform slices of zucchini that will grill evenly.

main dish salads

Sometimes a big salad—a perfectly balanced combo of crunchy and creamy textures, warm and cool temperatures—is the only thing you want for dinner.

bistro bacon & egg salad

4 servings

4 slices bacon, cut crosswise into thin strips
2½ tablespoons cider vinegar
2 teaspoons Dijon mustard
Kosher salt
Freshly ground black pepper
2 tablespoons extra-virgin olive oil
8 large eggs
8 cups mesclun salad greens (about 7 ounces)
4 to 8 slices crusty bread, toasted if desired

1. Cook the bacon in a medium skillet over medium heat, stirring occasionally, until crisp. Using a slotted spoon, transfer the bacon to a paper towel. Pull the skillet from the heat (leave drippings in the skillet) and stir in 1½ tablespoons cider vinegar, scraping up any browned bits clinging to the skillet. Pour the mixture into a large bowl and whisk in mustard, salt and pepper to taste, and olive oil.

2. Fill a nonstick skillet with about 2 inches of water and bring it to the barest simmer over medium heat; add the remaining 1 tablespoon vinegar. Crack the eggs, slipping them gently into the water, and cook until the whites are set but the yolks are still runny, about 4 minutes.

3. While the eggs poach, toss the greens with the vinaigrette and bits of bacon. Divide the salad among 4 plates or shallow bowls. Using a slotted spoon, gently scoop the eggs from the water, blot dry with a paper towel, and place 2 of them on top of each salad. Add bread to each plate and serve.

FROM THE KITCHENS
Our bistro salad cries out for a glass of crisp, fruity rosé.

quicky cobb salad | 4 to 6 servings

3 slices bacon, cut in half crosswise
1 ripe Hass avocado, halved, seeded,
    and diced
2 ripe medium tomatoes, cored and
    diced
2 hard-boiled eggs, peeled and
    chopped
  Kosher salt and freshly ground
    black pepper
8 cups mesclun salad greens
    (about 7 ounces)
2 cups shredded cooked chicken
    (about ½ of a rotisserie chicken)
2 ounces mild blue cheese (about
    ½ cup loosely packed crumbles)
3 tablespoons extra-virgin
    olive oil
1 tablespoon red wine vinegar

1. Spread bacon out on a paper towel on a microwave-safe plate and cover with another piece of paper towel. Microwave on high until crisp, 3 to 4 minutes. Cool.

2. Layer the avocado, tomato, and eggs in a large salad bowl, seasoning with salt and black pepper as you go.

3. Top with the mesclun greens, then scatter the chicken and cheese on top. Crumble the bacon over the salad. Season again with salt and black pepper. At the table, drizzle with the oil and vinegar and toss until the salad is evenly dressed.

FROM THE KITCHENS
• This salad got its start as a midnight snack when Hollywood restaurateur Bob Cobb got hungry one night in 1937 and raided the fridge. Raid your own fridge for this one—it's flexible. Add cooked potato or leftover roast turkey, or hit up the grocery store salad bar for grilled chicken, chopped eggs, or precut vegetables.
• If you pack this to go, put the dressing in a separate container and keep the avocado whole. Slice the avocado and toss it all together when you're ready to eat.

grilled chicken caesar salad

4 to 6 servings

CHICKEN
4 boneless, skinless chicken breast halves (about 1¾ pounds)
Lemon-Pepper Slather (see recipe, below)

SALAD
1 to 3 anchovy fillets
1 large egg
1 clove garlic, peeled
¾ teaspoon kosher salt, plus additional for seasoning
Juice of 1 lemon (about 3 tablespoons)
½ teaspoon Worcestershire sauce
¼ cup extra-virgin olive oil
Freshly ground black pepper
3 romaine lettuce hearts (1 package), torn into pieces
¼ cup freshly grated Parmigiana-Reggiano cheese
1 1- to 2-ounce wedge Parmigiana-Reggiano cheese, for garnish

CROUTONS
4 ¾-inch-thick slices sourdough bread
2 tablespoons extra-virgin olive oil
1 medium clove garlic, peeled and halved
Kosher salt

LEMON-PEPPER SLATHER
Makes ⅔ cup
1 teaspoon white peppercorns
1½ teaspoons coarse sea salt
1 teaspoon sugar
½ cup extra-virgin olive oil
¼ cup finely grated lemon zest (from 4 large lemons)
2 cloves garlic, smashed

1. For the chicken: Put the chicken in a self-sealing plastic bag, add the Lemon-Pepper Slather, seal, and turn the bag over a couple times to coat the chicken well. Refrigerate for 2 to 24 hours.

2. Prepare an outdoor grill with a medium-high fire.

3. For the salad: Soak anchovy fillets in cold water 5 minutes. Pat dry, chop coarsely, and put in a large salad bowl. Put the egg in a small saucepan with water to cover. Bring just to a boil over medium-high heat and drain. Crack the egg into the salad bowl (don't worry if some of the egg white remains attached to the shell; just discard it with the shell). Smash the garlic clove, sprinkle with the ¾ teaspoon salt, and, with the side of a large knife, mash and smear the mixture to a coarse paste. Add to the egg. Add lemon juice and Worcestershire, then slowly whisk in oil to make a creamy dressing. Season with salt and black pepper to taste and refrigerate.

4. Pat chicken dry; season with salt and black pepper to taste. Grill chicken, turning once, until cooked, about 4 minutes per side. Remove to a cutting board.

5. For the croutons: Brush the bread with the olive oil and grill until toasted, turning as necessary. After grilling, rub each toast with garlic and season with salt to taste. Break toasts into bite-size croutons.

6. Slice the chicken. Add the lettuce to the dressing in the salad bowl and toss to combine. Sprinkle with the cheese and croutons and toss again. Divide the salad among plates and top each with a sliced chicken breast. Use a vegetable peeler to shave large, thin pieces of Parmigiana-Reggiano over each. Serve immediately.

LEMON-PEPPER SLATHER
Pulse peppercorns in a spice grinder until coarsely ground. Add salt and sugar and pulse a few more times. Transfer to a bowl and stir in the olive oil, lemon zest, and garlic. Microwave until hot but not boiling, about 45 seconds. Let cool.

FROM THE KITCHENS
Extra-virgin olive oil—the most full-flavored of the olive oils— varies in flavor from peppery to aromatic to flowery to apple-sweet. It depends on the olive used and how ripe it was when it was picked. Intensely green oils, from underripe fruit, tend to be pungent; golden ones, from mature olives, more restrained. Buy small bottles of differently hued oils and sample to find the style that suits your taste.

southwestern cobb salad
with chili-rubbed steak

6 servings

DRESSING

- 2 cloves garlic
- ½ teaspoon kosher salt
- ⅓ cup mayonnaise
- ⅓ cup buttermilk
- 1 tablespoon chipotle hot sauce
- 3 tablespoons minced fresh cilantro
- 1 scallion (white and green parts), very thinly sliced
- 1 teaspoon finely grated orange zest

STEAK

- Kosher salt
- 1 tri-tip steak or other sirloin steak (about 1¾ pounds)
- 2 tablespoons chili powder
- 1 tablespoon extra-virgin olive oil

SALAD

- 1 ripe Hass avocado
- 1 head romaine lettuce, torn into pieces
- 3 ripe medium tomatoes, diced
- 1 orange, peeled and cut into segments (see tip, page 372)
- ½ medium jicama, peeled and diced (about 2 cups)
- 4 ounces Cotija (see tip, page 299) or feta cheese, crumbled (about 1 cup)
- Kosher salt and freshly ground black pepper

1. For the dressing: Smash the garlic cloves, sprinkle with the salt, and, with the flat side of a large knife, mash and smear the mixture to a coarse paste. Scrape the paste into a small bowl, add the mayonnaise, buttermilk, hot sauce, cilantro, scallion, and orange zest, and whisk well to make a creamy dressing. Set aside.

2. For the steak: Position a rack and broiler pan about 6 inches from the heat element and preheat the broiler to high. Season steak with salt to taste. Stir the chili powder into the oil in a small bowl and rub the spiced oil on both sides of the steak. Carefully lay the steak on the hot pan and broil, turning once, 8 to 10 minutes per side for medium-rare. Transfer the steak to a cutting board and let rest 5 minutes before cutting into bite-size cubes.

3. For salad: Cut to the seed around the midsection of the avocado. Hold avocado in both hands and twist gently to separate. Tap seed with a knife. When blade catches, rotate knife and lift out seed. Make cuts down the length of the avocado. Make cuts across the avocado. Scoop dice into a bowl. Put the romaine into a large salad bowl. Arrange the steak, avocado, tomatoes, orange, jicama, and cheese over the lettuce in wide stripes and season with salt and pepper to taste.

4. At the table, pour about 3 tablespoons of dressing over the salad and toss well. Pass the remaining dressing. Serve the salad with warm corn or flour tortillas, if desired.

FROM THE KITCHENS

Don't rush to slice meat directly after it's cooked, but let it rest— 5 minutes for a steak and up to 30 minutes for a large roast. This allows the juices to distribute throughout, and you avoid a bull's-eye of rare meat in the center of the cut.

southeast asian-style beef salad

4 servings

SALAD

- 12 ounces flank steak (about half of a full one)
- ¾ cup Sriracha-Miso Dressing (see recipe, below) or storebought ginger-miso dressing
- 1 head red leaf or 2 heads Boston or Bibb, washed and dried, or 10-ounce bag prewashed salad greens, preferably an Asian mix
- 3 scallions, thinly sliced (white and green parts)
- 1 medium carrot, peeled and thinly sliced
- 1 Kirby cucumber (see tip, page 75), thinly sliced
- 1 to 2 bird's eye chiles or 1 jalapeño, thinly sliced
- 1 bunch fresh cilantro or mint, washed and dried, tough stems discarded
- 1 large handful roasted peanuts or cashews (about ½ cup)
- 1 cup mung bean sprouts (optional)
- 1 lime, cut into thin wedges

DRESSING

Makes about 1 cup

- 1 1-inch piece fresh ginger, peeled
- 3 tablespoons yellow (shiro) miso
- 2 tablespoons water
- 1 tablespoon rice vinegar (not the seasoned kind)
- 1 teaspoon soy sauce
- ½ teaspoon Asian chile paste, such as Sriracha or sambal oelek
- ½ cup peanut oil

1. Brush the steak with about ¼ cup of the miso dressing. Marinate at room temperature for up to an hour or cook immediately. When ready to cook, position a broiler pan on the rack closest to the broiler and preheat to high.

2. Lay steak in the center of the hot pan and broil until steak is browned but still tender to the touch, about 4 minutes. Turn steak and broil another 2 to 3 minutes for medium rare (an instant-read thermometer inserted sideways into steak will register about 130°F). Transfer to a cutting board to rest for 5 to 10 minutes.

3. Arrange lettuce on a large platter or individual serving plates, along with the scallions, carrot, cucumber, chiles, cilantro, nuts, and sprouts, if using. Thinly slice the steak against the grain (see tip, page 190) and add to the platter. Garnish with the lime wedges. Serve, passing remaining dressing at the table.

SRIRACHA-MISO DRESSING

Drop the ginger into a blender and process until finely chopped. Add the miso, water, vinegar, soy sauce, and chile paste; puree. With the blender running, drizzle in the peanut oil to make a smooth, slightly thick dressing. Serve or refrigerate in a tightly sealed container for up to 3 days.

FROM THE KITCHENS

- Serve this with big lettuce leaves and extra dressing and have your guests make their own lettuce wraps.
- Asian-labeled mixed greens tend to have tangy, sharp add-ins like mizuna and tatsoi, which add mustardy zip to salads. If you can't find them, look for baby spinach or arugula.
- Bird's eye chiles, sometimes called piri-piri, are small, fiery chiles sold both fresh and dried. Taking the ribs (the white parts on the inside) and seeds out of fresh chiles lessens the burn. A chile's natural oils burn; don't rub your eyes when working with chiles, and always wash your hands after handling them.

Salads from grab-and-go items are terrific. Choose flavors and textures that flatter one another, and they make the ideal instant meal—tasty, surprising, and so, so easy.

roast beef salad
with pears, blue cheese & nuts | 6 servings

SALAD

8   cups mesclun salad greens
    (about 7 ounces)
2   endives, thinly sliced crosswise
2   ripe pears, preferably red Bartlett,
    Comice, or Forelle
10 ounces rare roast beef, thinly sliced
3   ounces blue cheese, such as
    Roquefort, Maytag, or Stilton
¼   cup toasted hazelnuts, skins
    removed (rub them in a clean
    cotton towel while still warm)
    Kosher salt
    Freshly ground black pepper
    Honey-Mustard and Hazelnut
    Vinaigrette (see recipe, below)

VINAIGRETTE
Makes 1 cup

2   tablespoons honey-Dijon mustard
2   tablespoons apple cider vinegar
1   teaspoon kosher salt
    Freshly ground black pepper
1   cup hazelnut oil or a mixture of half
    hazelnut, half extra-virgin olive oil

Toss the mesclun with the endives in a large bowl. Halve and core the pears and slice them very thin lengthwise—use a mandoline if you have one. Add the pear slices to the greens along with the roast beef, blue cheese, and hazelnuts. Season the salad with salt and pepper to taste and toss with all of the dressing. Divide the salad among 4 chilled plates and serve.

HONEY-MUSTARD AND HAZELNUT VINAIGRETTE
Whisk the mustard, vinegar, salt, and pepper to taste in a small bowl. Gradually whisk in the oil, starting with a few drops and then adding the rest in a steady stream, to make a smooth, slightly thick dressing.

FROM THE KITCHENS
Nut oils can be pricey, but the fast hit of deep flavor they bring to steamed vegetables, marinades, and cold sauces is worth every penny. Store them in your fridge to extend their life up to 3 months.

shrimp salad
with green goddess dressing | 4 to 6 servings

SALAD

1½	pounds cooked medium shrimp
1	medium cucumber
1	rib celery, peeled and diced
	Kosher salt and freshly ground black pepper
	Avocado Green Goddess Dressing (see recipe, right)
1	pound asparagus, trimmed and cooked
1	ripe medium tomato, cored and cut into 12 wedges
1	head Boston or Bibb lettuce, trimmed and washed
1	scallion (green part only), very thinly sliced

DRESSING

Makes about 1 cup

1	anchovy fillet
⅓	cup mayonnaise
1	ripe Hass avocado, seeded, peeled, and cut into chunks (see page 128, Step 3)
1	scallion, thinly sliced
1	tablespoon chopped fresh basil
1	tablespoon minced flat-leaf parsley
1	tablespoon minced fresh tarragon
2	teaspoons freshly squeezed lime juice
1	teaspoon kosher salt
	Freshly ground black pepper

1. Peel and devein shrimp and cut into ½-inch chunks. Peel and seed cucumber and cut into ¾-inch chunks. Toss the shrimp with the cucumber, celery, and salt and pepper to taste in a medium bowl. Fold in about half the dressing.

2. Arrange the asparagus and tomatoes on individual plates: Fan some asparagus spears on one side of the plate and some tomato wedges across. (If you prefer, you can arrange everything on 1 large serving platter.) Make a bed of lettuce in the center and top with the shrimp salad. Sprinkle the scallion over the salads and serve, passing the remaining dressing at the table.

GREEN GODDESS DRESSING

Soak the anchovy fillet in cold water for 5 minutes. Pat it dry and chop it coarsely. Puree the mayonnaise, anchovy, avocado, scallion, basil, parsley, tarragon, lime juice, and salt and pepper to taste in a blender until smooth. The dressing may be refrigerated in a tightly sealed container for 2 days.

FROM THE KITCHENS

People either love or hate anchovies. If you're in the latter group, skip them in the dressing. But if you're not sure, try the trick of soaking them in cold water first to temper their kick. The little bit used really adds dimension to the flavor of the dressing.

crab louis | 4 servings

DRESSING

- 2 ripe medium tomatoes
- 1 tablespoon extra-virgin olive oil
- ¾ teaspoon kosher salt
- ½ cup mayonnaise
- 2 tablespoons minced piquillo pepper (see tip, page 34) or jarred roasted sweet red pepper
- 1 tablespoon minced red onion
- 1 teaspoon chipotle hot sauce
  Freshly ground black pepper

SALAD

- 1 pound jumbo lump crabmeat
- ¼ cup peeled, diced jicama
- 1 teaspoon extra-virgin olive oil
- 1 lemon, halved
  Kosher salt
- 1 ripe Hass avocado
- 2 ripe tomatoes
- 1 head Boston lettuce, leaves separated
- ¼ cup fresh whole cilantro leaves

1. For the dressing: Halve the tomatoes crosswise to expose their seeds. Use your fingertip to pop the seeds out of the flesh and discard. Working over a small, shallow saucepan, grate the cut side of each tomato half against the large teeth of a box grater; discard the skins. Add the olive oil and ½ teaspoon of the salt and simmer over medium heat, stirring frequently, until thickened and reduced to about ⅓ cup, about 15 minutes. Set aside to cool.

2. Stir cooked tomatoes, mayonnaise, piquillo or red pepper, onion, hot sauce, remaining ¼ teaspoon salt, and black pepper to taste in a small bowl until combined. Refrigerate, covered, until ready to serve. (Dressing can be made up to 1 day ahead.)

3. For the salad: Spread the crabmeat on a pan and carefully pick out and discard any bits of shell. Place the crab and the jicama in a large bowl. Drizzle with the olive oil and some lemon juice, sprinkle with salt to taste, and use a rubber spatula or wooden spoon to very gently fold the ingredients together. Fold in ½ cup of the dressing.

4. Cut to the seed around the midsection of the avocado. Hold avocado in both hands and twist gently to separate. Peel avocado halves, then slice each half into thin wedges. Squeeze a bit of lemon juice over the avocado to keep the flesh from discoloring. Core the tomatoes and cut into wedges. Divide the lettuce leaves among 4 chilled plates and arrange the avocado and tomatoes attractively on top. Spoon some crab salad on each and drizzle with some of the dressing. Scatter cilantro leaves over each salad and serve, passing remaining dressing.

summer tomato bread salad
with scallops

4 servings

1½ pounds ripe tomatoes
1 shallot, minced
4 cloves garlic, minced
⅓ cup extra-virgin olive oil, plus
      additional for grilling
2 tablespoons red wine vinegar
1 slightly heaping tablespoon kosher
      salt, plus additional to taste
   Freshly ground black pepper
10 ounces stale country-style bread,
      torn into large pieces
1 cup fresh basil leaves
12 medium sea scallops
      (about 12 ounces)

1. Core the tomatoes and, if large, cut them into chunks; if small, halve or quarter them. Toss them gently with the shallot, garlic, oil, vinegar, 1 tablespoon salt, and pepper. Set aside until the tomatoes are very juicy, about 10 minutes.

2. Meanwhile, preheat a grill pan or heat an outdoor grill to medium heat. Fill a large bowl with ice water. Add the bread and set aside until soft, no more than 5 minutes. Using your hands, scoop the bread from the water, squeeze out as much water as possible, and rub it through your fingers into the tomatoes. Tear the basil over the salad and toss gently. (The bread salad can be served now or set aside at room temperature for a couple of hours.)

3. Lightly brush the scallops with olive oil and season with salt and pepper to taste. Grill the scallops, turning once, until firm but not tough, about 2 minutes per side. Cut the scallops in half, add to the bread salad, and serve.

FROM THE KITCHENS
It's easy to dry fresh bread. Tear it into chunks and microwave for 1 to 2 minutes. Or place the chunked bread on a baking sheet in a 250°F oven for a few minutes. Done.

In high summer, when the sun is strong and the tomatoes are ripe, make panzanella. An especially fine use for day-old bread, this meal begs to be eaten al fresco.

celery, tuna & white bean salad | 4 servings

SALAD
- 4 ribs celery, thinly sliced on an angle
- 1 15-ounce can white beans, drained and rinsed
- ½ cup pickled button mushrooms, with a little bit of their liquid
- ¼ cup chopped pitted kalamata olives
- 1 tablespoon capers, drained
- 1 rounded tablespoon whole-grain mustard

  Freshly squeezed juice from a good-size lemon wedge
- 1 teaspoon kosher salt

  Freshly ground black pepper
- 1 12-ounce can oil-packed tuna
- 1 cup ripe cherry or grape tomatoes, halved
- 5 cups mixed greens

  Grilled or toasted pocketless pita bread

  Lemon wedges (optional)

PITA BREAD
- 2 6-inch pocketless pita rounds

  Extra-virgin olive oil

  Kosher salt

1. Toss the celery with the beans, mushrooms and liquid, olives, capers, mustard, lemon juice, salt, and pepper to taste. Drain the tuna. Add the tuna and tomatoes; toss to break up the tuna and coat the salad with the dressing.

2. Spread the greens on a serving platter and spoon the salad on top. Arrange the pita and lemon wedges (if desired) around the greens and serve.

GRILLED POCKETLESS PITA BREAD
Preheat a grill pan over medium heat. Lightly brush both sides of the bread with olive oil and season with salt to taste. Grill until golden, turning once, about 4 minutes. Cut into wedges and serve warm. (The pita may be grilled on an outdoor gas or charcoal grill too.)

FROM THE KITCHENS
Oil-packed tuna is more flavorful and has a nicer consistency than its water-packed cousin.

french lentil & roasted beet salad

6 servings

SALAD

1	pound beets (about 3 medium), red, gold, striped, or a mixture
1	tablespoon olive oil
1	cup de Puy lentils (small, slate-green lentils from France)
1	sprig fresh rosemary, plus 2 teaspoons chopped leaves
1	bay leaf
2	large cloves garlic, peeled and smashed
½	onion, studded with a whole clove
½	teaspoon kosher salt, plus additional for seasoning
	Sherry Vinegar and Mustard Dressing (see recipe, below)
¼	cup minced fresh flat-leaf parsley
	Freshly ground black pepper
6	cups mixed greens
6	ounces aged goat cheese

DRESSING

Makes ½ cup

3	tablespoons aged sherry wine vinegar
2	tablespoons whole-grain mustard
1	teaspoon kosher salt
	Freshly ground black pepper
⅓	cup extra-virgin olive oil
2	shallots, minced

1. Preheat the oven to 400°F. Trim all but 1 inch of the beet stems. Put the beets on a large piece of aluminum foil, drizzle with olive oil, and seal the foil to make a tight package. Put the package in a small roasting pan. Roast the beets until easily pierced with a knife, about 1 hour. When the beets are cool enough to handle, peel them—the skins should slide right off with a bit of pressure from your fingers. If they don't, use a paring knife to scrape off any bits that stick. Dice the beets and set aside.

2. While you roast the beets, spread the lentils on a pan and pick out any pebbles or other foreign matter; rinse and drain. Put the lentils in a saucepan with cold water to cover by about 2 inches. Tie the sprig of rosemary and the bay leaf together with a piece of kitchen twine and add to the pan along with the smashed garlic, onion half, and ½ teaspoon salt. Bring to a boil over high heat; reduce the heat and simmer, uncovered, until the lentils are tender, about 25 minutes. Strain the lentils and discard herbs and onion.

3. Put the warm lentils in a bowl and stir in half the dressing. Cool the lentils completely, then add the beets, parsley, and chopped rosemary. Season to taste with salt and pepper. Lightly dress the greens with a bit of the dressing and divide among 6 plates. Spoon some of the lentil salad onto the greens, crumble goat cheese over each serving, and drizzle with some of the remaining vinaigrette.

SHERRY VINEGAR AND MUSTARD DRESSING

Whisk the vinegar with the mustard, 1 teaspoon salt, and pepper to taste in a small bowl. Gradually whisk in the olive oil, starting with a few drops and then adding the rest in a steady stream to make a smooth, slightly thick vinaigrette. Stir in the shallots. Use immediately or refrigerate in a tightly sealed container for up to 3 days.

Far from old-fashioned, this classic is spiced up with pickled jalapeño and served on a pile of fresh, peppery greens.

leslie's ham salad | 4 servings

1 small red onion, minced
1 pound cooked ham, cut
    into large pieces
2 ribs celery, quartered
6 cornichon or gherkin pickles
1 pickled jalapeño, seeded
    and stemmed
2 scallions (white and green
    parts), minced
⅓ cup mayonnaise
2 tablespoons Dijon mustard
¼ teaspoon freshly ground
    black pepper
1 bunch watercress, washed, dried,
    and stems trimmed (about 3 cups)
1 bunch arugula, washed, dried, and
    stems trimmed (about 2 cups)
4 to 8 slices rustic sourdough bread,
    toasted or grilled

1. To mellow the minced onion, soak it in cold water for 10 minutes, then drain it well, pat dry, and put it in a serving bowl. Pulse the ham in a food processor until chunky and add it to the red onion. Pulse the celery, pickles, and jalapeño in the processor until chopped and add to the ham.

2. Add the scallions to the ham mixture along with the mayonnaise, mustard, and pepper. Refrigerate the salad, covered, until thoroughly chilled, about 1 hour.

3. Toss the watercress and arugula together and divide among 4 plates. Divide the ham salad evenly on the greens and serve with the toasts.

FROM THE KITCHENS
This is just the thing to make with leftover holiday ham. (We don't recommend deli ham as a stand-in.) Our favorite smoked ham is neither too salty nor watery. Better hams still have a bone and most of their skin intact.

pasta & noodles

The world over, the craving for comfort leads to a big bowl of noodles. Find it—and some fun—in these globally inspired bowls of the saucy stuff.

spaghetti with meat sauce

makes 5 cups
(enough for 1 pound of pasta or 4 to 6 servings)

2   tablespoons extra-virgin olive oil
8   ounces ground beef (chuck is tastier
       and cheaper; sirloin is leaner)
1   medium onion, chopped
2   28-ounce cans whole
       peeled tomatoes
    Pinch sugar
    Freshly grated nutmeg (optional)
1½ teaspoons kosher salt, plus more for
       pasta-cooking water and to taste
    Freshly ground black pepper
1   pound spaghetti
1   sprig fresh basil leaves, stems
       discarded and leaves chopped
½   cup freshly grated grana-style
       cheese, such as Parmesan

1. In a large soup pot or Dutch oven, heat olive oil over medium heat. Add the meat, breaking it up with a wooden spoon, and cook until it loses its rosy color, about 3 minutes. Add onion to the meat and cook, stirring occasionally, until onion is golden brown, about 5 minutes.

2. Pour tomatoes and their juices into a large bowl and crush with your hands. Add the crushed tomatoes, sugar, nutmeg, if using, 1½ teaspoons salt, and some black pepper to the meat. Adjust the heat to maintain a simmer and cook the sauce, stirring occasionally, until it gets thick, about 25 minutes.

3. Meanwhile, bring a large pot of cold water to a boil over high heat and salt it generously. Drop the spaghetti into the boiling water and give it a stir. Cook, stirring occasionally, to make sure the noodles don't stick together.

4. Stir basil into the sauce.

5. When the pasta is almost done (taste it—it should still be a little chewy), carefully lift it out of the water with tongs; let most of the water drip off and transfer the pasta to the sauce. Stir and turn the pasta with the tongs to coat evenly with sauce. Cook over medium-high heat until the pasta absorbs some of the sauce and is just tender, 1 to 2 minutes. If the pasta seems dry, add a splash of a little pasta water to keep it saucy. Remove pan from heat; stir in cheese. Divide among 4 warm serving bowls and serve.

FROM THE KITCHENS
Canned tomatoes are perfect for sauce. They're super-handy to have around because they last forever; they come already peeled (you don't always have to peel tomatoes, but peeled tomatoes are best for cooking); and, since they're canned at the peak of ripeness, you don't lose out on flavor. Here we generally call for canned whole tomatoes and have you crush them with your hands (or kitchen scissors), but diced work just as well for quick sauces.

spaghetti
with spicy greens & garlic | 6 servings

1½ teaspoons kosher salt, plus
     additional for pasta water
16 cloves peeled garlic, thinly sliced
⅓ cup extra-virgin olive oil
2 medium yellow onions, halved
     and sliced
⅛ teaspoon crushed red pepper
12 cups torn greens, such as mustard,
     kale, chard, escarole, or a mix
12 ounces spaghetti
¼ cup grated Pecorino Romano cheese

1. Bring a large pot of cold water to a boil and salt it generously. Cook garlic in olive oil in a large skillet over medium-high heat, stirring occasionally, until golden brown and crispy, about 3 minutes; take care that the garlic doesn't get too brown or it will be bitter. Using a slotted spoon, transfer the garlic chips to a paper towel. Pour off and reserve all but 2 tablespoons oil. Add the onions and red pepper (add a little more if you like things spicy) to the skillet and cook, stirring, until light brown, about 10 minutes. Season with the 1½ teaspoons salt.

2. When the onions are almost done, add the greens to the boiling water and cook, uncovered, just until tender, about 2 minutes. Using tongs, lift the greens from the water, shake off the excess water, add them to the onions, and cook, stirring occasionally, until tender, about 5 minutes.

3. Using the same pot of boiling water, add the spaghetti and cook, stirring occasionally, until al dente, 8 to 10 minutes. Scoop out and reserve about 1 cup of the cooking water; drain the pasta. Transfer the pasta to a serving bowl and toss with the cheese. Add the greens and some of the reserved pasta water and toss, adding more water as necessary to keep the pasta from clumping. Scatter the garlic chips over the top and serve.

FROM THE KITCHENS
Speed-wash your greens like we do here in the Food Network Kitchens: Tear up the leaves, swish them in a big bowl of water, shake them semidry, and get cooking.

linguine
with mussels, herbs & wine | 4 servings

12 ounces linguine
8 tablespoons unsalted butter
4 shallots, thinly sliced
4 cloves garlic, chopped
1½ teaspoons kosher salt
½ teaspoon crushed red pepper flakes
¾ cup dry white vermouth
¼ cup water
¾ cup chopped fresh flat-leaf parsley
2 tablespoons chopped fresh tarragon
2 teaspoons chopped fresh thyme
1½ pounds farm-raised mussels
   (about 4 dozen)

1. Bring a large pot of cold water to a boil over high heat and salt it generously. Add the linguine and cook, stirring occasionally, until al dente, about 8 minutes. Drain.

2. While the linguine cooks, melt the butter in a large skillet. Add the shallots, garlic, salt, and red pepper flakes and cook, stirring occasionally, until the shallots are soft, about 8 minutes. Stir in the vermouth, water, parsley, tarragon, and thyme and bring to a boil. Add the mussels, cover, and steam, giving the pot a good shake every minute or so, until mussels open, about 5 minutes. Discard any mussels that remain shut.

3. Divide the pasta among 4 large, warm serving bowls. Spoon the mussels over the pasta and pour some of the broth over the tops.

FROM THE KITCHENS
Rinse the mussels in several changes of cold water and give them a scrub if they are muddy. Discard any raw mussels that don't close when tapped. Tug off any beard—the small, dark tuft that sticks out from the shell—before steaming. When possible, cook mussels the day you buy them.

penne with pesto | 4 servings

2 cups basil leaves
2 cloves garlic, smashed and peeled
¼ cup pine nuts
½ cup extra-virgin olive oil
½ cup freshly grated
   Parmesan cheese
½ teaspoon kosher salt, plus more for
   pasta-cooking water and to taste
   Freshly ground black pepper
1 pound penne rigate or other
   ridged small-tube pasta

1. Wash the basil leaves in a large bowl of cold water and dry in a salad spinner or gently pat dry with paper towels. Put the basil, garlic, and pine nuts in a food processor and pulse until coarsely chopped. With the food processor running, gradually add the olive oil and process until the pesto is smooth. Transfer the pesto to a large bowl and stir in the cheese. Season pesto with the ½ teaspoon salt and some black pepper to taste.

2. Bring a large pot of cold water to a boil over high heat and salt it generously. Add the penne and boil, stirring occasionally, until al dente, 8 to 10 minutes. Drain in a colander, saving about ¼ cup pasta-cooking water. Add the pasta to the bowl. Use tongs and toss with enough of the cooking water so the pesto coats the pasta evenly. Season with salt and black pepper to taste.

FROM THE KITCHENS
• Instead of basil in the pesto, try 1 cup parsley, 1 cup fresh spinach leaves, 2 tablespoons fresh rosemary leaves, and 2 tablespoons fresh thyme leaves. Substitute walnuts for pine nuts.
• Add ¼ cup ricotta cheese when processing basil, garlic, and pine nuts for a creamy pesto that's great with tortellini or ravioli.
• Upgrade this dish by topping the dressed pesto pasta with ½ pound chopped fresh mozzarella balls (bocconcini), 3 ripe medium tomatoes cut in large chunks, and ½ cup pitted, roughly chopped black olives (we like kalamata). Or, eliminate the cheese, tomato, and olives, and simply add 1 to 2 cups cooked chicken or shrimp.

farfalle with tomato & roasted red pepper sauce | 4 servings

1 teaspoon kosher salt, plus more
    for pasta-cooking water and
    to taste
1 28-ounce can plum tomatoes
2 tablespoons extra-virgin olive oil
3 large cloves garlic, smashed,
    peeled, and chopped
⅓ cup drained oil-packed sun-dried
    tomatoes, chopped
½ cup jarred roasted red
    peppers, chopped
⅛ teaspoon crushed red pepper flakes
1 teaspoon sugar
    Freshly ground black pepper
2 handfuls fresh basil leaves, chopped
1 tablespoon balsamic vinegar
12 ounces farfalle pasta (bowties)
    (about ¾ of a box)
½ cup fresh ricotta cheese (optional)

1. Bring a large pot of cold water to a boil over high heat and salt it generously.

2. Pour the canned tomatoes and their juices into a large bowl and crush with your hands.

3. Heat the olive oil in a large skillet over medium heat. Stir in the garlic, sun-dried tomatoes, roasted peppers, and red pepper flakes. Cook until the garlic is fragrant, about 1 minute. Add the crushed tomatoes, sugar, the 1 teaspoon salt, and some black pepper. Bring to a boil over high heat, then reduce to a simmer. Cook, uncovered, until thickened, about 10 minutes. Remove the sauce from the heat; stir in the basil and balsamic vinegar; cover and set aside for about 10 minutes to let the flavors come together.

4. Drop the farfalle into the boiling water. Stir occasionally to make sure they don't stick together. When the pasta is al dente, drain in a colander, saving about ½ cup cooking water. Over medium heat stir and turn the pasta in the skillet with tongs to coat with sauce. If the pasta seems dry, splash in a little pasta water to keep it saucy. Season with salt and black pepper to taste. Divide among 4 warm serving bowls. Spoon a generous dollop of fresh ricotta on each serving, if desired.

FROM THE KITCHENS
Ricotta, in Italian, means "recooked." It's made from whey left over from making mozzarella. It's a rich, sweet cheese textured like thick sour cream. It's got a short shelf life, so use it up quickly; drizzle it with honey for an easy dessert.

mac & cheese
with red peppers & tomatoes | 8 servings

1 pound ziti or penne pasta
4 tablespoons unsalted butter
1 clove garlic, smashed
2½ cups fresh bread crumbs, preferably
    from sourdough bread
1 tablespoon finely chopped
    fresh flat-leaf parsley
1 tablespoon finely
    chopped fresh thyme
6 ounces shredded sharp white
    Cheddar cheese (about 2 cups)
4 ounces shredded fontina cheese
    (about 1⅓ cups)
3 ounces shredded smoked Gouda
    cheese (about 1 cup)
1 recipe hot Béchamel Sauce,
    (see recipe, right)
10 Oven-Dried Tomato halves
    (see page 11)
1 roasted red pepper, seeded and diced
    (see tip, below)
1 teaspoon kosher salt
    Freshly ground black pepper

SAUCE
4 tablespoons unsalted butter
1 shallot, chopped
½ medium carrot, peeled and chopped
½ rib celery, chopped
6 tablespoons all-purpose flour
4 cups milk
3 sprigs fresh flat-leaf parsley
1 sprig fresh thyme
1 small bay leaf
½ teaspoons kosher salt
    Pinch freshly grated nutmeg
    Freshly ground black pepper

1. Preheat the oven to 400°F. Lightly butter a 9x13-inch gratin or casserole dish. Bring a large pot of cold water to a boil over high heat; salt it generously. Add the pasta and boil, stirring occasionally, until it is just barely al dente (it will finish cooking in the sauce), about 8 minutes. Drain the pasta, put it in a large bowl, and cool slightly.

2. While the pasta cooks, melt the butter with the garlic clove in a medium skillet over medium heat. Add the bread crumbs, parsley, and thyme and toss to coat the bread crumbs thoroughly with the butter. Remove the garlic clove and set the crumbs aside.

3. Toss the pasta with the cheeses. Fold in the béchamel sauce, then the tomatoes, red pepper, salt, and pepper. Transfer the mixture to the prepared baking dish and scatter the bread crumbs over the top. Bake until the sauce bubbles and the crumbs crisp and brown, 25 to 30 minutes. Let rest for 10 minutes before serving.

BÉCHAMEL SAUCE

Melt the butter in a medium saucepan over medium-high heat. Add the shallot, carrot, and celery, and cook, covered, until softened, about 5 minutes. Stir in the flour with a wooden spoon and cook until it lightens in color, about 2 minutes. Slowly whisk in the milk and bring to a boil. Add the parsley, thyme, and bay leaf. Reduce the heat to maintain a gentle simmer and cook, whisking occasionally, until the sauce is thick, about 15 minutes. Strain the sauce into a bowl and season with the salt, nutmeg, and pepper. Press plastic wrap on the surface of the sauce until ready to use.

FROM THE KITCHENS

Fire-roasted peppers—sweet or hot—can be prepared anywhere there's an open flame or very high heat. To use a gas burner, hold the pepper over the flame with tongs or a long fork and turn to roast it evenly. Or place the whole pepper (or peppers) on a grill, turning occasionally. To roast under a broiler, halve them and remove the stem and seeds. Place halves, cut side down, on a foil-lined baking sheet. When skins are evenly charred and blistered, place peppers under an inverted bowl and let cool for about 20 minutes. The steam that builds will make it easy to remove the skin with a paring knife. Discard skin.

weekday italian gravy

6 servings, plus extra sauce

2   tablespoons extra-virgin olive oil
1½ pounds hot Italian-style link sausage
2   tablespoons tomato paste
½   cup water
4   pieces beef shank, each 1 inch
    thick (about 3½ pounds)
2   28-ounce cans crushed tomatoes
6   sun-dried tomatoes, preferably
    not oil-packed
1   large onion, chopped
6   cloves garlic, smashed
2   teaspoons dried Italian herb mix
1   bay leaf
1   tablespoon kosher salt
    Freshly ground black pepper
1   pound tubular pasta, such
    as rigatoni or ziti
    Freshly grated Parmesan or
    pecorino cheese

1. Heat a heavy skillet over medium-high heat. Add the oil and then the sausage; cook, turning occasionally, until brown all over, about 5 minutes. Transfer the sausage to a slow cooker. Pour off and discard all the oil in the skillet and return it to the heat. Add the tomato paste and cook, stirring, until brick red, about 1 minute. Add the water and bring to a boil, stirring to scrape up the browned bits. Pour the mixture over the sausage.

2. Add the beef shank, crushed tomatoes, sun-dried tomatoes, onion, garlic, Italian herbs, bay leaf, salt, and pepper to taste. Set the slow cooker on LOW for 8 hours, cover, and cook until the beef is very tender. Remove and discard bay leaf.

3. When ready to serve, bring a large pot of water to a boil and salt it generously. Add the pasta to the boiling water and cook, stirring occasionally, until al dente, about 10 minutes. Transfer the sausage and beef to a cutting board, slice into serving portions, and arrange on a serving platter. Drain the pasta and toss with some of the sauce; transfer to a serving bowl. Serve the meat and pasta separately with sauce on the side. Freeze any leftover sauce for up to 3 months.

FROM THE KITCHENS

Uncover the essence of tomatoes fast by cooking the tomato paste to concentrate its flavor before adding liquid to the pan.

shiitake & sun-dried tomato lasagna

4 to 6 servings

SAUCE

16	sun-dried tomatoes
2	pounds fresh shiitake mushrooms
4	tablespoons unsalted butter
4	tablespoons extra-virgin olive oil
3	teaspoons kosher salt
	Freshly ground black pepper
2	shallots, thinly sliced
4	cloves garlic, minced
1	tablespoon tomato paste
3½	cups canned whole tomatoes
3	sprigs fresh thyme
3	sprigs fresh oregano
1	sprig fresh rosemary
1	bay leaf
6	fresh flat-leaf parsley stems and 3 tablespoons chopped

LASAGNA

12	dry lasagna noodles
½	cup freshly grated Parmesan cheese
½	cup freshly grated Pecorino Romano cheese (2 ounces) (see tip, below)
1	recipe Béchamel Sauce (see page 150)

1. For the mushroom and tomato sauce: Put the sun-dried tomatoes in a bowl and add boiling water to cover. Set aside until soft, about 20 minutes, and then drain and quarter. Stem and quarter mushrooms. Melt 1 tablespoon of the butter with 1 tablespoon of the olive oil in a soup pot or Dutch oven over medium-high heat. Add half of the mushrooms and cook, stirring occasionally, until well browned and soft, about 10 minutes. Repeat with another 1 tablespoon each of butter and oil and other half of mushrooms. When all the mushrooms are cooked, put them in a bowl and toss with 1½ teaspoons of the salt and pepper to taste.

2. Reduce heat to medium and melt remaining 2 tablespoons butter with remaining 2 tablespoons olive oil. Add shallots, remaining 1½ teaspoons salt, and some pepper and cook, stirring, until shallots are golden brown, about 10 minutes. Add garlic and cook, stirring, until lightly browned. Add sun-dried tomatoes and tomato paste and cook, stirring, until paste is brick red, about 3 minutes. Crush tomatoes through your fingers into the pot. Stir in tomato juices and mushrooms and bring to a boil. Tie thyme, oregano, rosemary, bay leaf, and parsley stems together with a piece of clean kitchen string and add to the pot. Reduce heat and simmer sauce, stirring occasionally, until thick, about 10 minutes. Remove from heat and stir in chopped parsley. Discard herb bundle.

3. Cook lasagna noodles according to package directions.

4. Preheat the oven to 350°F. Butter a 9x13-inch casserole. Mix Parmesan and Pecorino cheeses in a small bowl. Cover bottom of prepared dish with ⅓ of the noodles. Top with ¼ of the cheese, ⅓ of the mushroom-tomato sauce, and ⅓ of the béchamel. Repeat twice, and top with the remaining cheese. Bake, uncovered, until hot and bubbly, about 45 minutes. Let lasagna stand for 10 minutes before slicing.

FROM THE KITCHENS

While Parmigiano-Reggiano is the most famous Italian grating cheese made from cow's milk, Pecorino Romano is its sharp-flavored sheep's-milk parallel. Pecorino can be used the same way Parmesan is used.

Make this tangy vegetarian lasagna on Friday and serve it up Saturday night—if you can wait that long, that is.

tubetti
with crab, fennel & lemon | 4 to 6 servings

1   pound lump crabmeat
3   tablespoons extra-virgin olive oil,
        plus additional for drizzling
4   scallions (white and green parts),
        thinly sliced
1   rib celery, finely diced
½   medium fennel bulb, finely
        diced (about 1¼ cups)
1½   teaspoons kosher salt, plus
        additional for seasoning
2   tablespoons chopped fresh
        flat-leaf parsley
½   teaspoon finely grated lemon zest
     Pinch crushed red pepper flakes
     Freshly ground black pepper
1   pound tubetti pasta
2   tablespoons freshly squeezed
        lemon juice
2   heads Bibb or 1 head Boston
        lettuce, leaves separated
2   ripe medium tomatoes, cut
        into wedges
     Extra-virgin olive oil
     Lemon wedges, for serving

1. Spread the crabmeat on a pan and carefully pick out and discard any bits of shell. Heat the 3 tablespoons oil in a large skillet over medium heat. Add the scallions, celery, fennel, and the 1½ teaspoons salt and cook, stirring occasionally, until vegetables are softened and fragrant, about 8 minutes. Add the crab and cook just until heated through, tossing gently to keep the crabmeat in lumps, about 2 minutes. Transfer the crab mixture to a large bowl and very gently fold in the parsley, lemon zest, red pepper flakes, and black pepper to taste. Cover and refrigerate the crab mixture for about 1 hour to allow the flavors to come together.

2. Bring a large pot of cold water to a boil over high heat and salt it generously. Add the pasta and cook, stirring occasionally, until al dente, about 9 minutes. Ladle out ¼ cup of the cooking water, set aside, and drain the pasta. Gently toss the pasta, the reserved pasta cooking liquid, and the lemon juice with the crab mixture. Cool to room temperature.

3. Divide the lettuce leaves and tomato wedges among individual plates. Season with salt and pepper to taste and drizzle with olive oil. Spoon the pasta mixture over the salads, place a lemon wedge on each, and serve immediately.

wild mushroom stroganoff | 6 servings

STROGANOFF

2½ cups water
¼ ounce dried morel mushrooms
8 tablespoons unsalted butter
8 ounces button mushrooms, stemmed, caps left whole
8 ounces cremini mushrooms, stemmed, caps left whole
8 ounces shiitake mushrooms, stemmed, caps left whole
8 ounces oyster mushrooms, gently torn into medium pieces
3 teaspoons chopped fresh thyme
  Freshly ground black pepper
4½ teaspoons kosher salt
1 medium onion, cut in 1½-inch dice
5 cloves garlic, chopped
1 tablespoon tomato paste
2 tablespoons all-purpose flour
⅔ cup sour cream (not low-fat)
2 teaspoons Dijon mustard
2 teaspoons fresh-squeezed lemon juice
1 recipe Parslied Egg Noodles (see recipe, right)
2 tablespoons chopped fresh flat-leaf parsley

NOODLES

  Kosher salt
1 12-ounce package wide egg noodles
4 to 6 tablespoons cold unsalted butter, cut into bits
3 tablespoons chopped fresh flat-leaf parsley
  Freshly ground black pepper

1. Bring water to a boil in a saucepan, add morels, and set aside until soft, about 20 minutes. Scoop morels from liquid, squeeze out water, and set aside. Reserve 2¼ cups liquid.

2. Melt 2 tablespoons of the butter in a large skillet over medium-high heat. When the butter stops foaming, add half the fresh mushrooms, 1½ teaspoons of the thyme, and a generous amount of pepper. Let the mushrooms sizzle for a few minutes without stirring. Stir them once they brown and then cook, stirring only occasionally, until the mushrooms are a deep, rich brown and very fragrant, about 10 minutes. Transfer to a bowl and cook the remaining mushrooms, using 2 more tablespoons butter, remaining 1½ teaspoons thyme, and some pepper. When all mushrooms are cooked and in the bowl, toss with 2 teaspoons of the salt and set aside.

3. Reduce heat to medium and add remaining 4 tablespoons butter to the skillet. Add onion, 1 teaspoon of the salt, some pepper, and cook, stirring, until browned, about 15 minutes. Add garlic and cook, stirring, until lightly browned, about 2 minutes. Add tomato paste and cook, stirring, about 1 minute.

4. Sprinkle flour over onion mixture and cook, stirring, for 1 minute. Increase heat to high and add morels and their reserved soaking liquid. Whisking constantly, bring mixture to a boil, then reduce heat and simmer for 5 minutes, whisking frequently. Pull pan off the heat and whisk in sour cream, mustard, lemon juice, remaining 1½ teaspoons salt, and some pepper. Stir in cooked mushrooms and set sauce aside.

5. Prepare Parslied Egg Noodles: Bring a large pot of cold water to a boil over high heat and salt it generously. Add the noodles and cook, stirring occasionally, until al dente, about 5 minutes. Ladle ¼ cup of the noodle cooking water into a medium skillet. Whisk in the butter bit by bit over low heat, letting each piece melt completely before adding the next, to make a creamy sauce. Stir in the parsley and season with salt and pepper. Drain the noodles, toss with butter sauce, and serve immediately.

6. Reheat the mushroom sauce over medium heat until hot (don't let it boil) and stir in the 2 tablespoons chopped parsley. Divide noodles among serving plates and top with the mushrooms. Grind a generous amount of pepper over each serving and serve immediately.

Sopa seca means "dry soup" in Spanish. This traditional Mexican dish starts out soupy and ends up noodley and delicious.

sopa seca | 4 servings

¼ cup extra-virgin olive oil
12 ounces fideos (bundled vermicelli)
1 medium onion, chopped
3 cloves garlic, minced
1 teaspoon ground coriander
1 teaspoon dried oregano,
   preferably Mexican
1 teaspoon New Mexican chile powder
1 bay leaf
1½ cups canned whole peeled tomatoes
1 to 2 chipotles in adobo sauce,
   minced (see tip, below)
1½ cups chicken broth,
   low-sodium canned
1 teaspoon kosher salt
Freshly ground black pepper
2 cups shredded smoked turkey
1 cup coarsely shredded Cheddar
   cheese (4 ounces)
Mexican crema or sour cream thinned
   with a bit of milk (optional)

1. Preheat the oven to 375°F. Brush a 9-inch square baking dish with oil. Heat the olive oil in a large skillet over medium heat. Add the fideos and cook, turning them with tongs, until golden brown on both sides, about 5 minutes. Transfer the bundles and any broken pieces to a plate.

2. Add the onion to the skillet and cook over medium heat, stirring occasionally, until golden brown, about 8 minutes. Stir in the garlic, coriander, oregano, chile powder, and bay leaf and cook until fragrant, about 30 seconds. Crush the tomatoes over the pot with your hand and add them to the pot along with their juices. Add the chipotles, increase the heat to high, and cook until thickened, about 2 minutes. Stir in the broth, the toasted fideos, the salt, and pepper to taste. Bring mixture to a boil, reduce heat, and simmer gently, uncovered, breaking up the fideos with a spoon, for about 5 minutes. Stir in the turkey.

3. Remove the bay leaf. Transfer the mixture to the prepared baking dish, sprinkle the grated cheese over the top, and cover loosely with foil. Bake until the cheese melts and the casserole is hot through and through, about 20 minutes. If desired, serve with some crema drizzled over the top.

FROM THE KITCHENS
• Chile powder (with an "e") denotes a ground single pepper, such as New Mexican or ancho. Chili powder (with an "i") blends chile with other herbs and spices such as garlic, oregano, cumin, coriander, and clove. We remember it this way: Chili powders that end with "i" include other ingredients.
• Chipotles are dried, smoked jalapeño chiles that lend a little heat and a rich, chocolatey flavor to foods. The curing process mellows their heat a bit, compared to the fresh chile. You'll usually see them canned en adobo (a vinegary sauce made from pureed chiles, herbs, and vinegar) in the Latin section of your store, near the salsas and canned beans. They're also sold dried or pureed with vinegar in hot sauce form.

Forget takeout. With just a few pantry staples, you can deliver oodles of noodles to your table in no time.

sesame noodles with chicken

4 to 6 servings

Kosher salt
1 pound spaghetti or Chinese egg noodles
2 tablespoons toasted sesame oil
1 garlic clove, peeled
1 1-inch piece peeled fresh ginger
½ cup smooth peanut butter
¼ cup soy sauce
2 tablespoons dark brown sugar
1 tablespoon rice vinegar
¾ teaspoon crushed red pepper
¼ cup hot water
1 Kirby cucumber, halved and sliced
1 cup shredded cooked chicken
6 scallions (white and green parts), sliced
¼ cup dry-roasted peanuts, chopped

1. Bring a large pot of cold water to a boil over high heat. When the pasta water boils, salt it generously, add the spaghetti or noodles, and cook, stirring occasionally, until al dente. Drain and rinse under cold running water. Put the spaghetti in a large bowl and toss with the sesame oil.

2. To make the Peanut Sauce: In a blender drop in the garlic and ginger while the motor is running. When the chopping is complete, stop the machine and add the peanut butter, soy sauce, brown sugar, vinegar, and red pepper. Process until smooth, then—with the blender running—slowly pour in the water.

3. To serve, toss the spaghetti with the Peanut Sauce, then top with the cucumber, chicken, scallions, and peanuts.

FROM THE KITCHENS
Toasted sesame oil delivers richness and intensity to sesame sauce with just a drizzle. Maintain its punch by storing it in your fridge.

thai rice noodles | 4 servings

8   to 10 ounces medium-thick
    rice noodles (also called rice
    sticks or jantaboon)
3   tablespoons fish sauce
    (see tip, below)
3   tablespoons sugar
3   tablespoons soy sauce
2   tablespoons peanut oil
4   scallions, thinly sliced
    (white and green parts)
1   jalapeño, stemmed and finely
    chopped (see tip, below)
3   cloves garlic, smashed, peeled,
    and roughly chopped
1   cup mung bean sprouts
2   handfuls fresh mint or
    basil leaves (about 1 cup)
½   cup cashews or peanuts
1   lime, cut into wedges

1. Put the rice noodles in a bowl with hot water to cover. Soak until tender and pliable, about 30 minutes.

2. Meanwhile, in a small bowl whisk together the fish sauce, sugar, and soy sauce; set aside.

3. Drain the noodles and set aside. Heat a large skillet over high heat. Add the oil and, when hot, add the scallions, jalapeño, garlic, and bean sprouts. Cook, stirring, until the vegetables begin to brown and the garlic is fragrant, about 1 minute. Add the sauce mixture; gently swirl around the pan. Add the drained noodles and toss to coat them with the sauce. Remove the skillet from the heat and coarsely tear the mint into the skillet. Sprinkle in the nuts. Toss a few more times to incorporate the mint and nuts and mound into a large serving bowl. Garnish with lime wedges and serve.

FROM THE KITCHENS
• Fish sauce is the Southeast Asian equivalent of Worcestershire sauce: It's pungent, salty, and adds a hint of complexity to dishes. Despite the name, it doesn't taste fishy—it's got a unique, unmistakably authentic flavor. Look for the translucent, amber-color sauce in ethnic markets or the international aisle of your store. Keep it in a cool, dark cupboard for up to 2 years.
• For a milder dish, halve the jalapeño lengthwise and scrape out the seeds with the tip of your knife; for more heat, leave the seeds in.
• Upgrade this simple noodle dish in any one of these ways: Toss in 1 to 2 cups shredded cooked chicken, extra-firm tofu cubes, thinly sliced cooked pork tenderloin, or 1 pound ready-to-eat shrimp. Or, add a cup or so of quick-cooking vegetables, like snow peas, or sliced bell pepper or onion, along with the scallions. If you want to add longer-cooking vegetables, like broccoli or green beans, steam them most of the way before adding them to the pan. Or simply add some chopped ginger along with the garlic, ¼ cup canned coconut milk along with the sauce, or sprinkle on some chopped chiles before serving.

brothy japanese noodles
with mushrooms & tofu | 4 servings

⅓ cup soy sauce

3 tablespoons rice vinegar

2 tablespoons mirin (sweet Japanese rice wine)

2 tablespoons peanut oil

1 tablespoon toasted sesame oil

1 2-inch piece peeled fresh ginger, finely grated

2 blocks firm tofu (about 24 ounces), blotted dry

1 pound portobello mushroom caps (about 6 medium)

2 tablespoons gomashio (see tip, below), plus additional for garnish
Kosher salt

2 small bundles soba noodles (see tip, below) (about 11 ounces)

4 scallions (white and green parts), thinly sliced

1 teaspoon chile oil

1. Position an oven rack about 6 inches from the broiler and preheat. Line a large broiler pan with aluminum foil. Whisk the soy sauce with the vinegar, mirin, peanut oil, sesame oil, and ginger in a large bowl.

2. Stand the tofu blocks on end and halve top to bottom, then halve the slices to make 8 pieces. (If you like your tofu crispy, cut it into smaller pieces.) Arrange the tofu and mushroom caps on the broiler pan, pour about half the soy sauce mixture over, and turn the tofu and caps to coat thoroughly. Set aside for at least 5 or up to 30 minutes. Broil the tofu and mushrooms until the mushroom caps start to brown and shrink, about 5 minutes. Turn, sprinkle 1 tablespoon of the gomashio over the tofu and continue to broil until the mushrooms are soft and the tofu is glazed, about 5 minutes more.

3. Meanwhile, bring a medium saucepan of water to a boil. When the water boils, salt it generously, add the soba noodles, and cook until slightly tender, about 2 minutes. Add 1 cup of cold water to the pot, return it to a simmer, and cook the noodles until al dente, about 2 minutes more. Scoop out ¼ cup of the noodle cooking water and add it to the remaining soy mixture. Drain the noodles and add them to the soy mixture along with the scallions, chile oil, and remaining 1 tablespoon gomashio; toss to coat.

4. Slice the mushroom caps. Divide the noodles among 4 bowls and top them with the tofu and mushroom slices and more gomashio.

FROM THE KITCHENS
Japanese soba (buckwheat noodles) can be found in most supermarkets' ethnic or organic food aisle, which is where you'll also find gomashio, a sesame seed-sea salt (and sometimes seaweed flakes) spice blend that supplies big effects with little effort. It's great on soup or sprinkled over rice. You can substitute toasted sesame seeds in a pinch.

beans & grains

Humble at first glance, these earthy foods are transformed into a world of dishes and fabulous flavors that taste good—and make you feel good.

baked mexican black beans

4 to 6 servings

1 pound dried black beans
6 slices bacon, cut crosswise into
    thin strips
1 large onion, roughly chopped
5 cloves garlic, chopped
2 teaspoons ground cumin
1 bay leaf
6 cups water, chicken broth,
    or a combination
1 jalapeño
2 teaspoons kosher salt
   Freshly ground black pepper
1 14-ounce can diced tomatoes
1 tablespoon cider vinegar

TOPPING
1 red or yellow bell pepper, stemmed,
    seeded, and chopped
5 scallions, thinly sliced (white and
    green parts)
1 cup sour cream
½ teaspoon kosher salt
   Freshly ground black pepper

1. Preheat the oven to 350°F. Rinse the beans in a colander.

2. Cook bacon in a medium Dutch oven (or a soup pot with a tight-fitting lid that can go in the oven) over medium heat until almost crisp, about 10 minutes. Stir the onion, garlic, cumin, and bay leaf into the bacon. Cook, stirring occasionally, until onion is tender, about 8 minutes.

3. Add the beans, water, the whole jalapeño, the salt, and some black pepper. Stir with a wooden spoon to scrape up any brown bits in the pan. Bring to a boil, cover, and bake for 1 hour. Uncover, add the tomatoes and their juices, and bake until beans are tender and soupy, about 45 minutes to 1 hour. Stir in vinegar.

4. Meanwhile, make the topping: In a medium bowl combine the chopped bell pepper and scallions. Stir in the sour cream and season with ½ teaspoon salt and some black pepper.

FROM THE KITCHENS
• For a thicker bean dish, puree about half the beans in the Dutch oven with an immersion blender until creamy. Leftovers are great in burritos.
• Upgrade this rustic dish by adding 1 cup roughly chopped fresh cilantro, either to the cooked beans when you stir in the vinegar, or scattered over the fresh topping.

mexican rice casserole

4 servings

2 tablespoons olive oil, plus more for
   brushing in the baking dish
1 large onion, chopped
4 cloves garlic, chopped
2 teaspoons kosher salt
1 teaspoon dried oregano
1 teaspoon ground cumin
¼ teaspoon freshly ground
   black pepper
1 14.5-ounce can diced
   fire-roasted tomatoes
1 4.5-ounce can chopped
   roasted green chiles
2 cups cooked white rice
12 ounces Monterey Jack cheese, diced
1½ cups chopped or shredded cooked
   meat, such as chicken, chorizo,
   beef, or pork (optional)

1. Preheat the oven to 350°F. Grease an 8x8-inch casserole with a little olive oil. Heat the 2 tablespoons olive oil in a large skillet over medium heat. Add the onion, garlic, salt, oregano, cumin, and black pepper. Cook, stirring occasionally, until the onion is tender, about 5 minutes.

2. Add the tomatoes and chiles to the skillet, increase the heat to high, and simmer until thickened, 4 to 5 minutes.

3. Stir in the rice, cheese, and cooked meat, if using. Transfer to the prepared dish and bake until browned and bubbly, 30 to 35 minutes. Remove from the oven and let stand about 10 minutes before serving.

FROM THE KITCHENS

• Cook bell peppers, corn, or zucchini in a little olive oil and add them along with the rice or stir in some chopped cilantro or scallions before the casserole goes into the oven.

• This casserole, like most, can be assembled and refrigerated ahead of time. If you go that route, take it out of the fridge about 30 minutes before you bake it. Letting casseroles stand out of the oven for 10 minutes or so before serving makes them a little more solid and easier to cut.

• Canned roasted green chiles are a good bet for a mellow chile burn. Fire-roasted tomatoes give you a more concentrated tomatoey flavor with a hint of smokiness.

Here's to the humble chicken breast: No more dowdy sides for you. Rice takes on exotic flare when laced with spices, dried fruits, and nuts.

basmati rice pilaf
with apricots

4 servings

¼   cup chopped dried apricots

2   wide strips lemon zest

2   cups cold water

3   tablespoons unsalted butter

1   teaspoon garam masala
    (an Indian spice blend)

1   medium onion, diced

1¼   teaspoons kosher salt

1   cup basmati rice, lightly rinsed
    and drained

    Freshly ground black pepper

⅓   cup fresh mint leaves

¼   cup toasted unsalted pistachios
    or cashews

1. Put the apricots and lemon zest in the 2 cups of cold water. Melt the butter in a medium saucepan over medium heat, add the garam masala, and toast, stirring, until fragrant, about 1 minute. Add the onion and ¼ teaspoon of the salt and cook, stirring occasionally, until the onion is tender and translucent, about 6 minutes.

2. Stir in the rice and cook, stirring occasionally, until it begins to brown, about 4 minutes. Stir in the water along with the apricots, lemon zest, the remaining 1 teaspoon salt, and pepper to taste. Bring to a simmer. Reduce the heat to low, wrap a clean dish towel around the saucepan lid, and cover saucepan. Cook for 10 minutes, set aside for 5 minutes undisturbed, then remove lid and fluff with a fork. Mound the pilaf on a serving platter or in a shallow bowl, tear the mint over, and top with the nuts.

FROM THE KITCHENS

Wrapping the lid with a dish towel keeps the steam in the pot, encourages the rice grains to stay separate, and absorbs condensation that would otherwise collect on the lid and drip back into the pan.

middle eastern lentil & rice pilaf

4 servings

1/3 cup extra-virgin olive oil,
    plus 2 tablespoons
1 large onion, halved and thinly sliced
1 teaspoon kosher salt
Freshly ground black pepper
1/2 cup long-grain white rice
1/2 cup green (also called brown) lentils
2 cloves garlic, smashed and peeled
1/2 teaspoon ground allspice
3 cups water
1 large lemon, quartered

FOR SERVING
1/2 cup Greek-style yogurt, for serving
    (see tip, below) (optional)

1. Heat the 1/3 cup olive oil in a large skillet over medium heat. Add the onion and cook, stirring occasionally, until it is tender and golden brown, 30 to 45 minutes, adjusting the heat as needed if the onion starts to brown too quickly. Season with 1/2 teaspoon of the salt and some black pepper.

2. Heat the remaining 2 tablespoons olive oil in a Dutch oven over medium-high heat. Add rice and stir to coat. Cook, stirring occasionally, until rice is lightly toasted, about 5 minutes. Add the lentils, stirring to coat. Add the garlic, allspice, and remaining 1/2 teaspoon salt and cook, stirring until fragrant, about 1 minute. Add the water, increase heat to high, and bring to a rolling boil. Adjust the heat to maintain a low simmer, cover, and cook until the lentils are tender and all the water has been absorbed, about 20 minutes. (No peeking.)

3. To serve, toss the caramelized onions with the lentils and rice and sprinkle with the juice of 1 or 2 lemon wedges or to taste. Stir and mound onto a platter. Serve with the yogurt and the additional lemon wedges to pass at the table, if desired.

FROM THE KITCHENS
• Greek-style yogurt is thick and creamy. If you can't find it, drain plain whole-milk yogurt overnight through a coffee filter or paper towel in a strainer over a bowl in the fridge, discarding the liquid that accumulates.
• Cooking onions for a long time over low heat caramelizes the sugars and turns them rich and sweet. Make extra—leftovers are great in pasta, risotto, mashed potatoes, or on top of pizza or burgers.

singapore fried rice | 4 to 6 servings

¼ cup vegetable oil
8 ounces ham or smoked chicken or turkey, diced
Kosher salt
Freshly ground black pepper
3 cloves garlic
1 2-inch piece peeled fresh ginger
1 bunch scallions (white and green parts kept separate), thinly sliced
1 heaping cup frozen corn, peas, or carrots, or a mix
3 large eggs, lightly beaten
1 tablespoon hot Madras curry powder
4 cups cold cooked jasmine rice

1. Heat a large nonstick skillet over high heat. Add 1 tablespoon of the oil, then add the ham or other meats. Season with salt and pepper to taste and stir-fry until browned, about 2 minutes.

2. While the ham browns, finely chop the garlic and ginger together in a mini-chopper. Add the mixture to the ham, along with the scallion whites, and stir-fry until fragrant, about 30 seconds. Add the frozen vegetables, season with salt and pepper to taste, and stir-fry until vegetables are heated but still crisp, about 1 minute. Transfer the mixture to a large serving bowl.

3. Return the skillet to the heat and add 1 tablespoon of the oil. Add eggs and season with salt and pepper to taste. Cook, stirring constantly, until eggs are set but still tender. Tip eggs out of the pan into the bowl with the ham mixture and break eggs up with a wooden spoon or spatula.

4. Return the skillet to the heat and add the remaining 2 tablespoons oil and the curry powder. Stir until fragrant, about 30 seconds. Add the rice to the pan, breaking up any clumps, and stir-fry until coated evenly with the oil. Cook the rice undisturbed until the bottom is slightly crisp, about 3 to 4 minutes. Stir scallion greens into the rice. Add rice to the serving bowl, stir to distribute the ingredients evenly, and season with salt and pepper to taste.

cheese risotto | 4 servings

6 cups water or half water and
    half chicken broth
2 teaspoons kosher salt
2 tablespoons extra-virgin olive oil
1 medium onion, finely chopped
1½ cups Arborio rice
½ cup white wine or dry white
    vermouth
2 tablespoons unsalted butter
½ cup freshly grated Parmesan
    cheese, plus more for serving
Freshly ground black pepper

1. Put the water (or water and broth, if using) in a medium saucepan and add the salt. Bring to barely a simmer over low heat.

2. Heat the olive oil in a large soup pot or Dutch oven over medium heat. Add the onion and cook until tender, about 6 minutes. Add the rice and stir to lightly "toast" the rice and coat it with oil, about 2 minutes.

3. Add the wine and cook, stirring constantly with a wooden spoon, until the rice absorbs the wine, about 2 minutes.

4. Add just enough of the hot liquid to completely moisten the rice (about 1 cup or so) and adjust the heat so the risotto is at a brisk simmer but not boiling. Stir frequently until the rice absorbs the liquid, about 1 minute. When there is just a thin film of starchy liquid at the bottom of the skillet, add about 1 cup of liquid again. Cook, stirring, until it is absorbed. Repeat the process until the risotto is creamy but still al dente, 16 to 18 minutes. (You may not use all the liquid.)

5. Cut the butter into 4 or 5 pieces. Remove the risotto from the heat and vigorously beat in the butter. Stir in the cheese. Divide risotto among 4 warm bowls, grind a generous amount of black pepper over each, and serve, passing more cheese at the table.

FROM THE KITCHENS
• Risotto continues to cook after you take it off the heat, so even if it's still slightly underdone when you add the butter, it'll finish by the time it gets to the table.
• Boost the flavor of this simple risotto by using good vegetable, chicken, or fish broth in place of the water. Or, as you're beating in the butter, add the juice and zest of a lemon, ¼ to ⅓ cup of chopped fresh herbs, or try a different type of hard cheese.
• Add texture by stirring in a cup of cooked vegetables (asparagus, mushrooms, peas, zucchini, spinach, or artichokes), thawed frozen vegetables, or leftover roasted vegetables (beets, butternut squash, pumpkin) with the last addition of liquid. Or add a cup or so of cooked meat, poultry, or seafood.
• Add flavor and texture by using a cup of leftover sauce or stew in place of the water, about ⅔ of the way through cooking time. Marinara sauce is great here, as is any meat- or poultry-based stew (just chop any big pieces of meat or vegetables before you add them).

We love making risotto, but the last thing we want to do when we get home from a long workday is babysit a pot of rice. We wondered if a pressure cooker's high heat and concentrated steam could do the work for us. It was worth a shot.

shrimp & saffron risotto

4 servings

2 tablespoons extra-virgin olive oil
1 small onion, coarsley chopped
3 large cloves garlic, smashed
1 teaspoon fennel seeds
1 teaspoon kosher salt, plus additional for seasoning
  Freshly ground black pepper
1½ cups Arborio rice
2 tablespoons tomato paste
  Pinch saffron threads
¼ cup dry white vermouth
3 cups chicken broth, low-sodium canned or homemade
1 pound medium shrimp, peeled and deveined

1. Heat the olive oil in a 7-liter pressure cooker over medium-high heat. Add the onion, garlic, fennel seeds, the 1 teaspoon salt, and pepper to taste. Cook, stirring occasionally, until the vegetables soften a bit, about 5 minutes. Add the rice, tomato paste, and saffron and stir until the grains are evenly colored. Stir in vermouth and chicken broth. Close the pressure cooker lid and bring the pressure up to high (which can take up to 10 minutes), then reduce the heat, if necessary, to maintain an even pressure for 3 minutes. Remove from the heat and gently press the cooker's pressure indicator stem until no more steam comes out. This may take up to 2 minutes.

2. Carefully remove the lid—the risotto will look a bit soupy at this point. Stir in the shrimp and let the risotto stand, off the heat, until shrimp are pale pink and cooked through, about 2 minutes. Season with additional salt and pepper to taste.

risotto
with winter vegetables | 4 servings

4 tablespoons unsalted butter
1 medium onion, chopped
4 cloves garlic, smashed
1 teaspoon kosher salt, plus additional
   for seasoning
   Freshly ground black pepper
1½ cups Arborio rice
3 carrots, cut into large chunks
2 sprigs fresh thyme
1 small celery root (about 1 pound),
   peeled and cut into chunks
1 butternut squash, halved, peeled,
   seeded, and cut into large chunks
   (optional)
3 cups chicken broth, low-sodium
   canned or homemade
½ cup dry white wine
1 large bunch mustard greens, washed
   and torn (4 to 5 cups)
1 cup freshly grated pecorino cheese,
   plus additional for serving

1. Melt 2 tablespoons of the butter in a 7-liter pressure cooker over medium-high heat. Add the onion, garlic, the 1 teaspoon salt, and the pepper to taste and cook, stirring occasionally, until the vegetables soften a bit, about 5 minutes. Add the rice and stir to coat. Stir in the carrots, thyme sprigs, celery root, squash (if desired), chicken broth, and wine. Close the pressure cooker lid and bring the pressure up to high (which can take up to 10 minutes), then reduce the heat to maintain an even pressure for 3 minutes. Remove from the heat and gently press the cooker's pressure indicator stem until no more steam comes out. This may take up to 2 minutes.

2. Carefully remove the lid—the risotto will look a bit soupy at this point. Stir the mustard greens into the risotto, then let the mixture sit until the greens wilt, about 2 minutes. Stir in the remaining 2 tablespoons butter and the 1 cup cheese. Season to taste with salt and pepper, if you like. Pass additional grated cheese at the table.

FROM THE KITCHENS
Squash your prep time by buying peeled, seeded, and chopped butternut squash from your supermarket.

baked polenta
with broccoli rabe & sausage | 6 servings

POLENTA

- 5 cups water
- 1 cup coarse-ground cornmeal
  (see tip, below)
- 1 teaspoon kosher salt
- ½ cup freshly grated Pecorino Romano
  cheese (2 ounces) (see tip,
  page 152)

BROCCOLI RABE AND SAUSAGE

- 3 tablespoons extra-virgin olive oil
- 1 pound sweet Italian sausage links
- 2 tablespoons water
- 4 cloves garlic, thinly sliced
- ½ teaspoon crushed red pepper flakes
- 1 pound broccoli rabe, woody stems
  trimmed
- 1 cup canned crushed tomatoes
- ½ teaspoon kosher salt

1. For the polenta: Preheat the oven to 375°F. Pour the water into a Dutch oven, then whisk in the cornmeal and salt. Bake, uncovered, for 45 minutes. Remove from the oven and whisk. Return the polenta to the oven and bake until it thickens a bit more, about 10 minutes.

2. While the polenta bakes, cook the broccoli rabe and sausages: Heat the olive oil in a large skillet over medium heat. Add the sausages and water, cover, and cook until just firm, about 5 minutes. Uncover the skillet, increase the heat to high, and cook the sausages, turning as necessary, until browned all over and the water evaporates, about 4 minutes. Transfer to a plate and keep warm; leave about 1 tablespoon of drippings in the skillet and discard the rest.

3. Reduce the heat to medium, add the garlic to the drippings, and cook, stirring frequently, until golden brown, about 2 minutes. Stir in the red pepper flakes and cook for 30 seconds. Add the broccoli rabe, crushed tomatoes with juices, and salt; increase the heat to medium-high, cover, and cook, stirring occasionally, until the broccoli rabe is tender, about 4 minutes. Nestle the sausages in the greens, spoon sauce over and around them, and cook until heated through.

4. Just before serving, stir the polenta until smooth, then stir in the cheese. Spoon the polenta onto a serving platter and arrange the greens and sausages over the top.

FROM THE KITCHENS

- Broccoli rabe—also called rapini—is more assertive than broccoli and occasionally is downright bitter. Blanching it in salted water before sautéing will mellow it.
- Cornmeal comes in three textures: fine, medium, and coarsely ground. Although the three are generally interchangeable in recipes and can be used according to your own preference, polenta is traditionally made with a coarser grind.

This is
the perfect
one-pot
summer
supper,
garden
fresh with
a balance
of cool, fast
flavor.

beef & bulgur pilaf
with mint

4 servings

4	tablespoons extra-virgin olive oil
¼	cup pine nuts
8	ounces lean ground beef
¼	teaspoon ground allspice
1½	cups medium-grain bulgur
3½	cups chicken broth, low-sodium canned
1	medium zucchini, diced
1½	teaspoons kosher salt
	Freshly ground black pepper
2	cups cherry or grape tomatoes
2	scallions (green and white parts)
¼	cup chopped fresh dill
¼	cup coarsley chopped fresh mint
1	clove garlic, minced
	Finely grated zest and freshly squeezed juice of ½ lemon (about 2 tablespoons juice)

1. Heat 2 tablespoons of the olive oil and the pine nuts in a Dutch oven or soup pot over medium-high heat and stir occasionally until the nuts are toasted, about 2 minutes. Add the ground beef, breaking it up with a spoon. Sprinkle with the allspice and cook, stirring, until the meat is no longer pink, about 3 minutes. Stir in the bulgur and cook until lightly toasted, about 3 minutes. Add the chicken broth, bring the mixture to a boil, and then adjust the heat to maintain a gentle simmer. Scatter the zucchini over the surface of the pilaf (don't stir it in; it will steam on top) and sprinkle with 1 teaspoon of the salt and pepper to taste. Cook, uncovered, until the bulgur is tender but not mushy, 10 to 12 minutes.

2. Meanwhile, halve the tomatoes and thinly slice the scallions. Toss them with the dill, mint, garlic, lemon zest and juice, the remaining 2 tablespoons olive oil, the remaining ½ teaspoon salt, and pepper to taste.

3. Mound the pilaf on a serving platter and spoon the tomato salad evenly over the top. Serve warm.

FROM THE KITCHENS
Bulgur is quick-cooking cracked wheat that's most often used in the Middle Eastern side dish tabbouleh (see page 180). We take advantage of its chewy charm and healthy fiber content in our pilaf.

tabbouleh | 4 servings

1¼   cups water
1   cup medium-grain bulgur
2½   teaspoons salt, plus more
     for seasoning
2   large or 6 medium ripe plum
     tomatoes (about 1½ pounds),
     cored, seeded, and chopped
1   bunch fresh flat-leaf parsley
1   bunch fresh mint
4   scallions, thinly sliced (white and
     green parts)
2   lemons
¼   cup extra-virgin olive oil
     Freshly ground black pepper

1. Bring the water to a boil in a small saucepan. Add the bulgur and ½ teaspoon of the salt. Stir and remove from the heat. Cover with a tight-fitting lid and let the bulgur sit for 30 minutes. (No peeking.)

2. Toss the tomatoes in a colander with ½ teaspoon of the salt; set in the sink to drain.

3. Hold each bunch of herbs upside down over your cutting board and shave the leaves off using a very sharp knife. (See photo, page 38) Wash the leaves and dry well in a salad spinner or between paper towels. Finely chop the herbs and put in a large serving bowl.

4. Add scallions to the bowl. Juice the lemons through your fingers or a strainer (to catch the seeds) into the bowl. Stir in the olive oil, remaining salt, and black pepper to taste.

5. Fluff the bulgur with a fork and add to the salad bowl. Toss in the tomatoes and use a big spoon to mix everything together evenly. Taste and season with salt and black pepper, if necessary.

FROM THE KITCHENS
• The name "tabbouleh" comes from the Arabic verb for "to spice." Tabbouleh is common all over the Middle East, with regional variations in Lebanon and Syria. The Lebanese tend to prefer a greener (that is, more parsley-heavy) version of it; Syrian tradition bulks it up with more bulgur.
• Upgrade this grain-based salad by adding more veggies: diced cucumber, sliced radishes, pitted Kalamata olives, or diced red bell pepper. Or, add some protein: chickpeas, shredded cooked chicken, leftover salmon, crumbled feta cheese, or toasted pine nuts, almonds, or walnuts.

skillet cornbread pudding
with ham & pepper jack

4 to 6 servings

2 tablespoons unsalted butter
1½ cups cooked corn, thawed frozen or fresh
1 bunch scallions (white and green parts), sliced
1 6-ounce chunk Black Forest ham, diced (about 1¼ cups)
1 clove garlic, chopped
½ teaspoon chili powder
3 large eggs
2 cups half-and-half
4 ounces pepper Jack cheese, diced
¼ cup chopped fresh basil
1 teaspoon kosher salt
   Freshly ground black pepper
1 cup packaged cornbread stuffing cubes
   Pinch sugar

1. Preheat the oven to 350°F. Melt the butter in a 10-inch cast-iron skillet over medium heat. Add the corn, scallions, ham, garlic, and chili powder. Cook, stirring occasionally, until the scallions are soft, about 3 minutes. Meanwhile, lightly beat the eggs in a large bowl and stir in the half-and-half, cheese, basil, salt, and pepper to taste.

2. Pull the skillet from the heat. Stir the cornbread stuffing and sugar into the skillet. Pour the egg mixture over and stir gently to distribute all the ingredients evenly. Transfer the skillet to the oven and bake until lightly puffed and golden, about 30 minutes. Serve warm.

FROM THE KITCHENS
Lightly dressed mesclun mounded next to a serving of savory bread pudding transforms this country skillet dish from down-home to downtown.

sesame tofu stir-fry

2 to 4 servings

¼ cup soy sauce
1 tablespoon dark sesame oil
1 tablespoon rice vinegar
2 teaspoons sugar
1 block firm tofu (14 to 15 ounces), drained and cut into 1-inch cubes
2 teaspoons sesame seeds
3 tablespoons vegetable oil
1 1-inch piece fresh ginger, peeled and grated
1 clove garlic, finely chopped
2 scallions, chopped (white and green parts separate)
8 ounces snow peas, stemmed and tough strings removed
2 tablespoons water
2 to 4 cups cooked white or brown rice, for serving

1. Whisk soy sauce, sesame oil, vinegar, and sugar in a glass pie plate or baking dish. Add tofu, turn to coat, and set aside for 30 minutes.

2. Meanwhile, toast the sesame seeds in a small dry skillet over medium heat, stirring and tossing, until fragrant and a shade or two darker, about 4 minutes.

3. When you're ready to cook the tofu, reserve 1 tablespoon of the marinade in a small bowl and drain off the rest. Pat the tofu dry with paper towels. Heat 2 tablespoons of the oil in a large nonstick skillet or wok over medium-high to high heat. Working in batches if necessary, fry the tofu in the skillet, turning occasionally, until golden, about 7 minutes. Transfer the tofu with a slotted spoon or spatula; toss with the sesame seeds. Set aside.

4. Add the remaining oil to the skillet. Stir-fry the ginger, garlic, and scallion whites until fragrant, about 30 seconds. Add the snow peas and water and stir-fry until the snow peas are bright green and lightly glazed, about 2 minutes. Return the fried tofu and scallion greens to the pan, pour in reserved marinade, and stir gently to combine. Cook until the snow peas are crisp-tender, about 2 minutes more. Serve with rice.

FROM THE KITCHENS
• Tofu's a bean, sort of. Low-fat, high-protein, and really good for you, it's made from soybeans and comes in firm, soft, and silken forms, all available in individually wrapped blocks (usually found in the refrigerated section of the supermarket). Firm tofu is great for high-heat stir-fries, and soft and silken tofu tend to be better with more gentle cooking.
• Snow peas are sweet and crisp—buy vibrantly colored ones with no spots or discoloring. Usually their "strings" are removed before they're sold, but if you see prominent strings sticking out of one end when you get them home, snap back the stem end and pull off the string.
• Stir-frying works best on super-high heat. You don't need a wok to stir-fry; if you have one, use it, but if not, any wide-bottomed pan is fine. If you'd like to add other veggies, chop them up into bite-sized pieces. Add the slower cooking ones earlier than quick-cooking ones.

beef, pork & lamb

When nothing will do but a hearty, primal, meat-centered meal, here's a whole host of rib-sticking recipes to choose from.

steak frites | 2 to 4 servings

STEAK

1½ pounds bone-in rib-eye steak
    Kosher salt and freshly ground
       black pepper
 1 tablespoon oil, such as vegetable,
       soybean, or corn
    Spicy Red Pepper Sauce
       (see page 34)
 2 tablespoons minced fresh flat-leaf
       parsley

FRIES

 1 head garlic, loose skin rubbed off,
       halved horizontally
 6 cups vegetable oil
1½ pounds large boiling or baking
       potatoes, unpeeled, scrubbed
 ½ cup chopped fresh flat-leaf parsley
    Finely grated zest of 1 lemon
 ½ teaspoon kosher salt, plus additional
       for seasoning
    Lemon wedges, for garnish

Preheat the oven to 425°F. A half-hour before cooking, remove steak from refrigerator. Heat a large cast-iron skillet over high heat. Pat steak dry and season generously with salt and pepper. Add oil to hot skillet and when it begins to smoke add steak. Reduce heat slightly and cook steak until browned, about 4 minutes. Turn steak and transfer skillet to the oven. Roast until an instant-read thermometer inserted sideways into the steak registers 120°F for medium-rare, about 8 minutes. Transfer steak to a cutting board and let it rest for 10 minutes. Cut steak from the bone and carve meat across the grain. Arrange slices on 2 or 4 plates, drizzle some of the red pepper sauce over and around, and sprinkle with parsley.

GREMOLATA SHOESTRING FRIES

1. Put garlic halves and oil in a deep, heavy-bottomed pot and heat over medium heat until a deep-fry thermometer registers 320°F. Line a pan with paper towels. Use a slotted spoon to transfer garlic to prepared pan and heat oil to 360°F.

2. While oil heats, slice potatoes into shoestring fries with the thin julienne attachment of a mandoline or vegetable slicer. Swish cut potatoes in a bowl of tepid water, then spin them in a salad spinner. Spread on paper towels and blot with more paper towels—you want them bone dry so they don't spatter.

3. Increase heat to medium-high. Working in batches, add the potatoes to the oil, and fry until brown and crispy, about 4 minutes. Scoop fries from oil with a slotted spoon and drain on prepared baking sheet. Repeat with remaining potatoes, making sure oil returns to 360°F before adding each batch.

4. Squeeze cloves from one of the garlic halves and mince; reserve other half for garnish. Toss minced garlic with parsley, lemon zest, and ½ teaspoon salt in a large bowl. Dump fries on top and toss. Mound fries on a platter, season with salt to taste, and serve with reserved garlic and lemon wedges.

FROM THE KITCHENS

A rib-eye steak is from the same cut as a standing rib roast, which is why it is so nicely marbled (a lovely way to say it contains a fair amount of fat). The marbling makes rib-eye butter-knife tender and flavorful. Heads-up: The meat along the giant bone is beyond delicious.

Relish the smoky-charred flavor of grilled steak and tomatoes any time. A quick kiss from your broiler's flame is all it takes to awaken summertime flavor.

broiled flank steak
with tomato-scallion relish

4 to 6 servings

STEAK
1   flank steak (about 1½ pounds)
⅓   cup extra-virgin olive oil
1   tablespoon herbes de Provence
    Kosher salt
    Freshly ground black pepper

RELISH
3   ripe medium tomatoes
1   bunch scallions, trimmed
8   whole garlic cloves, unpeeled
1   tablespoon balsamic
    or red wine vinegar
¼   teaspoon Worcestershire sauce
    Toasted crusty bread, for serving

1. Position a broiler pan on the rack closest to the broiler and preheat to high. Rub the steak lightly with some of the olive oil and sprinkle with the herbes de Provence and salt and pepper to taste. Put the whole tomatoes, scallions, and garlic cloves in a large bowl, drizzle with about 1 tablespoon of the olive oil, and sprinkle with salt and pepper to taste. Turn the vegetables until they are lightly coated.

2. Carefully lay the steak in the center of the hot pan, arrange the vegetables around it, and broil until the steak is brown but still tender to the touch and the vegetables are charred, 5 to 6 minutes. Turn the steak and the vegetables and broil another 5 to 6 minutes, until the steak is medium rare (an instant-read thermometer inserted crosswise into the side of the steak registers 130°F) and vegetables are charred. Transfer the steak and vegetables to a cutting board.

3. Core the tomatoes, squeeze the garlic cloves from their skins, and chop them both with the scallions to make a chunky relish. Transfer the vegetables and all their juices to a bowl and stir in the remaining ¼ cup or so of the olive oil, the vinegar, and the Worcestershire sauce. Season with salt and pepper to taste. Slice the meat against the grain and on an angle, transfer to a plate or platter, and serve with the relish and toasted bread.

FROM THE KITCHENS
A broiler is a great tool for making food fast and healthy.
Here are some tips for making the most of it:
· The broiler pan is perfect for foods like steak and chicken because fat drips down through the vents and doesn't flare up. Line the bottom pan with foil for easy cleanup.
· Position your oven's rack as close as possible to the broiler.
· Preheat your broiler pan to cook food even faster.
· If your broiler shuts off when the door is closed, leave it open to keep air moving and the flame on.

flank steak with garlic mayonnaise (aioli)

4 servings

FLANK STEAK

2	tablespoons extra-virgin olive oil
1	tablespoon Dijon mustard
½	teaspoon Worcestershire sauce
2½	teaspoons freshly ground black pepper or pepper blend
1½	teaspoons kosher salt
1	flank steak, about 2 pounds

GARLIC MAYONNAISE (AIOLI)

1	large clove garlic, smashed and peeled
¼	teaspoon kosher salt
3	tablespoons mayonnaise
⅓	cup extra-virgin olive oil
½	lemon

1. For the flank steak: Line a broiler pan with foil and set insert on top. Position a rack so it's 5 to 6 inches from the broiler unit. Set prepared pan on the rack. The surface of the pan should be about 3 to 4 inches from the heat source. Heat pan for 10 minutes. Meanwhile, whisk together the oil, mustard, Worcestershire, black pepper, and salt in a small bowl. Rub onto both sides of the steak.

2. Carefully pull the preheated pan from the broiler. Set the steak in the center of the rack (it should sizzle when it hits the pan). Return pan to the broiler. Cook until the steak browns and feels somewhat firm but gives gently when pressed, 8 to 10 minutes for medium-rare. An instant-read thermometer inserted crosswise into the thickest part of the steak should read about 125°F. (If your broiler pan was preheated properly you won't have to turn the meat.) Remove meat from the broiler and let it rest on a cutting board for 5 to 10 minutes while you make the aioli.

3. For the aioli: Sprinkle the garlic clove with the salt, and, with the flat side of a large knife, mash and smear the mixture to a paste. Set aside. Put the mayonnaise in a small bowl. Gradually whisk in the oil, starting with a few drops and then adding the rest in a steady stream, to make a smooth, slightly thick dressing. Whisk in the garlic paste. Squeeze in about 1 teaspoon lemon juice to thin it out a bit.

4. Thinly slice the meat against the grain and arrange on a platter. Serve warm or at room temperature with the aioli.

FROM THE KITCHENS

• Whisk 1 teaspoon tomato paste into the mayo mix or add hot sauce or minced herbs. Or substitute freshly squeezed orange or lime juice for the lemon.

• Cuts like flank steak have long, chewy muscle fibers that need to be broken up for the best possible texture. When we say cut across the grain, look at the direction the muscle fibers are running, then slice across them.

• Aioli (also called garlic mayo) is a popular condiment throughout the Mediterranean. It's a great dipping sauce for fries, boiled or steamed vegetables, or crusty bread—and it's a classic with steak.

grilled shell steaks
with red wine butter

4 to 6 servings

8   tablespoons unsalted butter, softened
3   cloves garlic, minced
1   shallot, minced
1   teaspoon coriander seeds, cracked
½   teaspoon black peppercorns, cracked
½   cup ruby port
½   cup red wine
2   teaspoons red wine vinegar
2   tablespoons minced fresh flat-leaf parsley
1½ teaspoons kosher salt, plus additional for seasoning
    Vegetable oil for grill
4   10- to 12-ounce shell steaks (also called club steak or New York steak), about 1¼ inches thick
    Freshly ground black pepper

1. Melt 1 tablespoon of butter in a small saucepan over medium-high heat. Add the garlic and shallot and cook, stirring, until golden brown, about 3 minutes. Add the coriander seeds and peppercorns and cook until fragrant, about 30 seconds. Pull the pan from the heat and add the port and wine. Return the pan to the heat and, if cooking over a gas burner, tip the pan to let the alcohol ignite. (If cooking over electric or halogen, just keep cooking the mixture.) Bring the mixture to a boil, reduce the heat, and simmer briskly until syrupy, 20 to 25 minutes. Set aside to cool.

2. Beat the remaining butter in a medium bowl with a handheld electric mixer or whisk until smooth and light. Add the reduced wine mixture, vinegar, parsley, and 1½ teaspoons salt and beat until evenly mixed.

3. Spread a 12-inch-long piece of plastic wrap on a work surface. Mound the butter across the plastic wrap, about 2 inches from edge nearest you. Fold the bottom edge of the plastic wrap over the butter and roll it up to make a 1-inch-wide log. Twist the ends together in opposite directions (like a party favor) and refrigerate until firm.

4. Prepare an outdoor grill with a high fire.

5. Brush grill grate lightly with oil. Season the steaks on both sides with salt and black pepper to taste. Grill 3 to 5 minutes, turning once, until an instant-read thermometer inserted in the meat reads 120°F to 125°F for rare; 125°F to 130°F for medium- rare; or 130°F to 135°F for medium. Transfer the steaks to a cutting board and let rest for 5 minutes. Serve each steak topped with a ¾-inch-thick slice of the wine butter. Any leftover butter can be frozen and used with lamb and pork.

pan-seared t-bone steak
with red wine sauce

2 servings

1   1½-pound T-bone steak
2   to 4 tablespoons unsalted butter
    Kosher salt and freshly ground
        black pepper
1   tablespoon vegetable oil
2   shallots, thinly sliced
¾   cup dry red wine
¼   cup chicken broth

1. About ½ hour before you begin cooking, remove steak from refrigerator. Preheat the oven to 450°F. Cut the butter into small cubes and return to the refrigerator.

2. Heat a large, heavy-bottomed skillet over high heat. Pat the steak dry and season generously with salt and black pepper. Add the oil to the hot skillet. When it just begins to smoke, add the steak. Reduce heat slightly and cook until steak browns on one side, about 4 minutes. Turn and cook the other side for another 2 minutes, then transfer the steak to a baking dish and roast in the oven until an instant-read thermometer inserted sideways into the steak registers 120°F for medium rare, 6 to 8 minutes.

3. Meanwhile, add the shallots to the skillet and cook until brown and tender, about 2 minutes. Add the wine and broth and use a wooden spoon to scrape up any brown bits still left in the pan. Bring to a boil and cook about 2 minutes to let the shallots flavor the wine. Remove from the heat and whisk in the cold butter a piece at a time to make a glossy sauce. Season with salt and black pepper. Set aside and keep warm.

4. Transfer the steak to a cutting board and let rest for 10 minutes. Cut steak from the bone and slice across the grain.

FROM THE KITCHENS
· Shallots look like small, bulb-shaped, orangey-red onions. Look for smooth-skinned shallots with no black spots or sprouts coming out the top. Sometimes shallots will be split into two bulbs. If you've got a monster-size shallot, think of each bulb as one. They're mellow-tasting enough that you can eat them raw if you like, but they're also great in sauces. If you can't find them, use ¼ of a red onion.
· Here it makes sense to use a regular pan (that is, not nonstick) because that'll give you all the crusty little brown bits that flavor the sauce. Stainless steel works, as would cast iron.

grilled porterhouse
with roasted shallots and portobellos | 2 to 4 servings

STEAK

- 1   2-inch-thick porterhouse steak
  (about 3 pounds)
- 6   large shallots, unpeeled
- 2   tablespoons extra-virgin olive oil,
  plus additional for brushing
  Kosher salt
  Freshly ground black pepper
- 1   bunch fresh rosemary

MUSHROOMS

- 4   medium portobello mushrooms
  (about 1 pound total),
  stems discarded
- 3   tablespoons extra-virgin olive oil
- 2   tablespoons chopped fresh
  flat-leaf parsley
- 1   tablespoon balsamic vinegar
- 1   clove garlic, minced

1. Prepare an outdoor grill with a high fire for indirect grilling.

2. About 20 or 30 minutes before grilling, remove the steak from the refrigerator and set aside. On a large sheet of heavy-duty aluminum foil (or a doubled piece of regular), toss the shallots with the olive oil and some salt and black pepper to taste. Top with a generous sprig of rosemary and wrap and seal the foil into a tight package. Place package on the edge of the coals and roast, turning occasionally, until the shallots are very soft, about 25 minutes.

3. Season one side of steak generously with salt and black pepper to taste. Brush grill grate lightly with oil. If using charcoal, add the remaining rosemary sprigs to the fire. Grill the steak seasoned side down over the hottest part of the grill until seared, about 4 minutes. Rotate the meat 90 degrees to make clear grill marks, then continue to cook 2 minutes more. Season the top with salt and black pepper to taste, flip, and repeat on the other side. Once the steak is marked, move it to the cooler side of the grill with the eye (smaller end) away from heat and cover with a disposable aluminum pan. Cook until an instant-read thermometer inserted crosswise into the middle of the steak registers 120°F for rare. Transfer the steak to a cutting board and let rest for 5 minutes before slicing.

4. While the steak cooks, grill the mushrooms: Brush the mushroom caps with 2 tablespoons of the olive oil. Lightly oil the grill grate. Put the mushrooms cap side down on the edge of the charcoal, cover with a disposable aluminum pan, and cook until juices collect in the center of mushrooms, 6 to 7 minutes. Pour the juices into a bowl, flip the mushrooms, cover, and cook until soft and tender, about 6 minutes more. Slice mushrooms and toss with reserved juices, the remaining 1 tablespoon olive oil, the parsley, balsamic vinegar, garlic, and salt and black pepper to taste.

5. Slice the steak and serve with mushrooms and roasted shallots.

FROM THE KITCHENS

• Porterhouse and T-bone are similar cuts and have the best of all worlds—a tasty shell and a tender tenderloin, linked by the bone. The porterhouse has a larger eye of the tenderloin.
• Always pull your steak or whatever meat you are cooking from the refrigerator about 20 minutes before you cook it. If grilled cold straight from the refrigerator, it won't cook as evenly as it will if it's just cool.

mixed grill
with chimichurri sauce | 6 to 8 servings

SAUCE

- 4 cloves garlic, sliced
- 1 shallot, sliced
- 1 cup fresh flat-leaf parsley
- 2 tablespoons fresh oregano
- 1 tablespoon kosher salt
- ½ teaspoon crushed red pepper flakes
- ⅓ cup extra-virgin olive oil
- ⅓ cup red wine vinegar
- 3 tablespoons water

MEAT

- 2 beef blade steaks, each about 6 ounces
- 1 lamb leg steak, 1¼ to 1½ pounds
- 1 pork tenderloin, about 1¾ pounds
- 1 pound fresh chorizo sausage
  - Olive oil for brushing meats
  - Kosher salt and freshly ground black pepper

1. For the chimichurri sauce: Pulse the garlic, shallot, parsley, oregano, salt, and red pepper flakes in a small food processor until roughly chopped. Add the oil, vinegar, and water and pulse to make a textured sauce. Transfer to a serving bowl.

2. For the meat: Heat an outdoor grill to medium-high heat. (If you can hold your hand over the fire for 3 seconds, it's medium-high.) About 20 minutes before grilling, bring the meats to room temperature. Preheat the grate for 5 minutes; scrape it clean with a grill brush. Brush the beef, lamb, and pork with olive oil and season generously with salt and pepper. Grill all the meats, turning once, until an instant-read thermometer inserted into the sides of the steaks registers 125°F. For medium-rare, the beef takes about 2 minutes per side, the lamb about 4 minutes. Grill the pork tenderloin until the thermometer registers 145°F, about 15 minutes, and the sausage 160°F, about 10 minutes, turning both as needed to get nice grill marks on all sides. Transfer the meats to a cutting board and let them rest 5 minutes. Slice the beef and lamb steaks across the grain, slice the pork tenderloin, cut the sausage into chunks, and serve all the meats with the chimichurri sauce.

FROM THE KITCHENS

For the crosshatched marks of a master griller, lay your steaks at an angle across the grill grate and don't move them until they get a good sear. Then rotate them (don't turn them over yet) about 45 degrees from their original spot on the grill. Once you've made your mark, flip and repeat on the other side.

peppered beef tenderloin
with merlot

10 to 12 servings

BEEF

- 1 5-pound center-cut beef tenderloin, tied
  Kosher salt
- 4 tablespoons prepared coarsely ground peppercorn spice medley
- 3 tablespoons vegetable oil
- 10 unpeeled shallots
- 2 tablespoons extra-virgin olive oil

SAUCE

- 5 tablespoons unsalted butter, softened
- 3 medium shallots, peeled and sliced
- 1 750-milliliter bottle Merlot
- 2 cups vegetable broth
- ¼ cup all-purpose flour
  Kosher salt
  Freshly ground black pepper

1. For the beef: Preheat the oven to 450°F. Set a rack in a roasting pan. Heat a large skillet over medium-high heat until hot. While the pan heats, pat the meat dry and season it generously with salt. Roll the tenderloin in peppercorn mixture to coat, making sure to press the ends in mixture as well. Add vegetable oil to the skillet and heat just until smoking. Brown the meat all over, turning as each side reaches a deep mahogany, about 8 minutes in all. While the meat browns, toss the unpeeled shallots with the olive oil and scatter them in the roasting pan. Transfer the meat to the rack (save the skillet) and roast until an instant-read thermometer inserted in the center registers 125°F, about 30 minutes. Let the meat rest for 10 minutes before carving.

2. For the sauce: Wipe any burned bits from the skillet. Add 1 tablespoon of the butter and the sliced shallots to the skillet and cook over high heat until tender, about 2 minutes. Add wine and vegetable broth and scrape the brown bits from the bottom of the skillet with a wooden spoon. Bring to a brisk boil and cook until reduced by about half. Meanwhile, in a small bowl make a paste with remaining 4 tablespoons butter and the flour. Whisk the butter mixture into the reduced wine mixture a little bit at a time. Return to a full boil and cook until thickened, about 2 minutes. Season with salt and black pepper to taste.

3. Slice the beef and arrange it on a platter with the roasted shallots. Drizzle some sauce over the meat and serve, passing the remaining sauce.

FROM THE KITCHENS
Serve the tenderloin tightly shingled on an oblong platter and tuck less attractive pieces beneath the others.

Party on the fly!
Just because you're the one throwing the party doesn't mean you can't enjoy it. Here's a Friday after-work menu that gets appetizers, dinner, and dessert on the table without your even breaking a sweat.

6:00 PM. Dress the set: Preheat your oven to 450°F. Chill your wine (if it needs it), put on some fun music and an apron, and get cooking! Start with the Citrus-Spiced Mixed Olives.

6:30 PM. Make the tiramisú: Soak ladyfingers, fold together mascarpone cream, assemble, and chill. Put cheese out to warm up to room temperature. Prep and roast zucchini (it's fantastic when served at room temp).

MENU

Citrus-spiced mixed olives (page 29), cheese, crusty bread & roasted nuts • chicken saltimbocca (page 231) • polenta (page 324) • roasted zucchini with herbs (page 296)• tiramisú rapido (page 379)

INSIDER SECRETS

We asked our Food Network colleagues for some of their tried-and-true party tips.
• Always start a party with a clean kitchen and an empty dishwasher.
• Keep hors d'oeuvres simple—olives, crackers and cheese, and cheese straws are all great and simple starters.
• Make dessert ahead of time.
• Don't be afraid to delegate. Take people up on their "Can I bring anything?" offer. Request dishes that go with what you're serving as the main event, such as appetizers, bread, or dessert.

7:00 PM. Chop and roll: Once the zucchini's done, turn down the oven to 375°F. Slice mushrooms and chop parsley and herbs for chicken and zucchini. Roll chicken with prosciutto and sage, and chill. Grate cheese for polenta.

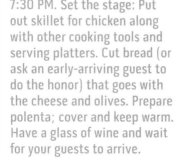

7:30 PM. Set the stage: Put out skillet for chicken along with other cooking tools and serving platters. Cut bread (or ask an early-arriving guest to do the honor) that goes with the cheese and olives. Prepare polenta; cover and keep warm. Have a glass of wine and wait for your guests to arrive.

slow-cooked beef provençale | 4 to 6 servings

1   3-pound beef chuck roast
2   teaspoons kosher salt, plus
     additional for seasoning
     Freshly ground black pepper
3   tablespoons vegetable oil
⅓   cup all-purpose flour
2   cups chicken broth
1   14.5-ounce can whole peeled
     tomatoes, with their juice
¼   cup cognac or brandy
1   tablespoon herbes de Provence
5   garlic cloves, peeled and smashed
4   medium carrots, peeled and
     cut into 2-inch pieces
1   fennel bulb, trimmed and thinly
     sliced
1   onion, halved and thinly sliced
⅓   cup prepared sun-dried tomato
     tapenade
⅓   cup coarsely chopped fresh
     flat-leaf parsley
1   packed teaspoon finely grated
     orange zest
     Hot buttered egg noodles, for serving

1. Heat a large, heavy-bottomed skillet over medium-high heat. Season the meat generously with salt and pepper to taste. Add the oil to the skillet and heat just until beginning to smoke. Brown the meat all over and sear the roast, turning as each side turns a deep mahogany, about 10 minutes. While the meat browns, put the flour in a medium bowl and whisk with about 1½ cups of the chicken broth until smooth.

2. Crush the tomatoes through your fingers into the slow cooker; stir in their juices, 3 tablespoons of the cognac, herbes de Provence, and the 2 teaspoons salt.

3. Transfer the browned meat to the slow cooker. Add the remaining ½ cup chicken broth to the skillet; let it bubble for a minute and then stir with a wooden spoon to scrape up the browned bits on the bottom of the pan. Pour over the meat, then scatter the garlic, carrots, fennel, and onion over and around the meat. Pour the flour mixture over. Cover the cooker, set it on HIGH, and cook for 4 hours. Set the cooker on LOW and cook until the meat is very tender, up to 2 hours more (for a total of 6 hours). Transfer the meat to a cutting board. Skim any excess fat off the top of the sauce in the cooker.

4. To finish the sauce: Stir the remaining 1 tablespoon cognac, the tomato tapenade, parsley, and orange zest into the vegetables and sauce in the slow cooker. Season with salt and pepper to taste. Slice the meat and lay the slices down the center of a serving platter. Arrange the vegetables around the meat and spoon some sauce over the top. Serve with hot buttered egg noodles. Pass the remaining sauce.

low & slow oven–barbecued brisket

8 to 10 servings

BRISKET

- 1 tablespoon pimenton (Spanish smoked paprika)
- 1 tablespoon ground coriander
- 1 tablespoon dried oregano
- 1 tablespoon kosher salt
- 2 teaspoons cayenne pepper
- 2 teaspoons ground cumin
- 1 teaspoon ground allspice
- 1 8-pound point-cut brisket (see tip, below)

SAUCE

- ¼ medium onion, chopped
- 4 cloves garlic, minced
- 1 tablespoon chile powder, preferably ancho (see tip, below)
- 2 cups canned whole peeled tomatoes in puree
- ½ cup firmly packed dark brown sugar
- ½ cup distilled white vinegar
- ¼ cup whole-grain mustard
- 1 tablespoon Worcestershire sauce
- 1 tablespoon kosher salt
  Freshly ground black pepper

1. For the brisket: Preheat the oven to 250°F. Combine the spices in a small bowl. Put the brisket in a shallow roasting pan and rub both sides with the spice mixture. Slow-roast until the top is browned and crusty and an instant-read thermometer inserted in the thickest part registers 200°F, about 10 hours. You don't need to baste or turn the brisket—just leave it alone. After a few hours, once a good amount of drippings and crispy bits have pooled in the pan, spoon them off and reserve ⅓ cup—with the bits—for the sauce.

2. For the barbecue sauce: Heat reserved drippings in a medium saucepan over medium heat. Add onion, garlic, and chile powder and stir until onions and garlic are lightly browned, about 5 minutes. Add tomatoes with puree, brown sugar, vinegar, mustard, Worcestershire sauce, salt, and pepper to taste and bring to a simmer. Whisk occasionally until sauce is deep red and thicker, about 5 minutes.

3. Transfer the brisket to a cutting board, cover loosely with foil, and let it rest for 15 minutes. Slice the brisket against the grain and arrange the slices on a serving platter. Serve with the barbecue sauce.

FROM THE KITCHENS

- A full brisket is very big and usually cut into two parts. The first cut is thin and lean; the second cut or point cut is well marbled, making it the perfect choice for slow and gentle cooking. The brisket will have a good layer of fat on one side, about ¼ inch or so—don't trim it, since it keeps the meat moist. Some will melt off as the brisket cooks. You can trim the remainder before you slice, if you wish, although it sure tastes good.
- Ancho chiles are the dried form of the poblano chile. The heat meter can range from slightly warm to downright lip-tingling. This slightly fruity chile also appears in the market ground into a powder.

grilled korean short ribs | 4 to 6 servings

CUCUMBER KIMCHEE

4	Kirby cucumbers
4	scallions (white and green parts), thinly sliced
5	cloves garlic, chopped
3	tablespoons grated peeled fresh ginger
3	tablespoons sugar
1½	teaspoons kosher salt
1½	teaspoons crushed red pepper, ground

RIBS

6	pounds beef short ribs, cut crosswise into twelve 2½-inch squares (ask your butcher to cut the ribs for you)
	Korean BBQ Marinade (see recipe, below)
	Vegetable oil for grill

MARINADE

Makes about 1½ cups

1	cup soy sauce
4	large cloves garlic, peeled and chopped (about 2 tablespoons)
2	tablespoons finely grated peeled fresh ginger
4	scallions (white and green), thinly sliced
¼	cup sugar
2	tablespoons dark sesame oil
	Freshly ground black pepper

1. A day before serving, halve the cucumbers crosswise, set them upright on the cut end, and slice lengthwise into quarters, stopping about 1/2 inch from the cut end. Mix the scallions, garlic, ginger, sugar, salt, and red pepper and stuff about a tablespoon of the mixture into each cucumber. Put the cucumbers in a small nonreactive baking dish, cover with plastic wrap, and refrigerate overnight.

2. Prepare ribs according to photo below. Place the ribs in one layer in a large nonreactive baking dish, pour in the Korean BBQ Marinade, and turn the ribs to coat. Cover and refrigerate. Marinate for 2 to 8 hours (longer makes the ribs too salty).

3. Prepare an outdoor grill with a high-heat fire.

4. Remove the ribs from the marinade. Brush the grill grate lightly with oil. Place the ribs on the grill meaty side down and cook, turning as needed, until well browned but still pink inside, about 10 to 12 minutes. Set ribs aside to rest for 5 minutes. Serve with Cucumber Kimchee.

KOREAN BBQ MARINADE

Whisk soy sauce, garlic, ginger, scallions, sugar, sesame oil, and black pepper to taste in a medium bowl. Use marinade immediately or refrigerate up to 2 days.

Remove any silver skin from the top of the meat. Butterfly the short ribs so they open like books, with the meat about ⅓ to ½ inch thick and still attached to the bone.

The perfect
date food—
romantic, just
right for two,
and simple
to do. Dazzle
with wit.
Charm with
your smile.
Then seduce
with your
scaloppini.

veal scaloppini with greens & radicchio

2 servings

5   slices white bread
3   cloves garlic, minced
2   tablespoons minced fresh
     flat-leaf parsley
2   teaspoons minced fresh rosemary
2   teaspoons minced fresh thyme
1   teaspoon finely grated lemon zest
    Kosher salt and freshly ground
     black pepper
2   large eggs, beaten
2   veal scaloppini, top-round
     center cuts preferred
     (about 8 ounces each)
1½ cups torn arugula
1½ cups torn frisee
1   cup torn radicchio
2   tablespoons unsalted butter
2   tablespoons extra-virgin olive oil
1   lemon, halved
    Small chunk Parmigiana-Reggiano or
     Pecorino Romano cheese
     (see tip, page 152)

1. Pulse the bread into coarse crumbs in a food processor; then spread them on a microwave-safe plate and microwave on high for 1 minute. (Alternately, spread the crumbs on a baking sheet and dry in a 200°F oven for 10 minutes.) Toss the bread crumbs with the garlic, parsley, rosemary, thyme, lemon zest, and salt and pepper to taste.

2. Put the bread crumbs in one shallow dish and the eggs in another. Pat the veal dry and season both sides with salt and pepper. Dip each piece into the egg, shaking off excess, and then press both sides into the breading to coat. Place on a baking sheet, cover, and refrigerate for at least 20 minutes or up to 2 hours to set the breading.

3. Toss the arugula, frisee, and radicchio in a bowl. Heat a medium nonstick skillet over medium heat and add 1 tablespoon each of the butter and olive oil. When the butter stops foaming, add 1 scallopine and cook (press down lightly with a spatula to help keep it from curling), turning once, until golden brown, about 2½ minutes per side. Repeat. After the veal is cooked, add the greens to the skillet, season with salt and pepper, and toss just until they begin to wilt, about 30 seconds. Squeeze the lemon over the greens and toss again. Pile some greens on top of each scallopine and shave the cheese over the greens.

pork chops
with pear chutney | 4 servings

CHUTNEY

1	shallot, diced
3	tablespoons cider vinegar
2	tablespoons light brown sugar
1	tablespoon unsalted butter
1	1-inch piece peeled fresh ginger, cut into coins
1	teaspoon Madras curry powder (see tip, page 68)
1	cinnamon stick
¼	teaspoon kosher salt
	Pinch crushed red pepper
3	pears, peeled, cored, and cut in large dice
2	tablespoons dried cranberries
2	tablespoons chopped fresh cilantro

CHOPS

8	thin bone-in pork chops, each about 4 ounces
	Kosher salt
	Freshly ground black pepper
2	tablespoons vegetable oil

1. For the chutney: In medium microwave-safe bowl, stir together the shallot, vinegar, brown sugar, butter, ginger, curry powder, cinnamon stick, salt, and red pepper. Cover and seal with plastic wrap and heat in the microwave oven on HIGH for 1 minute. Carefully remove the plastic wrap and stir in the pears and cranberries. Re-cover and microwave for 10 minutes more. Carefully poke holes in the plastic wrap to release the steam and set aside.

2. For the pork chops: Heat a large skillet over medium-high heat. Dry the pork chops well and season with salt and pepper to taste. Add 1 tablespoon oil to the pan and heat until shimmering. Lay 4 chops in the pan and sear until golden on one side, about 3 minutes. (Flatten the chops with a spatula if the edges curl.) Turn the chops over and cook an additional 1 minute. Remove from pan and set aside in a warm place; repeat with the remaining oil and chops. Add the chutney to the pan and, with a wooden spoon, scrape up any brown bits that cling to the pan. Simmer until thickened slightly. Stir in the cilantro. Serve 2 chops per person with the chutney.

FROM THE KITCHENS
Lower the heat if your chops start to balloon up in the center as they sear.

Stir, zap, and serve—that's how easy our Pear Chutney is. Besides being sinfully simple, it invokes the spicy sweetness of autumn—farm stands, hayrides, and falling leaves.

chinese peppered pork chops

4 servings

⅓   cup soy sauce
2   cloves garlic, minced
4   teaspoons sugar
2   teaspoons medium-cracked
     black pepper
½   teaspoon kosher salt
6   ¼-inch-thick loin pork chops
     (about 1½ pounds)
2   tablespoons vegetable oil

1. Put the soy sauce, garlic, sugar, pepper, and salt in a large self-sealing plastic bag, seal, and shake. Add the pork chops and rub them, through the bag, to work the spices into the meat. Marinate at room temperature for 30 minutes.

2. Heat 1 tablespoon of the oil in a large skillet over medium-high heat until shimmering. Add half the chops, shaking off excess marinade, and cook, turning once, until just cooked through, about 6 minutes. Repeat with the remaining oil and chops, wiping the skillet clean between batches.

FROM THE KITCHENS
Thin-sliced pork chops are frequently sold in family packs—plentiful and inexpensive. If you see 'em, buy 'em. Stick them in the freezer and keep this recipe in mind for those days when you have no time to shop and little time or inclination to cook. We're betting you have the rest of the ingredients in your pantry.

crispy pork medallions
with apple-horseradish sauce | 4 servings

PORK

- 2 large eggs
- 1 cup panko (Japanese coarse bread crumbs)
- 2 teaspoons kosher salt, plus additional for seasoning
- 1 teaspoon rubbed dried sage
- ½ teaspoon dried thyme
  Freshly ground black pepper
- 4 ½-inch-thick center-cut pork loin medallions (about 1 pound)
- 2 tablespoons vegetable oil
- 1 tablespoon unsalted butter

SAUCE

- 1 cup applesauce
- ¼ cup sour cream
- 3 to 4 tablespoons prepared white horseradish, excess vinegar squeezed out
- ½ teaspoon kosher salt

1. For the pork: Lightly beat the eggs in a shallow bowl. In another shallow bowl, toss the panko with the 2 teaspoons salt, the sage, thyme, and pepper to taste. Season the medallions with some salt and pepper to taste and dip them in the egg to coat completely. Press them gently into the panko mixture to coat both sides.

2. Heat a large skillet over medium heat. Add the oil and butter; when the butter stops foaming, add the medallions and cook until golden and crisp on the first side, about 4 minutes; turn and cook until the second side is crisp, about 3 minutes more.

3. Meanwhile, for the sauce: Combine the applesauce, sour cream, horseradish, and salt in a small bowl. Serve the medallions with the apple-horseradish sauce.

FROM THE KITCHENS
The goal is coating the pork—not your fingers. Keep your hands breading-free by using one hand to dip the pork in egg and panko.

We dare you not to go hog wild for our shortcut barbecued pork tenderloin. Oven broiled until golden, this is just the right cure for the cold weather no-'cue blues.

pork tenderloin
with chipotle-maple mop | 4 servings

PORK

2	teaspoons ground coriander
1	teaspoon garlic powder
½	teaspoon ground ginger
2	pork tenderloins, each about 12 ounces, silver skin removed
1	tablespoon vegetable oil
	Kosher salt
	Freshly ground black pepper

SAUCE

¼	cup pure maple syrup
2	tablespoons sherry vinegar
2	teaspoons chipotle chile hot sauce
½	teaspoon kosher salt

1. Position a rack closest to the broiler and preheat to high. Combine the coriander, garlic powder, and ginger. Brush the tenderloins with the oil and rub all over with spices. Season with salt and pepper to taste. Lay the pork on a small shallow pan and broil until golden, turning once, about 5 minutes per side. (An instant-read thermometer should register 130°F when inserted into the thickest part of the meat.)

2. Meanwhile, for the sauce: Whisk the syrup, vinegar, hot sauce, and salt together in a small bowl. Set about half the sauce aside. Generously brush the tenderloins all over with the remaining sauce. Return to the broiler and cook, turning once, until a deep rich brown, about 2 to 3 minutes. Set meat aside for 5 minutes to rest before slicing. Serve with reserved sauce for drizzling over the meat.

FROM THE KITCHENS
Be sure to remove the silver skin before cooking the tenderloin; otherwise, the meat will curl.

1. Lay the tenderloin on your work surface and slip a sharp knife under the surface of the silver skin. Keeping your knife flat against the meat, make your first cut by slicing away from you and toward the end of the tenderloin. **2.** Lift the unattached portion

of the silver skin up and place your knife at the point where the skin meets the tenderloin. Slice to separate.
3. Continue moving down the length of the tenderloin, pulling and slicing until the silver skin is completely removed.

grilled pork tenderloin
with quick cabbage slaw

4 servings

PORK

1	cup cold water
3	tablespoons kosher salt, plus more for seasoning
2	tablespoons dark brown sugar
4	cloves garlic, smashed
½	cup dark rum (optional)
2	pork tenderloins, about 12 ounces each
1	tablespoon olive oil
2	teaspoons ground cumin
	Freshly ground black pepper

QUICK CABBAGE SLAW

½	medium red onion, thinly sliced
½	head napa cabbage, very thinly sliced crosswise (about 6 cups)
	Large handful fresh cilantro, coarsely chopped
1	navel orange
2	tablespoons extra-virgin olive oil
1	tablespoon white wine vinegar
1½	teaspoons kosher salt
	Freshly ground black pepper

1. To brine the pork: Combine the water, 3 tablespoons salt, brown sugar, and garlic in a medium saucepan. Bring to a boil, remove from heat, and stir in the rum, if using. Cool to room temperature.

2. Put the tenderloins in a bowl or shallow container and pour the brine over them. (Or put the tenderloins and brine in a large resealable plastic bag.) Cover and refrigerate at least 1 hour or up to 4 hours.

3. For the slaw: Soak the onion in cold water for 10 minutes, then drain and pat dry. Toss the onion, cabbage, and cilantro together in a large bowl.

4. Finely grate ½ of the orange's zest into the slaw. Cut remaining peel and white pith off the orange. Quarter and then cut the orange segments crosswise into small pieces; toss into the vegetables. Dress the slaw with olive oil, vinegar, 1½ teaspoons salt, and black pepper to taste.

5. Preheat oven to 425° F. Heat a grill pan over medium-high heat. Brush the tenderloins with the olive oil and sprinkle with cumin and black pepper. Grill the tenderloins 5 minutes per side, then transfer to the oven and cook for an additional 10 minutes. (An instant-read thermometer should register 145°F when inserted in the thickest part of the meat.) Alternatively, broil the tenderloins: Position a rack closest to the broiler and heat to high. Lay the pork on a small shallow pan and broil until golden brown, turning once, about 5 minutes per side.

6. Set meat on a cutting board to rest for 5 minutes. Slice and serve with slaw.

FROM THE KITCHENS

• A brine is a solution of salt, sugar, and liquid (usually water) that makes lean meat (like pork, turkey, or shrimp) juicier and more tender. Brines are different from marinades; while marinades break down fibers in meat, brines make meat juicier. The smaller the piece of meat, the shorter the brining time. You can brine a pork tenderloin for up to 4 hours; don't brine shrimp for more than half an hour. Brining is optional here. If you skip it, rub the outside of the meat with chili powder for extra flavor and take care not to overcook.

• Napa cabbage, sometimes called Chinese cabbage, is mildly flavored and full of vitamin A. Look for compact, closed heads—also, the darker the leaves, the more nutritious.

pork chili verde | 6 servings

3 pounds trimmed pork shoulder,
    cut into 1-inch cubes
2 12-ounce bottles Mexican
    lager-style beer
2 to 3 chipotle chiles in adobo sauce,
    chopped (see tip, page 157)
1 tablespoon dried oregano,
    preferably Mexican
6 teaspoons kosher salt
2½ pounds fresh tomatillos (about 24),
    husks removed and rinsed
2 poblano chiles
2 medium white onions, quartered
5 cloves garlic, peeled
1 bunch cilantro, roots and some stem
    trimmed, plus sprigs for garnish
2 tablespoons freshly squeezed lime
    juice, plus wedges for garnish
1 tablespoon ground cumin
    Pinch sugar (optional)
¾ cup vegetable oil
1 cup whole unblanched almonds
4 slices sourdough bread, cubed
4 ounces crumbled queso fresco
    or farmer's cheese

1. Position an oven rack 6 to 8 inches from the broiler and preheat. Put the pork, beer, chipotles, and oregano in a Dutch oven or soup pot and season with 2 teaspoons of the kosher salt. Bring to a simmer, skimming off any foam as it rises to the surface, and cook, uncovered, until the meat is almost tender, about 40 minutes.

2. Meanwhile, spread tomatillos, poblanos, onions, and garlic on a foil-lined broiler pan. Broil the vegetables, turning as needed, until charred on all sides, about 20 minutes. Cool slightly. Transfer about half the tomatillos and onions, and the juices in the pan, to a blender and puree with the garlic, cilantro, lime juice, and cumin until smooth. Roughly chop the remaining tomatillos and onions. Seed and chop the poblanos, skin and all. Stir the vegetables into the puree. Taste, and if the sauce is very acidic, stir in a pinch of sugar.

3. Heat oil in a heavy-bottomed medium skillet over medium-high heat. When oil is hot but not smoking, stir in the almonds and fry until they just begin to brown, about 20 seconds. Transfer with a slotted spoon to a paper-towel-lined plate. Add the bread cubes to the oil and fry, stirring, until golden and crispy, about 30 seconds. Transfer to the plate with nuts and cool. Pull pan from the heat and let the oil cool somewhat.

4. Return the pan to medium heat. Very carefully add the tomatillo sauce to the oil (it will sizzle and can spatter dramatically) and fry, stirring, until thicker, about 5 minutes. Stir the sauce and the 4 teaspoons remaining salt into the pork and simmer until the meat is tender, about 40 minutes.

5. Chop the almonds. Divide the chili among bowls, scatter some of the cheese over each, and top with some of the bread and almonds. Garnish with a sprig of cilantro and a lime wedge and serve.

slow-cooker choucroute | 6 servings

1   large onion, peeled, root end
      left intact, and quartered
4   whole cloves
8   ounces thick-sliced smoked or pepper
      bacon, cut into 1-inch pieces
2   pounds sauerkraut, rinsed
      and drained
1   garlic head, halved
4   sprigs fresh thyme
4   sprigs fresh parsley
2   bay leaves
2   1-inch-thick smoked pork chops
      (about 10 ounces each)
1   pound kielbasa, cut diagonally
      into 2-inch pieces
2   Fuji or other baking apples, cored
      and cut into large chunks
1   pound small red-skinned
      potatoes, scrubbed
1½   cups dry white wine
¼   cup gin
      Pumpernickel rye bread, mustards,
      horseradish, and cornichons,
      for serving

1. Stud each onion quarter with a clove. Layer the bacon, sauerkraut, garlic, onion quarters, herb sprigs, bay leaves, pork chops, kielbasa, apples, and potatoes in the slow cooker in the order listed, then pour the wine and gin over the top. Cover the cooker and set it on LOW. Cook until the pork is falling off the bones and the potatoes are fork-tender, at least 6 and up to 8 hours. Remove and discard bay leaves.

2. Arrange the meats, potatoes, apples, onions, garlic, and sauerkraut on a large platter. Serve with pumpernickel rye bread, mustards, cornichons, and horseradish.

FROM THE KITCHENS
Bagged or jarred sauerkraut tastes livelier than the canned stuff.

stir-fried pork
with sugar snap peas | 4 to 6 servings

1 pound pork tenderloin,
    cut into ½-inch cubes
3 scallions, thinly sliced (white and
    green parts kept separate)
3 cloves garlic, minced
1 1-inch piece fresh ginger, peeled and
    minced (about 1½ tablespoons)
1 tablespoon soy sauce
2 teaspoons sugar
2 teaspoons cornstarch
1 teaspoon sherry or Shaohsing
    wine (see tip, below)
1 teaspoon dark sesame oil
5 tablespoons peanut oil
1 pound sugar snap peas, stringed
    Kosher salt
    Freshly ground black pepper
1 tablespoon hoisin sauce
    Hot cooked jasmine rice,
      for serving (optional)

1. Toss the pork with the scallion whites, half the garlic, half the ginger, the soy sauce, sugar, 1 teaspoon of the cornstarch, the sherry, and the sesame oil. Marinate at room temperature for 15 minutes. Mix the remaining 1 teaspoon cornstarch with 2 tablespoons water.

2. Heat a large skillet over high heat. Add 1 tablespoon of the peanut oil and heat. Add the sugar snap peas and the remaining garlic and ginger; stir-fry until the sugar snaps are bright green but still crisp, about 1 minute. (If the peas are still tough, add a tablespoon of water and cook for a minute longer.) Season with salt and pepper to taste and pour into a large bowl.

3. Heat the skillet over high heat again and add 2 more tablespoons oil. Add half the pork mixture, season with salt and pepper to taste, and stir-fry until lightly brown, about 2 minutes. Add the first batch of pork to the sugar snaps. Repeat with the rest of the oil and pork. Return the sugar snaps and pork to the pan. Add the hoisin and the cornstarch mixture. Cook until the juices thicken, about 1 minute. Mound the stir-fry on a serving platter or divide among 4 plates and scatter the scallion greens over the top. Serve with rice, if desired.

FROM THE KITCHENS
There are many varieties of Chinese rice wine, but we like to use Shaohsing, one of the higher-quality versions. If you can't find it use a good sherry (avoid what's called "cooking sherry").

chinese lacquered baby back ribs

4 main course servings,
up to 8 for party finger food

1   3-inch piece fresh ginger, roughly
        chopped (about ½ cup)
5   cloves garlic, roughly chopped
1   cup rice vinegar
¼   cup soy sauce
1   tablespoon dark sesame oil
2   racks baby back ribs
        (about 2 pounds total),
        inside membrane removed
      Kosher salt
      Freshly ground black pepper
1   teaspoon five-spice powder
        (optional)
½   cup hoisin sauce
3   to 4 teaspoons Asian chili sauce,
        such as Sriracha or sambal oelek
1   tablespoon water
4   scallions, thinly sliced (white
        and green parts)
1   teaspoon sesame seeds,
        for garnish (optional)

1. Whisk the ginger, garlic, vinegar, soy sauce, and sesame oil in a nonreactive dish (see tip, below). Add the ribs, turning to coat evenly. Cover and refrigerate for 1 hour.

2. Preheat the oven to 350°F. Remove the ribs from the marinade, brush off the ginger and garlic, and discard the marinade. Pat dry and season on all sides with salt, black pepper and the five-spice powder, if using. Place the ribs, bone side up, on a rimmed baking sheet and cover the sheet tightly with foil. Bake for 45 minutes.

3. Whisk the hoisin sauce, chili sauce, and water in a small bowl. Remove the ribs from the oven and brush all over with the sauce. Cook uncovered, meat side up, until the ribs are tender and nicely glazed, 30 to 35 minutes.

4. Transfer the ribs to a cutting board and let rest 5 minutes. Cut between the rib bones and place ribs on a serving platter. Scatter scallions and sesame seeds, if using, on top.

FROM THE KITCHENS
• A nonreactive dish is basically any dish not made out of aluminum.
• Five-spice powder is a Chinese spice mix containing more or less equal parts of cinnamon, cloves, fennel seeds, star anise, and Szechwan peppercorn, ground together to a fine powder.
• Hoisin sauce is a thick, rich, and sweet bean-based sauce. Look for it in an Asian market if you can't find it in the international aisle of your store. It's good brushed onto steaks, pork chops, or hamburgers before grilling or as a condiment for Asian noodle dishes.
• Asian chile sauces like sambal oelek are an easy way to add a quick hit of fire to a dish. Look for them in jars in the international aisle of your store and keep them in the fridge once open; they last forever.

pork rib roast
with cranberry-apricot stuffing | 4 to 6 servings

3 tablespoons cognac or other brandy
3 tablespoons water
⅓ cup dried cranberries
⅓ cup dried apricots, coarsely chopped
¼ cup whole almonds, toasted
   and chopped
1 medium shallot, minced
3 tablespoons unsalted butter,
   softened
1 teaspoon fennel seeds, toasted
   and crushed
½ teaspoon kosher salt, plus
   additional for seasoning
   Freshly ground black pepper
1 6-rib center-cut pork roast, backbone
   removed and ribs Frenched (see
   tip, below) (about 4 pounds
   after trimming)
2 tablespoons vegetable oil
1 cup crème fraîche or sour cream
½ cup Dijon mustard

1. Warm the cognac and water in a small saucepan, add the cranberries and apricots, and set aside until plump, about 10 minutes. In a small food processor, pulse the fruit and any unabsorbed liquid with the almonds, shallot, butter, fennel seeds, ½ teaspoon salt, and pepper to taste until the fruit and nuts are coarsely chopped.

2. With a boning knife or other long, thin knife, make a cut 3 inches across in the center of one end of the roast. Gently push and work the blade in and straight through the roast to the other end. (If your knife isn't long enough, make a cut at either end and work your way to the center, making sure that the cuts meet.) Insert the narrow end of a wooden spoon into the opening to widen it a bit all the way through. Push the stuffing into the loin, working first from one end and then the other, filling to the center.

3. Preheat the oven to 350°F. Pat the loin dry and season all over with salt and pepper. Heat the oil in a large ovenproof skillet over medium-high heat. Add the roast, holding the bones up so that the bottom gets well browned, then turn the roast to brown the meaty side, about 6 minutes total. Transfer the skillet to the oven and roast the pork meat side down for 30 minutes. Turn the roast over so it sits on the bones and roast until an instant-read thermometer inserted into the center of the meat registers 155°F, about 1 hour more. Transfer the roast to a carving board, tent loosely with foil, and let it rest for 10 minutes before carving.

4. Whisk crème fraîche or sour cream with the mustard in a small bowl and season with salt and pepper to taste. Slice roast between the bones to make individual chops, arrange on a platter, and serve, passing the mustard sauce.

FROM THE KITCHENS
• Roasting meat on the bone keeps meat moist and improves its flavor. Pan-searing before roasting is the way to get a great burnished crust on lean meats that would otherwise dry out if left to brown solely in the oven.
• To "French" means to remove the cartilage and fat between the rib bones on a rack of lamb, pork roast, or chops so that the clean bones are exposed. It makes for a striking and elegant presentation. Your butcher can French bone-in meats with a few quick cuts.

The WOW factor comes built into this glorious roast. The fall flavors are fabulous, and so are the Frenched ribs. It's an elegant adventure in home cooking that invites everyone to just dig in.

lamb chops
with rosemary-orange gremolata | 4 servings

LAMB

- 8 6-ounce loin lamb chops
- 2 tablespoons extra-virgin olive oil
   Kosher salt
   Freshly ground black pepper

GREMOLATA

- 2 garlic cloves, peeled
- ½ teaspoon salt
- 1½ cups flat-leaf parsley
- 2 sprigs fresh rosemary,
     leaves stripped
- 2 teaspoons finely grated orange zest
- 2 teaspoons red wine vinegar
- 2 tablespoons extra-virgin olive oil

1. For the lamb: Position a broiler pan on a rack 4 to 6 inches from the broiler and preheat to high. Brush the chops with the olive oil and season with salt and pepper to taste. Lay the chops carefully on the hot pan and broil, turning once— 7 minutes for rare, 8 minutes for medium, and 9 minutes for well-done. Remove from the oven and set aside for 5 minutes.

2. Meanwhile, for the gremolata: Smash the garlic cloves, sprinkle with the salt, and, with the side of a large knife, mash and smear the mixture to a coarse paste. Chop the parsley and rosemary leaves with the garlic paste; put the mixture in a small bowl and stir in the orange zest, vinegar, and the 2 tablespoons olive oil.

3. Divide the chops among 4 plates and spoon some of the gremolata over them; serve.

FROM THE KITCHENS
There are three kinds of lamb chops: rib, loin, and shoulder. Loin chops with their telltale T-bone are our favorites because they are tender, low in fat, and have a mild flavor.

grilled juniper & jalapeño jelly-glazed lamb chops

4 servings

8 juniper berries
1 teaspoon coriander seeds
2 tablespoons unsalted butter
4 cloves garlic, minced
1 10-ounce jar red jalapeño jelly
     (about 1 heaping cup)
2 tablespoons apple cider vinegar
¼ cup water
   Vegetable oil for grilling
8 rack lamb chops (about 1½ to
     2 pounds), Frenched
     (see tip, page 220)
1 teaspoon kosher salt
   Freshly ground black pepper

1. Prepare an outdoor grill with a medium-high fire for both direct and indirect grilling. Position a drip pan under grate on the cooler side of the grill.

2. Crack the juniper berries and coriander seeds in a mortar and pestle or with a small heavy pan. Melt the butter in a small skillet and cook the juniper, coriander, and garlic over medium heat until fragrant, about 3 minutes. Whisk in the jelly, vinegar, and water until smooth and simmer until slightly thick, about 5 minutes.

3. Brush the grill lightly with oil and season the chops all over with salt and pepper to taste. Lay the chops on the grate and grill, turning until nicely marked, about 3 minutes on each side. Move chops to the cooler side of the grill, over the drip pan, and brush generously with some of the jalapeño glaze. Cover and cook, brushing occasionally, until nicely glazed and an instant-read thermometer inserted into the chops registers 120°F for medium-rare. Set aside to rest for 5 minutes. Serve chops drizzled with more of the jalapeño glaze.

braised lamb shanks with herbs

4 servings

4   lamb shanks (about 1½ pounds each)
2   teaspoons kosher salt, plus
    additional for seasoning
    Freshly ground black pepper
    All-purpose flour, for dredging
¼   cup extra-virgin olive oil
2   ribs celery, sliced
1   medium onion, sliced
2   medium carrots, peeled and sliced
8   cloves garlic, smashed
2   tablespoons chopped fresh thyme
2   tablespoons chopped fresh rosemary
1   cup red wine
    About 4 cups low-sodium chicken
    broth
1   tablespoon water
1   tablespoon cornstarch
2   tablespoons minced fresh
    flat-leaf parsley
    Hot cooked polenta
    (see recipe, page 324) (optional)

1. Preheat the oven to 350°F. Season the shanks all over with some salt and pepper to taste. Put the flour in a pie plate and, 2 at a time, dredge the shanks. Heat the olive oil in a large Dutch oven until shimmering. Add the shanks and cook until they are a rich mahogany brown on all sides, about 15 minutes. Transfer the shanks to a plate.

2. Add the celery, onion, carrots, the 2 teaspoons salt, and some pepper to the Dutch oven. Cook until tender and starting to brown, about 20 minutes. Stir in the garlic, thyme, and rosemary and cook until fragrant, about 3 minutes more. Add the wine, increase the heat to high, and with a wooden spoon scrape up any of the browned bits that cling to the pan. Cook until the wine reduces enough to lightly coat the vegetables. Return the shanks to the pan along with enough broth to cover by about two-thirds. Simmer, then transfer the pot to the oven and cook, uncovered, turning the shanks every 30 minutes, until meat is fork-tender, about 2½ hours. Transfer shanks to a foil-lined pan and keep them in the oven while making the sauce.

3. Let the braising liquid stand about 10 minutes, then skim off the fat that comes to the surface. Strain the sauce into a bowl, pressing down on the solids to get as much liquid as possible, and skim again, if needed. Return the sauce to the pot and bring it to a boil over high heat. Whisk the water into the cornstarch until smooth, then whisk into the sauce until thickened, about 1 minute. Taste, and add salt and pepper if desired. Stir in the parsley. Put the shanks in the sauce and turn to coat. To serve, divide the shanks among 4 plates with cooked polenta, if desired, and spoon some of the sauce over; pass the remaining sauce.

lamb curry with chickpeas

4 servings

1　2-inch piece fresh ginger, peeled and roughly chopped
4　garlic cloves, peeled and smashed
3　tablespoons vegetable oil
1¾　teaspoons garam masala (see tip, page 227), plus additional for serving
1　teaspoon cumin seeds
1　teaspoon ground turmeric
¼　teaspoon crushed red pepper flakes
2¼　pounds lamb stew meat cut into 1¼-inch cubes
1　butternut squash (about 2¼ pounds), halved, seeded, and cut into large chunks, with or without skin
1　15½-ounce can chickpeas, drained and rinsed
1　cup water
¼　cup golden raisins
2　teaspoons kosher salt
1　cup roughly chopped cilantro
¼　cup plain yogurt (optional)
Naan bread or rice pilaf, for serving

1. Put the ginger and garlic in a minichopper and pulse into a textured paste. Heat the oil in a 7-liter pressure cooker over high heat. Add the garam masala, cumin seeds, turmeric, and red pepper; cook, stirring, until fragrant, about 30 seconds. Stir in the ginger mixture and cook, stirring, until brown, 2 to 3 minutes.

2. Stir in the lamb, squash, chickpeas, water, raisins, and salt. Close the pressure cooker lid and bring the pressure up to high (this can take up to 10 minutes), then reduce the heat to maintain even pressure for 15 minutes. Remove from heat and cool until the pressure gauge drops. This can take up to 10 minutes.

3. Carefully open the cooker and stir in the cilantro. Ladle the curry into 4 large bowls. Garnish with yogurt, if you like, and sprinkle with more garam masala. Serve with warm naan or rice pilaf.

FROM THE KITCHENS
There's no need to peel the squash before cooking. The skin cooks up nice and tender.

masala-yogurt-marinated boneless leg of lamb

6 to 8 servings

5   cloves garlic
1   3-inch piece peeled fresh ginger
2   teaspoons ground turmeric
2   tablespoons water
3   tablespoons vegetable oil
1   3-inch cinnamon stick
1   bay leaf
1   tablespoon ground coriander,
        plus 2 teaspoons
1   tablespoon ground cumin,
        plus 1 teaspoon
1   tablespoon curry powder
1   teaspoon cayenne pepper
½   medium onion
1½ cups whole milk yogurt
    Grated zest of 1 orange
        (about 2 tablespoons)
1   butterflied leg of lamb
        (5 to 6 pounds)
3   teaspoons kosher salt, plus
        additional for seasoning
    Grilled naan or other Indian flat
        bread (optional)

1. Process the garlic, ginger, turmeric, and water to a paste in a small food processor. Heat the oil in a medium skillet over high heat. Add the cinnamon and bay leaf and stir-fry until the cinnamon unfurls, about 30 seconds. Add the garlic paste, coriander, cumin, curry powder, and cayenne and stir-fry until browned and almost dry, about 1 minute. Scrape the mixture into a large, shallow baking dish and cool slightly. Using the large holes of a box grater, grate the onion into the paste. Whisk in the yogurt and orange zest.

2. Pierce the lamb all over with a fork. Cut the lamb in half following a natural seam that runs across the center of the meat. Put the lamb in the marinade and turn to coat well. Cover with plastic wrap and refrigerate overnight, turning occasionally when possible.

3. About 45 minutes before cooking, take the lamb from the refrigerator. Position an oven rack 4 to 6 inches from the broiler and preheat. Line a broiler pan with aluminum foil. Put the lamb on the prepared broiler pan, smooth side down, and season with 1½ teaspoons of the salt. Broil until just charred, about 15 minutes. Turn the lamb, season with the remaining 1½ teaspoons salt, and broil until an instant-read thermometer inserted into the thickest part of the meat registers 130°F for medium-rare, 5 to 10 minutes more. Transfer the lamb to a cutting board, loosely cover with foil, and let it rest for 10 minutes before slicing. Slice the lamb across the grain, season the slices with salt to taste, and serve with grilled naan or other flat bread, if desired.

FROM THE KITCHENS
Masala means "blend." There are many different kinds of masala, but the term refers to some combination of black pepper, cinnamon, cloves, coriander, cumin, caradamom, dried chiles, fennel, mace, and nutmeg. For this recipe, you make your own blend, but garam masala is readily available at most supermarkets. If you can't find it at your market, look for it at an Indian market.

poultry

When it comes to inspired preparations on the simple bird, our imaginations soar. We like them roasted, fried, grilled, or stewed—and on any day of the week.

This easy twist on the classic veal dish is a total winner. Guests love it, and it impresses with minimal effort.

chicken saltimbocca | 4 servings

Instant flour for dredging,
   such as Wondra
4 boneless, skinless chicken breast
   halves (about 1 to 1½ pounds)
Freshly ground black pepper
16 fresh sage leaves
4 thin slices prosciutto
   (about 2 ounces)
1 tablespoon extra-virgin olive oil
1 tablespoon unsalted butter
5 ounces cremini mushrooms, sliced
2 cloves garlic, smashed
½ cup dry Marsala wine
3 tablespoons water
⅓ cup crème fraîche
2 tablespoons chopped fresh
   flat-leaf parsley (optional)
Kosher salt

1. Preheat the oven to 375°F. Put the flour in a shallow dish. Lay the chicken breasts smooth side up on a piece of waxed paper and season lightly with pepper. Lay 3 sage leaves across the top of each chicken breast and then wrap with a slice of prosciutto, tucking the ends of the prosciutto underneath. Heat a large skillet over medium-high heat; add the oil and butter. Dredge the wrapped chicken in the flour, shaking off excess. Place the chicken in the pan with the prosciutto seam side down and cook, turning once, until lightly browned on both sides, about 5 minutes in all. Transfer the chicken to a roasting pan and bake, uncovered, for 10 minutes.

2. Turn the heat under the skillet to high. Add the mushrooms and garlic and cook, stirring, until the mushrooms brown, about 4 minutes. Add the Marsala and the remaining 4 sage leaves and bring to a boil, scraping up any browned bits with a wooden spoon; cook until the liquid is almost gone. Add the water, pull the pan off the heat, and swirl in the crème fraîche and parsley, if using. Season the sauce with salt and black pepper to taste. Pool the mushroom sauce on individual plates or on a serving platter and arrange the chicken pieces on top.

FROM THE KITCHENS
Crème fraîche is a cultured cream—sort of a rich yogurt. It's perfect for adding luster to sauces in a flash. If you can't find it, add heavy cream stirred with a drop or two of lemon juice.

These chicken fingers feed more than just the K-12 crowd. Made from meaty chicken breasts, our juicy fingers will have you licking your digits clean.

chicken fingers with apricot sauce

4 servings

CHICKEN

4	boneless, skinless chicken breast halves (about 1½ pounds)
2	cups panko (see tip, below)
2	teaspoons finely grated lemon zest
2	teaspoons kosher salt, plus additional for seasoning
3	large eggs
	Vegetable oil for frying
	Freshly ground black pepper
1	lemon, cut into wedges

SAUCE

Makes 1 cup

²⁄₃	cup apricot preserves
2	tablespoons soy sauce
2	teaspoons ketchup
6	slices unpeeled fresh ginger
	Freshly squeezed juice from half a lemon (about 2 tablespoons)

1. Set a rack on a baking sheet, put it in the oven, and preheat to 200°F. Cut each chicken breast into 4 thick, even pieces. Toss the panko, lemon zest, and 2 teaspoons salt in a shallow bowl or pie plate. Beat the eggs lightly in another.

2. Heat about ½ inch oil in a large, heavy skillet over medium-high heat. Season the chicken all over with salt and pepper to taste, dip in the eggs, and then press into the panko mixture to coat evenly, shaking off any excess. Carefully place the chicken in the hot oil, taking care not to crowd the pan. Adjust the heat as necessary to maintain a constant sizzle. Fry the chicken, a few pieces at a time, turning once, until evenly brown, about 5 minutes total. Keep cooked fingers warm in the oven on the rack. Repeat with the rest of the chicken. Serve the chicken hot with lemon wedges and the dipping sauce.

APRICOT SAUCE

Combine the preserves, soy sauce, ketchup, and ginger in a small microwave-safe bowl. Cover with plastic wrap and microwave on HIGH until the preserves melt, about 30 seconds. Stir in lemon juice and cool before serving.

FROM THE KITCHENS

Panko are Japanese coarse bread crumbs—and our top choice for coating pan-fried cutlets, fish, and vegetables. The coating stays crisp and browns beautifully.

chicken curry | 4 servings

5   cloves garlic, smashed and peeled
1   medium red onion, quartered
       and peeled
1   2-inch piece fresh ginger, peeled
2   cups cold water
2   tablespoons vegetable oil
2   teaspoons Madras-style
       curry powder (see tip, page 68)
½   teaspoon ground cumin
½   teaspoon ground cardamom
       (optional)
       Pinch cayenne pepper
1   tablespoon tomato paste
1   bay leaf
½   teaspoon kosher salt
3   pounds skinless, bone-in chicken
       thighs and drumsticks
       (about 5 each)
2   tablespoons plain yogurt
       Freshly ground black pepper
½   lemon
       Small handful fresh cilantro, chopped

FOR SERVING
Cooked basmati rice (optional)
Mango chutney (optional)

1. Put the garlic, onion, and ginger in a blender or food processor with ¼ cup of the water. Blend to a coarse puree.

2. Heat the oil in a large skillet over medium-high heat. Add the onion mixture, curry powder, cumin, cardamom, if using, and cayenne. Cook, stirring, until the mixture begins to stick to the bottom of the pan, about 5 minutes. Stir in tomato paste and cook until brick red, about 1 minute. Add the remaining 1¾ cups water, the bay leaf, salt, and chicken. Bring to a boil, cover, and reduce heat to medium-low. Simmer until the chicken is tender, about 30 minutes.

3. Transfer the chicken to a bowl. Raise the heat to high and boil the curry uncovered, stirring occasionally, until it gets thick and saucy, about 10 minutes more. Stir in yogurt. Reheat the chicken in the sauce without boiling it; finish with some black pepper, a squeeze of fresh lemon juice, and the cilantro. Serve with rice and chutney, if desired.

FROM THE KITCHENS
Add chunks of cooked potatoes or carrots to the curry to round out the meal.

grilled soy & ginger chicken

4 to 6 servings

¾ cup soy sauce
½ cup sugar
¼ cup mirin (see tip, below)
¼ cup sake
10 coin-size pieces fresh ginger
12 boneless chicken thighs
   (about 2½ pounds)
   Sansho pepper (optional)
   (see tip, below)
   Grilled scallions (see tip, below)

1. Prepare an outdoor grill with medium-high fire for both direct and indirect grilling.

2. Combine the soy sauce, sugar, mirin, sake, and ginger in a small saucepan and simmer until sweet and syrupy, for 15 to 20 minutes.

3. Put the chicken skin side down on the direct heat side of the grill and brush with some glaze. Cook until the skin crisps, about 5 minutes, moving the chicken occasionally to keep it from charring. Turn chicken over and move it to the indirect heat side of the grill, brush the skin side with some glaze, and cover. Continue to cook the chicken, brushing occasionally with the glaze, until firm to the touch and an instant-read thermometer inserted into the thickest part registers 170°F, about 20 to 25 minutes.

4. Sprinkle the skin side with sansho pepper, if desired, and serve with grilled scallions.

FROM THE KITCHENS
• Sansho pepper, a Japanese spice that comes from the prickly ash, has a bright peppery taste similar to that of Szechwan peppercorn. It is a common Japanese condiment and adds just the right zing to this simple chicken dish. A shake on plain white rice is fabulous too. It comes in small jars and can be found in Asian and health food markets.
• Mirin is the "sweet" component in many Japanese dishes. If you can't find this mild rice wine, substitute a few pinches of sugar.
• To grill scallions, trim the white roots and the ragged ends of the greens (or, you can grill them whole). Drizzle with olive oil and season with salt. Cook on a grill, uncovered, over medium-high direct heat, turning occasionally, for 2 to 3 minutes.

chicken
with mustard pan sauce | 4 servings

4   boneless chicken breast halves,
      with skin (about 2 pounds)
    Kosher salt and freshly
      ground black pepper
2   tablespoons vegetable oil
½   cup white wine or dry white
      vermouth
1½ cups low-sodium chicken broth
      (about ¾ small can)
1   tablespoon all-purpose flour
2   tablespoons water
2   tablespoons whole-grain mustard
1   tablespoon unsalted
      butter (optional)

1. Preheat the oven to 350°F.

2. Heat a large skillet over medium-high heat. Pat chicken dry with paper towels and season all over with salt and black pepper. Add the oil to the hot pan and swirl to evenly coat. Lay the chicken pieces in the pan, skin side down, and cook without moving them until the skin crisps and browns, about 5 minutes. Flip and cook for another 3 minutes. Transfer chicken to a baking dish, skin side up, and bake until cooked through, about 10 minutes.

3. Pour the wine into the hot skillet. Use a wooden spoon to scrape up the browned bits in the bottom of the pan. Boil until almost all the wine evaporates and it gets a little syrupy, about 3 minutes. Add the broth and bring to a boil.

4. Mix the flour and water together to make thin paste (that's a "slurry"). Then whisk the slurry and mustard into the broth and boil until the sauce thickens, 1 to 2 minutes more. Remove pan from the heat. Swirl in the butter, if using, to give the sauce a little richness; season with salt and black pepper to taste. Add any collected juices from the chicken to the sauce. Put chicken on a plate, pour the sauce on top, and serve.

FROM THE KITCHENS
- A major reward of sautéing is a pan sauce—it's easy, tasty, fancy-looking, and impressive, with minimal cleanup and a lot of room for improvisation. Instead of white wine use red or substitute a smaller amount of lemon juice or wine vinegar. Add a sprig or 2 of chopped fresh herbs, like thyme, sage, or rosemary with the broth. Or, add 2 to 4 tablespoons heavy cream intead of the butter for a cream sauce; skip the slurry, then, and just boil until thick. (You can cook pork chops the same way.)
- If the wine flames when you add it, it's fine. Step back and shake the pan until the flames die down. If the sauce is sticky and too thick, add a splash of water.

Fire up the grill, watch the sunset, and rediscover why it's called the great outdoors.

grilled chicken
with avocado cucumber salad | 4 servings

CHICKEN

4   chicken paillards, about
      6 ounces each (see tip, below)
      Extra-virgin olive oil
1   teaspoon ground coriander
      Kosher salt
      Freshly ground black pepper

SALAD

1   Kirby cucumber with peel,
      coarsely chopped
1   cup grape or cherry tomatoes and/or
      yellow pear tomatoes, halved
¼   red onion, diced
1   tablespoon chopped fresh tarragon
1   teaspoon grated lemon zest
      (about ½ lemon)
      Freshly squeezed juice of half a
      lemon (1 to 2 tablespoons)
½   teaspoon kosher salt
      Pinch cayenne pepper
1   ripe Hass avocado

1. For the chicken: Preheat a grill pan or heat an outdoor grill to medium-high. Brush the chicken paillards lightly with olive oil and season with the coriander, salt, and black pepper to taste. Grill the chicken, in batches if necessary to avoid crowding the pan, turning once, until cooked through, about 2 minutes per side.

2. For the salad: While the chicken cooks, toss the cucumber, tomatoes, onion, tarragon, lemon zest and juice, salt, and cayenne pepper in a serving bowl. Halve the avocado; press a knife into the pit, twist, and lift out. Score the flesh with the tip of a knife, and then use a spoon to scoop it from the skins and into the salad; toss gently to combine. Put a paillard on each of 4 plates and spoon some salad over the chicken.

FROM THE KITCHENS

To butterfly chicken breasts for paillards: Turn the breast over and pull away the tenderloin. Flip over and slice into two halves horizontally, leaving the far edge intact. Open the breast. Using the flat side of your chef's knife, pound chicken (as you would smash a garlic clove) so that it is an even thickness. This is called a paillard.

chili-rubbed pan-roasted chicken with pico de gallo

4 servings

CHICKEN

2	tablespoons peanut or corn oil
4	bone-in chicken breast halves (about 10 ounces each), skin on
2	teaspoons chili powder
	Kosher salt

PICO DE GALLO

2	cups cherry or grape tomatoes, halved
½	to 1 jalapeño, stemmed and minced with seeds
¼	medium red onion, grated
½	teaspoon kosher salt, plus pinch for garlic
1	clove garlic, peeled
2	tablespoons extra-virgin olive oil
½	cup chopped fresh cilantro
	Warm corn tortillas (optional)

1. Preheat the oven to 400°F. Heat a large ovenproof skillet over medium-high heat. Add the oil and heat until shimmering. Season the chicken with chili powder and salt to taste. Lay the chicken in the skillet skin side down and cook until brown, about 4 minutes. Turn the chicken, transfer the pan to the oven, and cook until firm, basting occasionally with the pan drippings, 15 to 20 minutes.

2. While the chicken cooks, make the pico de gallo: Toss the tomatoes with the jalapeño, onion, and the ½ teaspoon salt. Smash the garlic clove, sprinkle with a pinch of salt, and, with the flat side of a large knife, mash and smear the mixture to a coarse paste. Stir the paste into the salsa with the olive oil and the cilantro.

3. To serve, divide the chicken among 4 plates, drizzle with pan drippings, and spoon some salsa over and around. Serve with warm corn tortillas, if desired.

FROM THE KITCHENS

We don't love grape tomatoes because they're cute (though they are), but because they taste like a tomato even in the off-season. They also don't require a lot of chopping because they're already small—and they hold their shape nicely when halved.

lemon-herb-marinated broiled chicken

4 servings

2 lemons
½ cup extra-virgin olive oil, plus additional for brushing
2 cloves garlic, smashed and peeled
½ cup chopped mixed fresh herbs, such as flat-leaf parsley, sage, oregano, thyme, and rosemary (see tip, below)
2 teaspoons kosher salt, plus more for seasoning
Pinch crushed red pepper flakes
Freshly ground black pepper
1 3- to 4-pound chicken, cut into 8 pieces

1. Juice 1½ lemons into a dish large enough to hold the chicken. Cut the remaining half into wedges for garnish, if desired. Whisk the olive oil, garlic, herbs, the 2 teaspoons salt, the crushed red pepper flakes, and some black pepper into the lemon juice. (Or just put the marinade together in a large resealable plastic bag and add the chicken pieces.) Trim away any excess fat from the chicken pieces before adding the chicken to the marinade, turning to coat evenly. Marinate at room temperature for 1 hour, turning once, or cover and refrigerate up to 12 hours.

2. Position a rack 6 to 8 inches from the broiler and, if you have the option, turn the broiler to medium-low. Line a broiler pan with foil and set insert on top.

3. Remove the chicken from the marinade and season with some salt and black pepper. Arrange the chicken pieces, skin side down, on broiler pan with the largest pieces in the center so they'll be under the hottest part of the broiler. Broil until the chicken loses its raw color, about 10 minutes. Turn chicken skin side up, and continue to cook until the skin is crispy and golden brown and an instant-read thermometer inserted in the thickest part of each piece registers 170°F, 15 to 20 minutes more. Transfer to a large platter. Garnish with lemon wedges, if using, and serve.

FROM THE KITCHENS
• Microwave lemons (or any citrus) for 5 seconds on low heat to make them easier to juice.
• Mixed fresh herbs (also sometimes called poultry herbs) are a blend of parsley, sage, oregano, thyme, and rosemary. If you can't find a mix, make your own: Use more leafy herbs (like parsley and sage) than woody ones (thyme, oregano, and rosemary), because a little of the woody ones goes a long way.

chicken
with apricots, olives & couscous | 4 servings

CHICKEN

8   chicken thighs (2 to 2½ pounds)
      Kosher salt and freshly ground
         black pepper
3   tablespoons extra-virgin olive oil
2   medium onions, each cut into
         6 wedges
4   cloves garlic, smashed
¾   teaspoon dried mint
¼   teaspoon crushed red pepper
         flakes or to taste
8   ounces dried apricots
         (about 2 dozen)
¾   cup small green olives, such
         as picholine (a small, crisp
         Provençal olive)

COUSCOUS

¾   teaspoon ground cumin
½   teaspoon caraway seeds
3   cups chicken broth,
         low-sodium canned
1   teaspoon kosher salt, plus
         additional for seasoning
      Pinch cayenne pepper
      Freshly ground black pepper
1½ cups uncooked couscous
2   to 3 tablespoons water or
         chicken broth

1. For the chicken: Position a rack in the middle of the oven and preheat to 450°F. Season chicken thighs generously with salt and pepper. Heat a large ovenproof skillet over medium heat, add oil, and heat until shimmering. Cook chicken skin side down until golden and crispy, about 8 minutes. Turn chicken and brown for another 2 minutes. Transfer chicken to a plate. Pour off 2 tablespoons of the pan drippings and reserve; leave remaining drippings in the skillet.

2. Add the onions, garlic, mint, and red pepper flakes to the skillet and cook until the onions are tender, about 8 minutes. Stir in the apricots and olives. Arrange the chicken, skin side up, on top of the onion mixture and bake, uncovered, until the chicken is cooked through, about 30 minutes.

3. While the chicken bakes, make the couscous: In a small saucepan, toast the cumin and caraway seeds over medium heat, swirling the pan frequently, until fragrant, about 2 minutes. Add the chicken broth, reserved drippings, the 1 teaspoon salt, and cayenne and black peppers to taste and bring to a boil. Stir in the couscous, pull the saucepan off the heat, cover, and set aside until the liquid has been absorbed and the couscous is plump, about 5 minutes.

4. When ready to serve, fluff the couscous with a fork and mound it on a warm serving platter. Arrange the chicken around the couscous. Stir 2 to 3 tablespoons water or broth into the onions so they look glazed. Season with salt, if desired, and spoon onions over the couscous and chicken.

philippine chicken adobo | 4 servings

3 tablespoons vegetable oil
   (or half butter and half oil)
8 skinless, bone-in chicken thighs
   (about 2¾ pounds)
1 teaspoon kosher salt, plus
   additional for seasoning
15 cloves garlic, smashed and peeled
2 bay leaves
2 cups water
¾ cup distilled white vinegar
2 tablespoons soy sauce
1 tablespoon sugar
¾ teaspoon coarsely ground
   black pepper
¼ teaspoon crushed red pepper
1 tablespoon cornstarch mixed with
   1 tablespoon cold water
   Hot cooked rice, for serving
   (optional)

1. Heat a large skillet over medium-high heat. Add the oil (or oil and butter, if using). Pat chicken dry and season with some salt to taste. Add the chicken smooth side down and cook until brown, about 4 minutes. Scatter the garlic and bay leaves around the chicken, then add the water, vinegar, soy sauce, sugar, the 1 teaspoon salt, black pepper, and red pepper. Bring the liquid to a boil; adjust heat to maintain a simmer. Cook, uncovered, turning the chicken occasionally, until tender, about 25 minutes.

2. Transfer the chicken to a bowl. Remove and discard bay leaves. Whisk the cornstarch mixture into sauce and simmer, whisking constantly, until it thickens a bit. Return the chicken and any juices to the sauce and simmer gently, turning the chicken occasionally, until it is very tender and glazed, about 10 minutes more. Serve over rice, if desired.

FROM THE KITCHENS
Rather than chopping, breeze through 15 cloves of garlic in no time by smashing them with the flat side of your knife.

chicken-n-biscuits potpie | 4 to 6 servings

FILLING

4	bone-in chicken breast halves (about 3 pounds)
4	cups chicken broth, low-sodium canned
4	tablespoons unsalted butter
3	medium carrots, peeled and cut into ½-inch slices
5	button mushrooms, quartered
1	rib celery (with leaves), cut into ½-inch slices
1	tablespoon kosher salt
1	cup frozen pearl onions, thawed
⅓	cup all-purpose flour
1	tablespoon minced fresh flat-leaf parsley
1	tablespoon chopped fresh dill
	Freshly ground black pepper

DOUGH

2	cups all-purpose flour, plus additional for dusting
1	tablespoon baking powder
1	teaspoon sugar
1	teaspoon fine salt
8	tablespoons cold unsalted butter, sliced
1	teaspoon finely grated lemon zest
¾	cup milk, plus additional for brushing

1. For the chicken filling: Put the chicken breasts in a medium saucepan, add the broth (it should just cover the chicken), and bring to a boil. Cover, turn the heat very low, and poach chicken until just firm to the touch, about 20 minutes. Remove chicken from the broth and, when cool enough to handle, shred or dice it into large bite-size pieces, discarding the skin and bones. (If some of the pieces are still a bit pink, they will finish cooking in the pie.) Reserve the broth.

2. Melt the butter in a 9-inch cast-iron or other heavy ovenproof skillet over medium-high heat. Add carrots, mushrooms, celery, and salt and cook until vegetables are light brown, about 4 minutes. Add the onions and cook about 1 minute more. Stir the flour into the vegetables and cook for 1 minute. Pour in the reserved chicken broth and whisk until it comes to a boil. Reduce the heat slightly and simmer, uncovered, until thick, about 3 minutes. Stir in chicken and remove skillet from heat. Stir in parsley, dill, and pepper.

3. For the biscuit dough: Preheat the oven to 450°F. Whisk the flour, baking powder, sugar, and salt in a large bowl. Using your fingers, rub 3 tablespoons of the butter into the flour until the mixture is sandy. Work in the remaining 5 tablespoons butter until it forms pea-size pieces. Stir lemon zest into the milk and stir milk into the flour mixture to make a soft dough. Turn the dough onto a lightly floured work surface and pat into a ½-inch-thick rectangle. Fold the dough in thirds as you would a business letter, then pat into a 10-inch-wide disk. You may leave the dough in one piece or cut into pieces.

4. Bring chicken filling to a simmer. If using a large biscuit round, cut a small hole in the center and lay the biscuit on the hot filling; if using pieces, arrange them on the filling. Brush the biscuit(s) lightly with milk. Put the skillet on a baking sheet and bake until golden brown, about 20 minutes. Let the potpie rest for 5 minutes before serving.

our favorite fried chicken | 6 to 8 servings

1 quart buttermilk

¼ cup kosher salt

2 tablespoons dried thyme

2 tablespoons dried oregano

1 tablespoon hot pepper sauce

2 cloves garlic, smashed

16 pieces chicken, half each white and
    dark meat, or whatever you prefer
    (about 6 pounds)

4 cups all-purpose flour

1 tablespoon sweet paprika

1 tablespoon freshly ground
    black pepper

Solid vegetable shortening or
    vegetable oil for frying

1. Whisk the buttermilk with salt, thyme, oregano, hot pepper sauce, and garlic in a large nonreactive bowl. Add the chicken pieces, turn to coat, cover the bowl, and refrigerate overnight.

2. Shake the flour, paprika, and pepper in a large, clean plastic or paper bag. Set a large rack over a baking sheet. Drain the chicken in a colander. Shake 2 or 3 pieces at a time in the bag with the flour mixture, shake off any excess, and set on the rack.

3. Set another rack over another baking sheet. Fill 2 large heavy skillets with ¾ inch of shortening. Heat over medium-high heat until a deep-frying thermometer registers 340°F. Working in batches, carefully add the chicken skin side down, with white meat in one skillet and dark in the other. The oil temperature will drop precipitously to about 250°F as you slip in the chicken. Adjust the heat as necessary to keep the temperature right around 250°F—the oil should be bubbling gently around all of the chicken pieces. Fry the chicken until it is a deep golden brown, about 10 minutes. Turn and fry until the other side is a deep golden brown, another 10 minutes for the white meat and 15 minutes for the dark meat. Transfer the cooked chicken to the clean rack. Serve immediately or at room temperature.

FROM THE KITCHENS

The ¼ cup salt serves not only as flavoring but as a brine. Some fried-chicken aficionados claim chicken should be covered while it cooks to stay juicy, but we found that the moisturizing steam also steamed the crispy coating right off our bird. Brining makes the meat juicier. So you have a no-compromise situation on your hands: You get succulent chicken and a crunchy coat.

We love
the way the
spices, chiles,
and smoke of
the grill go
together in
jerked foods.

grilled jerk chicken

4 to 6 servings

⅓ cup cider vinegar

¼ cup dark rum

3 tablespoons firmly packed dark brown sugar

1 bunch scallions (white and green parts), roughly chopped

4 cloves garlic, chopped

1 Scotch bonnet chile, stemmed, seeded, and minced

2 tablespoons Pickapeppa sauce (see tip, below)

1 tablespoon freshly grated peeled ginger

1 tablespoon ground allspice

¼ teaspoon pumpkin pie spice

3 tablespoons vegetable oil

4 chicken halves (about 6 pounds)

1. Pulse the vinegar, rum, brown sugar, scallions, garlic, chile, Pickapeppa sauce, ginger, allspice, and pumpkin pie spice in a food processor to make a slightly chunky sauce. Heat the oil in a medium skillet and cook the sauce over medium heat, stirring, until the oil is absorbed and the sauce thickens slightly, about 3 minutes. Cool.

2. Rub the jerk paste all over the chicken halves, cover, and refrigerate for 2 to 24 hours.

3. Prepare an outdoor grill with a medium-high fire for both direct and indirect grilling. Position a drip pan under the grate on indirect side. Place the chicken, skin side down, over direct heat and cook until skin crisps and has definite grill marks, about 4 minutes per side. Move to indirect heat over the drip pan and cook skin side up, covered, until an instant-read thermometer inserted into the thickest part of the thigh registers 165°F, about 35 to 40 minutes. Let the chicken rest about 5 minutes, then cut into pieces and serve.

FROM THE KITCHENS

Pickapeppa—the celebrated Jamaican bottled sauce—is a blend of tomatoes, onions, sugar, cane vinegar, mangoes, raisins, tamarind, peppers, and spices. Fans use this "Jamaican ketchup" on all manner of grilled foods. It adds a distinct punch to this version of the island's spicy jerk marinade.

Delight
yourself with
a culinary
trip to
Provence
with the
romantic
scent of
honey and
thyme.

provençal roasted chicken
with honey & thyme

4 servings

CHICKEN

- 1   3- to 4-pound chicken, excess fat trimmed and giblets removed
-      Kosher salt and freshly ground black pepper
- 1   shallot, sliced
- 1   bunch fresh thyme
-      Zest from 1 lemon, peeled in large strips
- 3   tablespoons extra-virgin olive oil
- 1   tablespoon honey

SAUCE

- 3   tablespoons water
- 1   tablespoon freshly squeezed lemon juice
- 1   tablespoon extra-virgin olive oil
- 1   tablespoon honey
- 2   tablespoons minced shallot
- 2   teaspoons chopped fresh thyme
- ¼   teaspoon kosher salt
-      Freshly ground black pepper

1. For the chicken: Preheat the oven to 425°F. Season the chicken cavity with salt and pepper to taste. Stuff the chicken cavity with the shallot, half the thyme, and lemon zest. Set a v-rack or regular rack in a roasting pan and brush with a bit of the olive oil. Whisk the honey and remaining oil in a small bowl. Dip the remaining thyme in the honey mixture and use it to brush the chicken all over. Set the thyme aside; you'll use it later as a basting brush. Season bird with salt and pepper to taste.

2. Tuck the wings under the back, cross the legs, and tie them with kitchen twine. Place the chicken breast side down on the rack and roast until the back is golden brown, 35 to 40 minutes. Remove the pan from the oven and turn the chicken breast side up. Cut the string where it holds the legs together and open up the legs a bit. Baste the chicken with the pan drippings, using the thyme sprigs as a brush. Roast the chicken again until the breast is golden brown and a meat thermometer inserted in the thigh registers 170°F, 20 to 25 minutes more. Transfer chicken to a carving board and let it rest for 10 minutes before carving.

3. For the sauce: Remove the rack from the roasting pan. Put the pan over medium-high heat, add the water, and stir with a wooden spoon to release the brown bits that cling to the pan. Strain the pan drippings into a small bowl and spoon off the fat. Whisk in the lemon juice, olive oil, honey, shallot, thyme, salt, and pepper to taste. Carve the chicken and serve drizzled with the sauce.

roast turkey | 8 to 10 servings

1 8- to 10-pound turkey, neck
    and giblets removed
   Kosher salt
   Freshly ground black pepper
1 medium onion, quartered
1 head garlic, halved
   Several sprigs of fresh herbs, such as
    thyme, parsley, rosemary, or sage
2 bay leaves
8 tablespoons unsalted butter, melted

1. Adjust a rack to lowest position and remove other racks. Preheat the oven to 325°F. Dry bird well with paper towels inside and out. Season the inside of the breast cavity with salt and pepper to taste and stuff with the onion, garlic, herbs, and bay leaves. Set the bird on a roasting rack in a roasting pan breast side up and brush generously with half the butter and season again with salt and pepper to taste. Tent bird with aluminum foil.

2. Roast turkey for 2 hours. Remove the foil and baste with remaining butter and some of the pan drippings. Increase oven temperature to 425°F and continue to roast until an instant-read thermometer registers 170°F in the thigh of the bird, about 45 minutes more. Remove turkey from the oven and set aside to rest 20 minutes. Before carving, remove and discard onion, garlic, herbs, and bay leaves.

FROM THE KITCHENS

It is best to remove the breast meat, legs, and wings from the carcass before storing. Cut through the wing joints and reserve the first two joints; save the tips for broth. Remove each side of the breast in one piece by cutting straight along the top of the breast and then down along the rib bones. Pull legs back and away from the carcass and cut along the thigh to free them from the frame. Store turkey, tightly covered, for 3 to 4 days in the refrigerator. If freezing, store the pieces in broth in resealable plastic bags. Use the bones for turkey broth.

What's fast and easy about roasting a turkey? The leftovers! A big bird cooked on the weekend provides the base for weekday meals. This is cooking smart.

turkey enchilada casserole | 4 servings

2 tablespoons vegetable oil
1 tablespoon unsalted butter
1 small onion, roughly chopped
2 cloves garlic, roughly chopped
1 jalapeño pepper, seeded and minced
1 slightly heaping teaspoon
  ground cumin
  Kosher salt
3 7-ounce cans tomatillo sauce
8 6-inch corn tortillas, preferably
  white, cut into quarters
2 cups cooked turkey meat, in bite-size
  pieces (about 10 ounces)
1 15½-ounce can black beans,
  rinsed and drained
2 cups shredded Cheddar
  or Monterey Jack cheese or a mix
  Sour cream (optional)
  Chopped fresh cilantro (optional)

1. Preheat the oven to 375°F. Heat the oil and butter in a large ovenproof skillet over medium heat. Add the onion, garlic, jalapeño, cumin, and salt to taste and cook until tender and fragrant, about 8 minutes. Stir in the tomatillo sauce, tortillas, turkey, and beans. Bring to a boil and stir in half the cheese.

2. Scatter the remaining cheese over the top and bake until casserole is bubbling and cheese has melted, about 20 minutes. Serve with sour cream and cilantro, if desired.

FROM THE KITCHENS
If you're faced with the decision of buying yellow or white corn tortillas, always opt for the white ones. They taste better, have a less cottony texture, and are more pliable.

turkey hoppin' john | 6 servings

6   slices bacon (about 4 ounces)
1   bunch scallions, sliced (white
     and green parts kept separate)
1   rib celery, sliced
4   cloves garlic, smashed
2   teaspoons kosher salt, plus
     additional for seasoning
1   teaspoon freshly ground black
     pepper, plus additional
     for seasoning
1   cup Southern long grain rice such as
     pecan, popcorn, or Texas basmati
6   cups chicken broth,
     low-sodium canned
2   cups roughly torn cooked
     dark-meat turkey
1   10-ounce package frozen
     black-eyed peas, thawed
1   bay leaf
2   tablespoons apple cider vinegar

1. Preheat the oven to 350°F. Crisp the bacon in a Dutch oven over medium-high heat, about 7 minutes. Remove the bacon, crumble it coarsely, and set aside; leave the pot over the heat.

2. Add the scallion whites, celery, garlic, 2 teaspoons salt, and 1 teaspoon pepper to the bacon fat in the pot and cook until tender and fragrant, 3 to 4 minutes. Stir in the rice. Raise the heat to high and stir in the chicken broth, turkey, black-eyed peas, bay leaf, and bacon. Bring the mixture to a boil, cover, and transfer to the oven. Bake until the rice is tender but not mushy, about 20 minutes.

3. Remove rice from the oven and let it rest 5 minutes—don't open the pot. Remove and discard bay leaf. Stir in the cider vinegar, adjust the seasonings, and scatter the scallion greens over the top.

FROM THE KITCHENS

For the biggest, freshest flavor, use aromatic long grain basmati rice hybrids such as pecan (also called popcorn) or Texmati and frozen black-eyed peas instead of canned.

Our rustic
Turkey
Turnovers
are proof that
good things
come in small
packages.
Gift-wrapped
in a flaky
triangle, they
deliver the
best of turkey
day any day.

turkey turnovers | 4 servings

2 tablespoons unsalted butter
8 ounces fresh shiitake mushrooms,
   stems removed and discarded,
   caps sliced
1 medium onion, diced
½ teaspoon dried thyme
½ teaspoon kosher salt
   Freshly ground black pepper
3 tablespoons cognac or other brandy
½ cup heavy cream, plus additional
   for brushing
1 teaspoon Dijon or
   whole-grain mustard
2½ cups cooked turkey, torn into bite-
   size chunks (about 12 ounces)
2 9-ounce, 9¼x10-inch sheets
   frozen puff pastry, thawed
   Cranberry sauce, for
   serving (optional)

1. Preheat the oven to 425°F. Line a baking sheet with parchment paper. Melt the butter in a medium skillet over medium-high heat. Add the mushrooms, onion, thyme, salt, and pepper to taste. Cook, stirring occasionally, until the onion softens and the mixture is dry, about 5 minutes. Carefully add the cognac (if working over gas, pull the skillet from the heat) and simmer until slightly syrupy. Add the cream and mustard, bring to a boil, and cook until the cream thickens slightly. Stir in the turkey and remove from the heat. Cool slightly.

2. Lay 1 puff pastry sheet on the baking sheet. Using a pastry wheel or sharp knife, cut it in half diagonally. Mound a quarter of the turkey mixture into the center of each half. Wet the edges of the pastry with water and then fold the pastry over the filling to make a large, triangular turnover. Press the edges with the tines of a fork to seal and cut a small hole in the top to vent the steam. Repeat with the other pastry sheet and the remaining filling. Space the turnovers on the parchment-lined pan so they brown evenly. Brush the turnovers lightly with cream and bake until golden, about 25 minutes. Serve warm or at room temperature with cranberry sauce, if desired.

1. Cut 1 sheet of puff pastry in half diagonally.
2. Mound one-quarter of the turkey mixture in center of each half. Wet pastry edges and fold top half over filling to meet edges of bottom half.
3. Press edges with fork tines to seal. 4. Make a slit in top to vent steam. Repeat with other pastry.

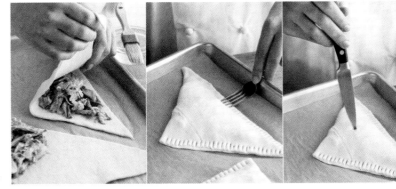

roasted duck
with orange-molasses glaze | 3 to 4 servings

DUCK
1   Pekin (Long Island) duckling
     (about 5 pounds)
     Kosher salt and freshly ground
     black pepper
3   1x3-inch strips orange zest
1   small onion, halved
1   cup water

GLAZE
3   1x3-inch strips orange zest
1½   tablespoons dark molasses
1½   tablespoons honey
2   tablespoons freshly squeezed
     orange juice
2   tablespoons balsamic vinegar
2   large garlic cloves, smashed
8   whole black peppercorns,
     lightly crushed
¼   teaspoon coriander seeds,
     lightly crushed

1. The day before roasting, remove the giblets and neck from the cavity of the bird and discard. Trim the neck flap and excess fat from around the cavity. Rinse the bird inside and out and pat dry with paper towels. Set the duck on a rack on a baking sheet and refrigerate, uncovered, for 24 hours.

2. The next day, preheat the oven to 300°F. Pierce the duck all over at ½-inch intervals with a skewer or small knife; be sure to pierce the skin on the back. Season the cavity with salt and pepper and stuff it with the orange zest and the onion. Set the duck breast side up on a rack in a roasting pan and pour the water in the pan. Roast 3 hours; remove the duck every hour to again pierce the skin so that the fat drains from the bird. After 3 hours, increase the temperature to 450°F and continue roasting until the skin is crisp and brown, about 30 minutes more.

3. While the duck is roasting, make the glaze: Put orange zest, molasses, honey, orange juice, vinegar, garlic, peppercorns, and coriander in a small saucepan. Heat over medium-high heat until the honey dissolves. Set aside while duck roasts.

4. When the duck is cooked, transfer it to a cutting board and let it rest for 10 minutes before carving. Brush the skin with glaze 4 to 5 five times during the resting period—don't cover it or you will forfeit its lovely crisp skin. Carve the duck and arrange pieces on a warm serving platter. Drizzle a bit more of the glaze over the pieces and pass the rest at the table.

FROM THE KITCHENS
We pierce the skin while roasting a duck to let the fat run free. The rendered fat can be saved. It adds fabulous flavor to sautéed greens and a crisp, flavorful crust to fried or roasted potatoes.

grilled greek mountain hens

4 servings

6 cups roughly chopped escarole, tough outer leaves removed (about 1½ heads)
16 sun-dried tomatoes packed in oil, drained and roughly chopped
½ cup pitted green olives, such as Picholine, roughly chopped
½ cup toasted walnut pieces, roughly chopped
5 cloves garlic, minced
2 tablespoons dried oregano, preferably Greek
½ teaspoon finely grated lemon zest
¼ teaspoon ground cinnamon
¼ cup extra-virgin olive oil
⅓ cup honey
Freshly ground black pepper
10 ounces Greek feta cheese, crumbled (about 2½ cups)
4 Cornish game hens (about 1½ to 1¾ pounds each)
Kosher salt

1. Prepare an outdoor grill with a medium-high fire for both direct and indirect grilling.

2. For the stuffing: Mix the escarole, tomatoes, olives, walnuts, garlic, oregano, lemon zest, and cinnamon in a large bowl. Add 2 tablespoons of the olive oil and 1 tablespoon of the honey and season with black pepper to taste. Mix in the feta, taking care not to break up the cheese too much.

3. To butterfly a Cornish hen: Cut the backbone out of the hen with poultry shears. Turn the bird over and snip along either side of the breast bone but not through the bird. Lift out the breast bone. Repeat with remaining birds. Slip a finger under the skin, from the neck end to loosen the skin over the breasts, thighs, and legs, making a pocket for the stuffing. Stuff ¼ of the stuffing under the skin of the breast and thighs of each hen. Brush with the remaining olive oil and season with salt and black pepper to taste.

4. Grill the hens skin side up over the direct heat until the underside is just browned, for 3 to 5 minutes. Transfer to indirect heat skin side up and cook, covered, until skin is golden brown (it does brown, although not directly on the heat) and an instant-read thermometer inserted in the thigh registers 155°F, about 15 to 25 minutes. Brush the skin generously with the remaining honey and cook, covered, until glazed and thermometer registers 160°F, about 5 minutes. Transfer hens to a cutting board and let rest 10 minutes before serving.

FROM THE KITCHENS
You'll notice a variety of honey in stores. The color and flavor of a honey depends totally on the flowers the bee visits. Some honeys come from the nectar of just one flower and have distinct flavors, while the regular honey you buy at the grocery store is a blend from many flowers. Our favorite honey for this dish is a floral one such as clover, thyme, or orange.

fish & shellfish

Feeling virtuous is just one reason to eat fish. It's also fresh, fast, and absolutely fabulous.

Our fennel
and orange
salad is
great any
time, but we
especially like
it in winter.
Fresh, bright,
and lively,
it takes only
minutes to
make and is
guaranteed
to chase away
the winter
blahs.

indoor-grilled salmon
with fennel & orange

4 servings

SALAD

- ½ medium red onion, thinly sliced
- ¾ teaspoon kosher salt, plus additional for seasoning
- 2 medium fennel bulbs (about 1½ pounds), trimmed and halved through the core
- 2 to 3 tablespoons basil-flavored olive oil
- 1 tablespoon white wine vinegar
- 2 navel oranges
  Freshly ground black pepper

SALMON

- 4 5-ounce center-cut salmon fillets (about 1 inch thick)
- 2 tablespoons olive oil
  Kosher salt
  Freshly ground black pepper
- 3 tablespoons dry English-style mustard
- 3 tablespoons honey
- 1 tablespoon water

1. Preheat the oven to 450°F. For the salad: Soak the onion in salted ice water for 10 minutes. Meanwhile, thinly slice the fennel lengthwise, using a mandoline if you have one. Put the fennel in a serving bowl and toss with the ¾ teaspoon salt, olive oil, and vinegar. Trim all of the peel and white pith from the oranges, halve them top to bottom, and slice into thin half-moons. Add the oranges to the fennel. Drain the onion, pat dry, and add it to the salad; season with salt and pepper to taste and toss.

2. For the salmon: Heat a grill pan or cast-iron skillet over medium-high heat. Brush the salmon lightly with the olive oil and season both sides with salt and pepper to taste. Lay the fillets skin side up in the pan and grill for 5 minutes.

3. Meanwhile, whisk mustard, honey, and water in a small bowl until smooth. Turn the salmon over, brush generously with the sauce, and transfer the grill pan to the oven. Bake the fish 2 to 3 minutes if you like it pink, or 5 minutes for fish that is cooked through but still moist.

4. Transfer salmon to a platter and let it rest for a couple minutes to finish cooking. Serve with the fennel salad.

FROM THE KITCHENS
For crisscross grill marks, give the salmon a quarter turn when it's halfway cooked on each side.

grilled pesto-stuffed salmon | 4 servings

SALMON
½ cup loosely packed fresh basil
½ cup loosely packed fresh parsley
2 tablespoons blanched whole almonds
¼ teaspoon minced garlic
¼ teaspoon kosher salt, plus
　　additional for seasoning
Freshly ground black pepper
3 tablespoons extra-virgin olive oil,
　　plus additional for brushing
1 1½-pound center-cut skinless
　　salmon fillet
Vegetable oil for grilling

SALAD
1 pound ripe mixed small tomatoes,
　　halved or diced
1 cup cooked fresh corn kernels
　　(from 2 ears)
3 tablespoons extra-virgin olive oil
1 tablespoon white wine vinegar
2 teaspoons minced fresh
　　marjoram or oregano
Kosher salt
Freshly ground black pepper

1. For the salmon: Pulse the basil, parsley, almonds, garlic, ¼ teaspoon salt, and black pepper to taste in a food processor to make a coarse paste. With the motor running, drizzle in the olive oil until incorporated. Lay the salmon fillet on a work surface. With a cut side facing you, cut a wide pocket with a narrow-bladed knife, taking care not to cut through the top or bottom of the fish. Hold the pocket open, season the inside with salt and black pepper to taste, and spread the pesto evenly inside the fish with a flat metal spatula. (The fish can be prepared up to this point a day ahead of grilling, then covered and refrigerated.)

2. Prepare an outdoor grill with a medium-high fire.

3. For the salad: Toss the tomatoes with corn. Add the olive oil, vinegar, marjoram, and salt and black pepper to taste. Toss again, taking care not to break up the tomatoes.

4. Lightly brush the grill grate with oil. Brush the fillet on both sides with olive oil and season the flesh side with salt and black pepper to taste. Lay the fish flesh side down on the grill and cook until there are distinct grill marks and you can lift the fish without its sticking, about 3 to 5 minutes. (Test it by gently lifting a corner—if it sticks, let it cook a bit longer.) When it lifts cleanly, carefully turn it about 45 degrees from its original position (don't turn it over). Cook for another 3 minutes, until marked. Season the skin side with salt and black pepper to taste, turn the fillet over, and cook about 3 to 5 minutes more or until an instant-read thermometer inserted in the side registers about 125°F. Transfer the fish to a plate and let it rest for 5 minutes. Cut salmon into 4 equal pieces and transfer to serving plates. Serve salmon warm or at room temperature topped with the Tomato-Corn Salad. Drizzle with any extra juices from the salad.

FROM THE KITCHENS
We like to use the microwave to cook corn. Just cut the kernels from the ears into a bowl and scrape the cobs with a knife to get out the juices. Cover and microwave on high for 1 minute.

grilled
planked salmon | 4 servings

SAUCE

- 10 tablespoons cold unsalted butter, cut into pieces
- 2 medium shallots, peeled and sliced
- 3 thick slices bacon, diced
- 3 cloves garlic, peeled and smashed
- 1 bottle Pinot Noir
- ¼ ounce dried porcini mushrooms (about 2 tablespoons)
- 3 sprigs fresh thyme
- 1 bay leaf
- 2 tablespoons demi-glace (see tip, below)
- 2 teaspoons red wine vinegar
- 1½ teaspoons kosher salt
  Freshly ground black pepper

SALMON

- 2 tablespoons unsalted butter, melted
- 1 teaspoon dry English-style mustard
- 1 tablespoon finely ground porcini powder (dried porcini mushrooms ground in a spice mill or coffee grinder)
- 1 3-pound side salmon fillet, pin bones removed
  Kosher salt
  Freshly ground black pepper

1. Soak a cedar or alder plank in cold water for 2 to 4 hours (see tip, below). Pat dry.

2. Prepare an outdoor grill at medium-high heat for indirect grilling.

3. For the sauce: Melt 1 tablespoon of the butter in a medium skillet, then add shallots, bacon, and garlic and cook over medium heat until the bacon renders its fat and the vegetables turn golden-brown, about 8 minutes. Pour off the fat and discard. Add the wine, dried mushrooms, and herbs, bring to a brisk boil, and cook until reduced by about half. Whisk in the demi-glace and heat until combined. Pull the pan from the heat and whisk in the remaining butter 1 tablespoon at a time. Add the vinegar and season with the salt and black pepper to taste. Strain the sauce and keep warm in a double boiler until ready to serve.

4. For the salmon: Whisk the melted butter, mustard, and porcini powder together. Lay the salmon skin side down on the plank and brush with butter-mustard mixture. Season with salt and black pepper to taste. Place the plank on the cooler side of the grill and cover. Cook until an instant-read thermometer inserted crosswise into the thickest part of the salmon registers 135°F, about 20 to 30 minutes.

5. Transfer fish, on the plank, to the table and let rest for 5 minutes. Serve each portion of the salmon drizzled with the warm Pinot Noir Sauce. Pass extra sauce at the table.

FROM THE KITCHENS

- Pacific Northwest Native Americans were the first to cook salmon on planks of wood. This ingenious technique has caught on. Cedar and alder planks specifically for cooking (they shouldn't be treated) are sold in sporting goods stores, cooking equipment and home improvement stores, and online.
- Demi-glace is a finely concentrated meat broth. We found ours at the meat counter, but it also can be found in specialty markets and on the web. To make your own, simply boil down a hearty homemade beef, veal, or chicken broth until it is a syrupy glaze.

Our 10-minute express coleslaw is in a class of its own. Plate it like a pro with grilled tuna and our spicy sauce, and dinner guests will want to reserve a seat at your table.

grilled tuna
with napa slaw & wasabi mayo | 4 servings

WASABI MAYONNAISE
- 4 teaspoons wasabi powder
- 4 teaspoons water
- ½ cup mayonnaise

SLAW AND TUNA
- ½ head (about 1 pound) napa cabbage, quartered, cored, and thinly sliced (6 cups)
- 6 ounces fresh snow or sugar snap peas, cut in thirds crosswise
- ¼ cup pickled ginger, drained and chopped
- 1½ teaspoons kosher salt, plus additional for tuna
- Freshly ground black pepper
- ¼ cup rice wine vinegar
- 2 tablespoons peanut oil, plus additional for tuna
- 1 1¼-pound tuna steak (about 2 inches thick)
- 2 teaspoons gomashio (see tip, page 162) (optional)

1. Heat an outdoor grill or preheat a grill pan to medium-high. Whisk the wasabi and water in a small bowl to make a thick paste; turn the bowl over and set aside for a couple minutes. Whisk in the mayonnaise until smooth. Cover until ready to use.

2. For the slaw: Toss the cabbage, snow peas, pickled ginger, 1½ teaspoons salt, and pepper to taste in a large bowl. Add the vinegar and the 2 tablespoons peanut oil and toss again to coat.

3. For the tuna: Brush the tuna lightly all over with peanut oil and season generously with salt and pepper. Grill the tuna until it looks cooked about ⅓ inch up the side, about 3 minutes; then turn and cook another 3 minutes. Using tongs, hold the tuna on its sides to brown, about 1 minute on all sides. (If you like your fish medium, add 1 to 2 minutes per side to the cooking time.) Set aside for 5 minutes before cutting.

4. Cut the tuna into bite-size chunks. Mound some slaw on each of 4 plates and arrange the tuna on top. Sprinkle some gomashio over each serving, if desired, and serve with a dollop of wasabi mayonnaise.

FROM THE KITCHENS
When buying tuna, ask for sushi-grade tuna, the highest quality available, and look for glossy, bright red steaks.

grilled tuna with mojo

4 servings

MOJO
- ½ to 1 small fresh jalapeño or serrano chile, halved and stemmed
- 4 cloves garlic, chopped
- ¼ cup extra-virgin olive oil
- Juice of 4 limes
- Handful fresh cilantro, coarsely chopped
- 1 teaspoon kosher salt

TUNA
- 2 12-ounce tuna steaks (about 1¼ inches thick)
- 1 tablespoon extra-virgin olive oil
- Heaping ½ teaspoon kosher salt
- Freshly ground black pepper

1. Heat an outdoor grill or a stovetop grill pan to medium-high.

2. For the mojo: For a milder mojo, scrape out the seeds with the tip of your knife; for maximum heat, leave the seeds in. Slice the chile very thinly; set aside. Stir the garlic and olive oil together in a medium microwave-safe bowl, cover loosely with plastic wrap, and microwave on HIGH until the garlic is soft and aromatic, about 2 minutes. Add the chile, lime juice, cilantro, and salt to the hot oil. Set aside to cool until ready to serve.

3. For the tuna: Brush the tuna with olive oil and season generously with the salt and some black pepper. Grill until there are distinct grill marks on both sides, turning once, 3 to 5 minutes per side for medium rare or 4 to 6 minutes for cooked through. (If cooking on an outdoor grill, the fire should be hotter than a grill pan, so use the shorter cooking times.) Let rest for 5 minutes.

4. Slice each tuna steak in half, divide among plates, and drizzle with some of the mojo, passing more at the table.

FROM THE KITCHENS
Grill pans are fantastic if you can't grill outdoors.
If you don't have one, use a flat, heavy-bottomed pan.

halibut steaks
with tapenade, tomatoes & herbs | 4 servings

FISH

1	bunch flat-leaf parsley
½	bunch fresh thyme, about 20 sprigs
2	bay leaves, preferably fresh
8	cloves garlic, smashed
2	1-pound halibut steaks, 1¼ inch thick
	Kosher salt and freshly ground black pepper
¾	cup dry white vermouth
4	tablespoons extra-virgin olive oil
12	red and yellow cherry, grape, or pear tomatoes, halved
2	teaspoons freshly squeezed lemon juice

TAPENADE

½	cup kalamata olives, pitted and finely chopped
1	tablespoon extra-virgin olive oil
1	teaspoon chopped fresh thyme
1	teaspoon finely grated lemon zest
	Kosher salt and freshly ground black pepper

1. Preheat the oven to 450°F. Set aside 4 sprigs of the parsley. Line a medium gratin or baking dish with the remaining parsley, the thyme, and bay leaves; scatter the garlic on top.

2. For the fish: Season both sides of the halibut steaks with salt and pepper and lay them on the herbs. Pour vermouth around fish and drizzle 2 tablespoons of the olive oil over the steaks. Cover tightly with aluminum foil and bake just until steaks are firm to the touch and opaque, 20 to 25 minutes. Check after 20 minutes—it is best to remove the fish from the oven when it is slightly underdone because it will continue to cook as you make the sauce. While the fish cooks, toss the tomatoes with salt and pepper to taste in a small bowl.

3. For the tapenade: Stir together the olives, the 1 tablespoon olive oil, thyme, and lemon zest in another small bowl. Season with salt and pepper to taste and set aside.

4. After removing the fish from the oven, carefully pour the juices from the pan into a small saucepan. Remove the garlic, thyme, and bay leaves and set aside. Re-cover the fish and set aside. Boil the juices over high heat until reduced by about half and slightly thickened, about 5 minutes. Pull the saucepan from the heat and whisk in the remaining 2 tablespoons olive oil and the lemon juice. Taste and season with salt and pepper.

5. To serve, run the tip of a paring knife between the bone and the flesh and gently lift out the bone to separate each steak into 4 portions. Peel the skin from the sides of the steaks. Put 2 pieces on each of 4 plates, top with the tapenade and tomatoes, and drizzle with the sauce.

FROM THE KITCHENS
Fish cooked on the bone is juicier and more full-flavored than filleted.

steamed sea bass
with citrus & herbs | 6 servings

1   medium bunch fresh herbs such as dill, parsley, thyme, tarragon, or a mix
1   lemon
1   lime
1   small orange
4   6-ounce sea bass or red snapper fillets
¼   cup extra-virgin olive oil
½   teaspoon kosher salt, plus additional for seasoning
   Freshly ground black pepper

1. Chop enough herbs to make ¼ cup and set aside. Finely grate about 1 teaspoon zest from each citrus fruit and add to the chopped herbs. Pour an inch or more of water in a wok or skillet and bring to a boil over medium-high heat.

2. Make a bed of the remaining whole herbs in a bamboo or collapsible steamer and cover with 3 or 4 slices of each citrus fruit (reserve the remaining lemon and lime halves for juice). Lay 2 of the fish fillets skin side down on top of the herbs, drizzle with some of the oil, and season with some salt and pepper to taste. Place the 2 remaining fillets skin side up on top of the other fillets. Set the steamer over the water, cover, and cook for 10 minutes or just until the fish is barely cooked through. Turn off the heat and leave fish covered in the steamer over the hot water for 5 more minutes to finish cooking.

3. Meanwhile, squeeze about 1 tablespoon each of juice from the lemon and lime into a medium bowl. Season with the ½ teaspoon salt and pepper to taste. Gradually whisk in the remaining olive oil, starting with a few drops and then adding the rest in a steady stream to make a smooth dressing. Stir in the reserved herbs and zest.

4. Divide the fish among 4 plates, discarding the whole herbs and citrus slices, and drizzle some dressing over the fish. Pass extra dressing at the table.

Perfumed in a steam bath of citrus and herbs, this light fish dish is a welcome reward after a taxing day.

Cook like a pro: plan ahead.

Mise en place may sound chef-y, but all it really means is "putting in place." Have all of your ingredients ready up to the point of cooking, and there's no stopping you.

grilled mahi tacos
with escabeche

6 servings

SALSA

2   ancho chiles, stemmed and seeded
3   tablespoons fresh orange juice
2   teaspoons honey
¾   teaspoon kosher salt
2   tablespoons extra-virgin olive oil

ESCABECHE

4   tablespoons extra-virgin olive oil
6   cloves garlic, thinly sliced
2   to 3 jalapeños, thinly sliced
3   carrots, peeled and sliced
1   red onion, halved and sliced
3   whole cloves
2   bay leaves (fresh, if available)
1   stick cinnamon
2   teaspoons kosher salt
1   teaspoon coriander seeds, cracked
½   teaspoon dried thyme
½   teaspoon dried Mexican oregano
     Freshly ground black pepper
½   cup apple cider vinegar

FISH

6   5- to 6-ounce mahi-mahi fillets
     Extra-virgin olive oil
     Kosher salt and ground pepper

TACOS

12   to 24 corn tortillas
12   sprigs fresh cilantro

1. For the salsa: Toast the chiles in a dry skillet over medium-high heat, turning and flattening with a spatula, until fragrant, about 1 minute. Put the chiles in a bowl, cover with very hot water, and set aside until soft, about 30 minutes. Drain, roughly chop, and puree the chiles in a blender with the orange juice, honey, salt, and a bit of water, if needed. Blend in olive oil. Set aside.

2. For the escabeche: Heat olive oil in a medium skillet over medium-high heat. Add remaining ingredients except cider vinegar and cook until carrots are crisp-tender, stirring, about 5 minutes. Add 1 cup water and the cider vinegar, bring to a boil, reduce heat, and cook at a gentle simmer until just soft, about 15 minutes. Cool.

3. For the fish: Preheat a grill pan over medium-high heat or prepare an outdoor grill. Brush the fillets all over with a little olive oil and season generously with salt and pepper. Lay the fish on the grill and leave it until you see distinct grill marks and can lift the fish without it sticking to the grill, 5 to 6 minutes. Test it by gently lifting a corner—if it sticks, cook it a bit longer and try again. Carefully turn the fish over and cook until firm to the touch, another 5 to 6 minutes. Brush with some of the salsa and transfer to a platter.

4. To assemble tacos: Grill tortillas until slightly charred but still pliable, about 10 seconds per side. Lay a sprig of cilantro on a single or double tortilla and top first with some of the escabeche and then a piece of fish—half of a fillet per taco will do. Top with sour cream, if desired, and additional salsa.

FROM THE KITCHENS
Escabeche is a spicy pickle popular in Latin America. Use it on any poached, grilled, or fried fish.

Add an authentic south-of-the-border relish to a time-honored fish taco and feel your taste buds come alive. Great for the grill or a day at the beach.

spicy pecan fish | 4 servings

5 tablespoons unsalted butter
¼ cup all-purpose flour
½ teaspoon chili powder
1 teaspoon kosher salt, plus more
     for seasoning
4 6-ounce skinless scrod or
     haddock fillets
⅓ cup pecans, roughly chopped
5 fresh sage leaves, roughly chopped
3 tablespoons cider vinegar
1 teaspoon honey
½ teaspoon hot pepper sauce
     Freshly ground black pepper

1. Position a rack 4 to 6 inches from the broiler and preheat broiler. Melt the butter in a small skillet and lightly brush a baking dish with some of the butter.

2. Mix the flour and chili powder together on a plate. Season the fish with the 1 teaspoon salt and roll in the seasoned flour to coat. Shake off the excess flour and place the fish in a single layer, skinned side down, in the prepared baking dish. Drizzle another tablespoon or so of the butter over the fish. Broil the fish until firm to the touch, 8 to 10 minutes.

3. Meanwhile, cook the pecans in the remaining butter over medium heat, swirling the pan occasionally, until they are toasted and fragrant, about 5 minutes. Remove skillet from the heat and let cool slightly. Carefully whisk in the cider vinegar, honey, hot sauce, and sage. (Be careful—the butter may foam and bubble when you add the liquids.) Season with salt and black pepper to taste. Put the fish on serving plates, pour the pecans and butter over the fish, and serve.

FROM THE KITCHENS
• Browned-butter sauces are one of the best things that ever happened to fish. When you heat butter, the milk solids burn slightly, giving the butter a toasty brown color and a nutty, rich taste. It can go from brown to black in seconds, though, so be sure to stand there and watch it as it cooks.
• Scrod, despite the urban legend to the contrary, isn't a made-up word for "catch of the day"—it's young cod.

cajun corn-crusted catfish with remoulade | 4 servings

FISH

- 4 6-ounce catfish fillets
- 2 cups buttermilk
- 1 teaspoon kosher salt, plus additional for seasoning
- 1 cup cornmeal
- ½ cup all-purpose flour
- 2 tablespoons Cajun seasoning (see recipe, below)
  Vegetable oil for shallow frying
- 2 ripe large tomatoes, sliced
- 2 to 3 cups mixed salad greens (optional)
  Freshly ground black pepper
- 1 cup Remoulade (see recipe, below)

SEASONING
Makes ⅓ cup

- 1 tablespoon dried oregano
- 1 tablespoon dried thyme
- 1 tablespoon sweet paprika
- 1 tablespoon kosher salt
- 2 teaspoons garlic powder
- 1 teaspoon onion powder
- 1 teaspoon cayenne pepper
- 1 teaspoon English-style dry mustard
- ½ teaspoon freshly ground black pepper

REMOULADE
Makes 1 cup

- ¾ cup mayonnaise
- ¼ cup minced sweet pickles
- 3 tablespoons minced celery
- 2 tablespoons Creole mustard
- 1 tablespoon minced fresh flat-leaf parsley
- 1 scallion, thinly sliced
- ½ teaspoon sweet paprika
- ½ teaspoon kosher salt
- ¼ teaspoon finely grated lemon zest
- 1 dash hot pepper sauce

1. Soak the catfish in the buttermilk with 1 teaspoon salt, cover, and refrigerate for 1 hour. Whisk the cornmeal, flour, and Cajun seasoning together in a shallow bowl.

2. Heat 2 heavy skillets (we like cast-iron) over medium heat with about ½ inch of oil. Remove catfish from the buttermilk, shaking slightly so the excess buttermilk drains from the fish. Dredge the fillets in the cornmeal mixture. Lay the catfish rounded side down in the pans and cook until golden brown, about 5 minutes. Flip and cook until the fish feels firm to the touch, about 5 minutes more. Divide the tomatoes and salad greens, if desired, among 4 plates and lay the fish on top. Season with salt and pepper. Spoon a dollop of Remoulade on top. Serve, passing additional sauce at the table.

CAJUN SEASONING
Combine oregano, thyme, paprika, salt, garlic powder, onion powder, cayenne pepper, dry mustard, and black pepper thoroughly in a small bowl. Store in an airtight container.

REMOULADE
Stir together mayonnaise, pickles, celery, mustard, parsley, scallion, paprika, salt, lemon zest, and hot pepper sauce in a medium bowl. Refrigerate for 1 hour before serving.

FROM THE KITCHENS
Coarsely ground Creole mustard has a kick but also enough of a rounded sweet flavor to make it a great all-purpose mustard.

This is fast, easy, and impressive. Don't be intimidated by the whole fish—this is the way fish are meant to be served.

grilled trout in grape leaves

4 servings

FISH

4   whole rainbow trout
    (each about 14 ounces)
    Kosher salt
    Freshly ground black pepper
2   tablespoons unsalted butter, diced
1   bunch fresh thyme sprigs
    About 20 jarred grape leaves
    Extra-virgin olive oil

VINAIGRETTE

1   lemon
1   tablespoon chopped fresh thyme
    Kosher salt
    Freshly ground black pepper
3   tablespoons extra-virgin olive oil

1. For the fish: Heat an outdoor grill or preheat a grill pan to medium. Season the fish cavities with salt and pepper to taste. Stuff each fish with a quarter of the butter and thyme sprigs. Season the outside of the fish with salt and pepper to taste.

2. Rinse the grape leaves in a colander and pat them dry. Lay 3 leaves sideways and slightly overlapping on the work surface. Lay 2 more leaves along the far edge of the line of leaves to make a large sheet of grape leaves. Lay a fish across the leaves and wrap around the fish. Tie the fish in 2 or 3 places with kitchen twine. Repeat with the remaining fish and leaves.

3. Brush the wrapped fish lightly with oil. Grill the trout until an instant-read thermometer inserted into the thickest part of the fish registers 125°F, turning once, about 5 to 7 minutes per side. Set aside for 5 minutes before serving.

4. For the vinaigrette: Squeeze the lemon juice into a small bowl and stir in thyme and salt and pepper to taste. Gradually whisk in the oil to make a dressing. Snip off the string and serve each fish with a bit of the dressing.

FROM THE KITCHENS

Cushion a platter with parsley and thyme, then lay the whole fish on their herb bed and surround them with lemon wedges.

sole gratin
with tomatoes, capers & olives | 4 servings

5   tablespoons extra-virgin olive oil,
        plus additional for pan and fish
4   6-ounce fillets of sole
¼   teaspoon kosher salt, plus
        additional for seasoning
     Freshly ground black pepper
4   to 5 canned plum tomatoes, drained
1   small onion, halved and sliced
4   to 5 pitted kalamata olives, chopped
1   heaping teaspoon capers, drained
½   cup flat-leaf parsley,
        coarsely chopped
¼   cup dried bread crumbs

1. Preheat the oven to 400°F. Lightly brush a 1½-quart oval gratin dish with olive oil. Lay the fish out on the work surface skin side up, drizzle with a bit of the oil, and season with some salt and pepper to taste. Fold the fillets in half (thick end over thin) and lay the pieces down the center of the prepared pan, slightly overlapping.

2. Crush the tomatoes through your fingers into a small bowl. Stir in 3 tablespoons of the olive oil, the onion, olives, capers, the ¼ teaspoon salt, and pepper to taste. Stir in the parsley and spoon the mixture over the fish.

3. Toss remaining 2 tablespoons olive oil with the bread crumbs until evenly moistened and scatter them over the fish. Bake until the fish is cooked through and the crumbs get crispy and brown, about 25 minutes.

FROM THE KITCHENS
Can you tell which end is up? Let the herringbone pattern be your clue—this is the skin side, so keep it facing up and center.

cioppino | 4 to 6 servings

¼ cup extra-virgin olive oil
1 medium onion, diced
½ teaspoon fennel seeds
6 cloves garlic, minced
1 tablespoon kosher salt
  Freshly ground black pepper
1 tablespoon tomato paste
½ cup red wine
2½ cups canned plum tomatoes,
  with their juice
1 cup clam juice
1 cup water
1 bay leaf
½ cup torn fresh basil
1 pound monkfish, preferably on
  the bone, sliced into 4 steaks
1 medium live Dungeness crab
  (see tip, right, for preparation)
8 ounces cleaned squid, cut into
  ½-inch pieces
3 tablespoons roughly chopped
  fresh flat-leaf parsley

1. Heat the olive oil in a large soup pot over medium heat. Add the onion and fennel seeds and cook until golden brown, about 15 minutes. Add the garlic, salt, and pepper to taste and cook 2 minutes more. Stir in the tomato paste and cook for 1 minute. Stir in ¼ cup of the wine and simmer until reduced to a glaze. Add the remaining ¼ cup wine and reduce by half. Crush the tomatoes through your fingers into the pot; stir in their juices, the clam juice, water, and bay leaf, cover, and simmer 30 minutes. (The cioppino may be prepared up to this point and refrigerated overnight in a tightly sealed container.)

2. Adjust the heat so that the cioppino simmers briskly. Stir in the basil and monkfish, cover, and cook 5 minutes. Add the crab and cook 1 minute; finally, add the squid and cook until just firm, about 2 minutes. Remove bay leaf. Transfer the cioppino to a large bowl, scatter the parsley on top, and serve.

FROM THE KITCHENS
To prepare the Dungeness crab: Add the crab to a pot of boiling water. Boil for 5 minutes; remove from the pot and cool. Remove the top shell and discard. Remove the gills from the sides of the crab, trim off the face, and scoop out the yellow matter and discard. Cut the body with legs attached into 4 pieces and reserve for the stew.

shrimp
with tomatoes, basil & garlic | 4 servings

1½ cups cherry or grape tomatoes
(about ¾ of a pint container),
halved or quartered

Handful of fresh basil leaves,
roughly chopped

¾ teaspoon kosher salt, plus
more for seasoning

Freshly ground black pepper

1¼ pounds peeled and deveined
medium or large shrimp
(see tip, page 78)

2 tablespoons extra-virgin olive
oil or unsalted butter

1 large clove garlic, minced

1 lemon, cut into wedges

1. Toss the tomatoes and basil in a medium bowl and season with the ¾ teaspoon salt and some black pepper. Set aside so the tomatoes get juicy.

2. Spread the shrimp out on a clean pan or cutting board and pat them completely dry with a paper towel. Heat a large skillet over high heat. Season the shrimp with some salt and black pepper. Add a little less than half the olive oil or butter to the skillet. Lay half the shrimp in the pan relatively quickly so they cook evenly. Cook the shrimp, undisturbed, until they turn golden brown on the bottom, about 2 minutes. Add a bit more oil and scatter half the garlic in the skillet. Turn the heat off and turn the shrimp over with tongs. Cook for 1 minute in the residual heat of the skillet. Transfer the shrimp to the bowl with the tomato mixture and toss to combine. Reheat the pan and repeat with the remaining oil, shrimp, and garlic.

3. Divide the shrimp among 4 plates or mound on a serving platter. Serve, with the lemon wedges, hot or at room temperature.

FROM THE KITCHENS

▪ Shrimp really don't need tons of heat; too much can turn them tough. The pan's still going to be hot after you turn the burner off—just hot enough to cook the shrimp through without toughening them up. Shrimp cook so fast that it's key to get all of them in the pan at once so they cook evenly. If you crowd the pan, they won't brown, so do a layer at a time.

▪ Instead of basil, try dill, parsley, or mint. Toss over pasta.

pan-seared shrimp
with romesco sauce

4 servings

SAUCE

1	small ancho chile, stemmed and seeded (see tip, page 131)
¼	cup extra-virgin olive oil
¼	cup whole blanched almonds
½	medium onion, thinly sliced
2	cloves garlic, smashed
2	teaspoons kosher salt, plus additional for seasoning
	Freshly ground black pepper
2	teaspoons sweet paprika
¾	cup roughly chopped jarred, drained piquillo peppers (see tip, page 34)
½	slice stale white bread, roughly torn
2	tablespoons sherry vinegar

SHRIMP

1½	pounds large shrimp, peeled, deveined, and patted dry (see tip, page 78)
	Kosher salt and freshly ground black pepper
3	tablespoons extra-virgin olive oil

1. For the sauce: Toast the ancho chile in a small dry skillet over medium-high heat, turning and flattening with a spatula, until fragrant, about 1 minute. Put the chile in a medium bowl, cover with very hot water, and set aside until soft, about 10 minutes. Drain, chop roughly, and set aside.

2. Heat the olive oil in a large skillet over medium heat. Add the almonds and cook, stirring, until toasted, about 3 minutes. Transfer the almonds to a plate, leaving the oil in the skillet. Add the softened chile, the onion, garlic, the 2 teaspoons salt, and pepper to taste. Cook, stirring, until onions are lightly browned, about 3 minutes. Add paprika and cook until fragrant, about a minute more. Scrape onion mixture into a sieve set over a bowl; reserve 3 tablespoons strained oil.

3. Pulse the onion mixture, almonds, piquillo peppers, bread, and vinegar in a food processor until coarse. With the motor running, drizzle in the reserved oil. Scrape the sauce into 4 small serving bowls, cover, and set in a warm place while you cook the shrimp.

4. For the shrimp: Spread shrimp on a pan or a piece of aluminum foil. Heat 2 large skillets over medium heat. Sprinkle salt and pepper over the shrimp. Add 1 tablespoon of the olive oil to each skillet and increase the heat to high. Add the shrimp seasoned side down, taking care not to crowd them. (Even with two pans, you may need to cook the shrimp in batches; if you crowd the skillets the shrimp will steam and get soggy.) Cook the shrimp undisturbed until they turn golden brown on the bottom, about 3 minutes. Add a bit more oil to each skillet and season the shrimp with salt and pepper. Turn the heat off and flip the shrimp with tongs. Leave shrimp in the skillets another minute; the residual heat will finish cooking them. Place a bowl of sauce on each of 4 serving plates and arrange some of the shrimp around each bowl.

thai shrimp curry | 4 servings

2 tablespoons peanut oil
1 pound medium shrimp, peeled, deveined, and tails removed (see tip, page 78)
1 13.5-ounce can unsweetened coconut milk
2 teaspoons prepared Thai red curry paste
1 stalk lemongrass, sliced (see page 78)
1 tablespoon fish sauce
2 teaspoons dark brown sugar
1 teaspoon kosher salt
8 ears canned baby corn (about ½ can)
4 scallions (white and green parts), chopped
½ cup sliced canned water chestnuts, drained
½ cup canned straw mushrooms, drained
¼ cup fresh basil leaves, torn
2 tablespoons torn mint leaves
1 lime
Hot cooked jasmine rice
Sliced scallions (white and green parts) (optional)

1. Heat the oil in a large skillet over medium-high heat. Add the shrimp and stir-fry just until pink and curled but not cooked through, about 2 minutes. Transfer the shrimp to a plate and set aside.

2. Skim the thick cream from the surface of the coconut milk and add it to the skillet along with the curry paste. Cook, stirring, until smooth and fragrant and a bit shiny, about 1 minute. Stir in the remaining coconut milk, the lemongrass, fish sauce, brown sugar, and salt; simmer for 3 minutes, uncovered. Return the shrimp to the skillet along with the baby corn, scallions, water chestnuts, and straw mushrooms. Simmer until the shrimp finish cooking, about 3 minutes more. Pull the pan off the heat. Stir in the basil and mint, and squeeze in the lime's juice. Serve with jasmine rice. Sprinkle with sliced scallions, if desired.

FROM THE KITCHENS
We love Thai curry pastes. Based on chiles along with other spices, prepared pastes are used in tandem with liquid—usually coconut milk—to tame their spiciness. Buy them in a jar or can in any hue—red, yellow, or green. They're all instant flavor boosters.

veggies & sides

Round out dinner with a simple vegetable dish, a fresh and inspired side salad, or one of our favorite carb-loaded accompaniments (we love 'em!).

asparagus
with asiago & prosciutto | 4 servings

2 pounds medium asparagus
2 tablespoons extra-virgin olive oil
½ teaspoon kosher salt
  Freshly ground black pepper
1- to 2-ounce chunk Asiago or
   Parmesan cheese
1 ounce thinly sliced prosciutto

1. Preheat the oven to 450°F. Trim the woody ends from the asparagus. Spread the spears in a single layer in a shallow baking pan, drizzle with olive oil, sprinkle with salt, and roll to coat thoroughly.

2. Roast the asparagus until lightly browned and tender, about 10 minutes, giving the pan a good shake about halfway through. Spread the roasted asparagus on a serving platter. Grind a generous amount of pepper over and shave the Asiago into wide flakes on top of that. Tear the prosciutto into ragged pieces and scatter on top. Serve warm or at room temperature.

FROM THE KITCHENS
Buy asparagus with tightly closed, slightly purple-tipped heads and healthy, hydrated stem ends. The thicker the asparagus, the stronger the flavor.

green beans with shallots | 4 servings

½ teaspoon kosher salt, plus more for
   the cooking water
1 pound fresh green beans, trimmed
1 to 2 tablespoons extra-virgin olive oil
1 large shallot, finely chopped
   Freshly ground black pepper

1. Bring a medium pot of water to a boil over high heat and salt it generously.

2. Drop the green beans into the boiling water and cook, uncovered, until crisp-tender, about 4 minutes. Drain in a colander and rinse with very cold water until cool. Drain well and pat dry with paper towels. (The vegetables can be prepared up to this point up to 4 hours ahead.)

3. Heat the olive oil in a large skillet over medium heat. Add the shallot and cook, stirring occasionally, until the shallot is just golden, about 2 minutes. Add the green beans, increase the heat to high, and cook, stirring occasionally, until the beans are heated through, about 4 minutes. Season with the ½ teaspoon salt and some black pepper and serve immediately.

FROM THE KITCHENS
Look for smooth, crisp green beans with velvety skin. If they're pretrimmed, make sure the trimmed end is moist-looking.

wilted spinach | 4 servings

2 pounds spinach
   (about 2 big bunches), stemmed,
   leaves torn into large pieces
2 to 3 tablespoons extra-virgin olive oil
1 large clove garlic, smashed and
   peeled
   Kosher salt and freshly ground
   black pepper
4 lemon wedges (optional)

1. Fill a large bowl with cold water and wash the spinach, lifting it out of the water to leave the dirt and grit in the bowl. Repeat with fresh water 2 or 3 times or until the spinach is clean. Drain in a colander.

2. In a large skillet over medium heat add half the oil. Add the garlic and stir until it begins to turn golden, about 3 minutes. Remove the garlic and discard. Add the spinach in batches, stirring with tongs to wilt before adding more. When all the spinach has been added, raise the heat to high, season with salt and black pepper, and cook, covered, for 3 minutes. Drain the spinach in a colander or remove with tongs, taking care to shake excess water into the pan. Serve in a medium bowl, drizzled with the remaining oil and garnished with lemon wedges, if desired.

FROM THE KITCHENS
Two pounds of spinach might seem like a lot for 4 people, but a mountain of spinach wilts down almost totally once cooked. Always go with more than you think you need when you're cooking leafy greens.

broccoli hash

4 servings

Kosher salt
1   head broccoli (about 1 pound),
        cut into florets, stems peeled
        and diced
3   tablespoons unsalted butter
2   tablespoons pine nuts
1   shallot, chopped
2   cloves garlic, minced
    Freshly ground black pepper
    Coarsely grated aged Asiago or other
        grating cheese (optional)

1. Bring a medium saucepan of water to a boil over high heat, then salt it generously. Add the broccoli and boil, uncovered, until tender, about 2 minutes. Drain the broccoli and pat very, very dry with a double layer of paper towels; chop coarsely.

2. Meanwhile, melt the butter in a large skillet over medium heat. Add the pine nuts and swirl the pan until the nuts are toasted, about 1 minute. Use a slotted spoon to transfer the pine nuts to a small dish. Add the shallot, increase the heat to high, and cook until lightly browned, about 1 minute. Add the garlic and stir until fragrant, about 30 seconds. Add the broccoli and cook, tossing every so often, until the edges of the broccoli are brown and crispy. Add the pine nuts and season with salt and pepper to taste—go easy with the salt if you plan to garnish with the Asiago, which is pleasantly salty as well. Mound the broccoli on a platter and serve as is or scatter the grated cheese on top, if desired.

mushrooms
with rosemary & garlic | 4 servings

1½ pounds mixed fresh mushrooms,
   such as shiitake, cremini, or oyster,
   trimmed and cleaned
6 garlic cloves, smashed
3 sprigs fresh rosemary
½ cup extra-virgin olive oil
1½ teaspoons kosher salt, plus
   additional for seasoning (optional)
   Freshly ground black pepper
¼ cup water

1. Preheat the oven to 450°F. Toss the mushrooms, garlic, and rosemary with the olive oil in a shallow baking pan. Season with the 1½ teaspoons salt and pepper to taste and toss again. Roast the mushrooms until golden, 20 to 25 minutes. Stir in the water, scraping up the brown bits on the bottom of the pan and tossing until the mushrooms are glazed. Season with more salt, if desired, and serve warm or at room temperature.

FROM THE KITCHENS
Never wash mushrooms. Wipe or brush dirt off with a paper towel or mushroom brush. Shiitake stems are too tough to eat, so they must be removed. Cremini and oyster stems are fine left on.

Mushrooms are the ultimate fall guy. They're always available and, when roasted, always delicious.

maple-roasted butternut squash

serves 4

1 butternut squash, about 2½ pounds
¼ cup real maple syrup
1 tablespoon unsalted butter
1 teaspoon chipotle hot sauce
1 teaspoon kosher salt

1. Preheat the oven to 425°F. Cut the stem off the squash. Halve the squash lengthwise, then halve again lengthwise to make quarters. Scoop out the seeds with a spoon. Lay the quarters, cut sides up, on a foil-lined baking sheet.

2. Combine the maple syrup and butter in a microwave-safe bowl or measuring cup. Cover with plastic wrap. Microwave on HIGH until the butter melts. Carefully remove the plastic wrap and stir in the hot sauce and salt.

3. Pour half the sauce over the squash, making sure it pools in the seed cavity. Roast for 10 minutes. Remove from the oven, turn the squash to coat it in the sauce, and arrange the pieces with cut sides down. Return to the oven and cook until the sides in contact with the pan begin to caramelize, 10 to 15 minutes. Turn the other cut side down and continue to cook until browned and tender, about 15 minutes more. Transfer wedges to a platter and drizzle with the remaining sauce.

FROM THE KITCHENS
Add fresh sage, rosemary, or thyme to the butter intead of hot sauce or try another variety of winter squash, like acorn, delicata, or sweet dumpling.

roasted zucchini with herbs

6 servings

4 medium zucchini (about 2 pounds)
2 tablespoons extra-virgin olive oil
½ teaspoon kosher salt
    Freshly ground black pepper
1 tablespoon chopped fresh herbs such as basil, dill, mint, flat-leaf parsley, or a mix

1. Preheat the oven to 450°F. Trim the zucchini and halve or quarter them lengthwise, taking care that the wedges are all about the same thickness. Toss the wedges with the olive oil on a baking sheet and space them evenly with a cut side down. Roast, turning once, if necessary, so that any other cut sides are against the pan, until tender and brown, 15 to 20 minutes.

2. Transfer the zucchini to a serving platter. Season with salt and pepper to taste and scatter the fresh herbs over the top. Serve warm or at room temperature.

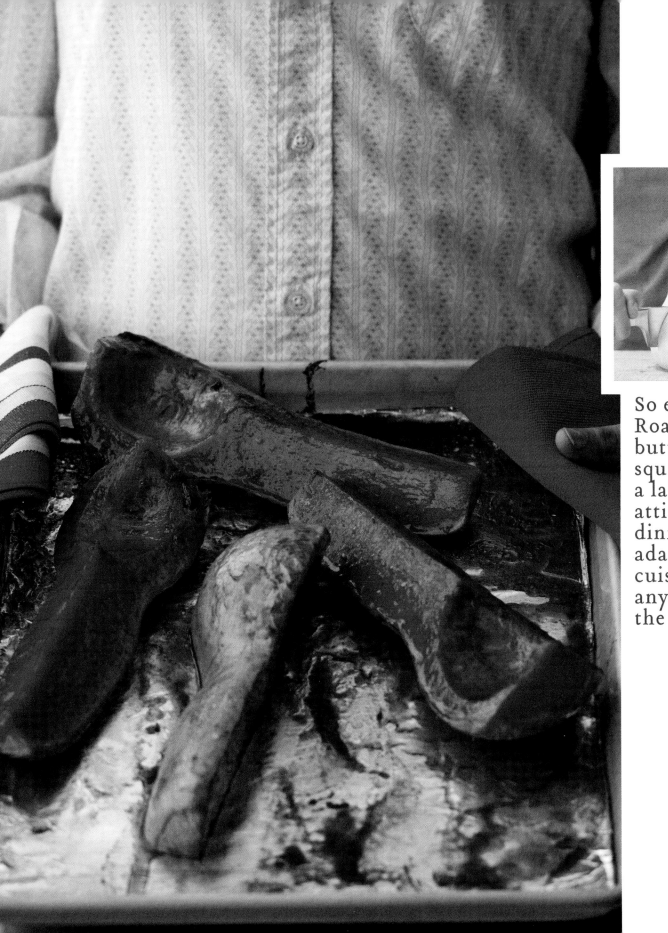

So easy.
Roasted
butternut
squash brings
a laissez-faire
attitude to
dinner and
adapts to
cuisine from
any corner of
the globe.

cilantro

We found this recipe at a location taping in Mexico where we not only had to shop for pottery and pans—but had to build our own stove out of bricks. It was one of our best shoots.

grilled corn
with cotija cheese & cilantro | 4 servings

4   ears fresh-picked corn, yellow
      or white, with husks (each
      about 8 ounces)
1   tablespoon extra-virgin olive oil
      Kosher salt
1¼   cups crumbled Cotija cheese
      (see tip, below)
½   cup chopped fresh cilantro
¼   cup mayonnaise
      Chile powder for sprinkling,
      preferably ancho
      (see tip, page 201)
2   limes, cut into wedges

1. Preheat an outdoor grill to medium-high. (If you can hold your hand over the fire for 3 seconds, it's medium-high.) Peel back the husks from the corn, leaving them attached at the ends and twisting to make handles. Strip the silk. Brush each cob with olive oil and season with salt. Arrange the cobs on the grill with the husks dangling over the side so they won't burn. Grill, turning occasionally, until lightly charred all over, about 20 minutes.

2. Spread the cheese on a medium plate and the cilantro on another. When the corn is done, slather the cobs with mayonnaise and then roll them first in the cheese and then in the cilantro. Sprinkle liberally with chile powder and serve with lime wedges and lots of napkins.

FROM THE KITCHENS
Often called the Parmesan of Mexico because of the way it's used, Cotija is a pleasantly salty, crumbly, semi-sharp aged Mexican cheese that actually more closely resembles feta (which you can use if you can't find Cotija). It's available in Mexican and specialty food stores.

provençal vegetable gratin

serves 4 to 6

3   to 4 sprigs fresh thyme
4   tablespoons extra-virgin olive oil
2   medium onions, sliced
3   cloves garlic, smashed and peeled
2   teaspoons kosher salt
3   ripe medium plum tomatoes, thinly sliced crosswise
3   medium zucchini, yellow, or other summer squash (or a combination), thinly sliced crosswise
    Freshly ground black pepper
⅓   cup finely grated grana-style cheese, such as Parmesan

1. Preheat the oven to 375°F.

2. Strip thyme leaves from stems; discard stems. Heat 2 tablespoons of the olive oil in a large skillet over medium heat. Add the onions, garlic, 1 teaspoon of the salt, and the thyme. Cover and cook, stirring occasionally, until the onions are wilted, about 5 minutes; uncover and cook over high heat until most of the excess moisture evaporates (but don't let the onions brown), about 10 minutes. Spread cooked onions on the bottom of an 8x11-inch baking dish.

3. Toss sliced tomatoes and zucchini in a large bowl with remaining 2 tablespoons olive oil, 1 teaspoon salt, and some black pepper. Scatter the vegetables over the onions, spreading them out in an even layer. Scatter the cheese evenly over the vegetables. Cover the dish with aluminum foil and bake until the vegetables get juicy, 30 to 40 minutes. Uncover and cook until cheese begins to brown, 20 to 30 minutes more. Serve hot or at room temperature.

FROM THE KITCHENS

• The word "gratin" comes from the 16th-century French for "to scrape" and originally referred to the cooked-on crust certain dishes left on pots and pans. In the 19th century the meaning changed to refer to any dish with a deliberately browned crust on top.
• Many different herbs work here; if you've got basil, use that, or even fresh marjoram, if it's available. Dress it up by arranging the vegetables in patterns or strips, or by adding some thinly sliced eggplant for another layer of color.

We're inspired by the magical touch Italians have with vegetables. Keep it simple, and their flavors will sing out like a fine tenor.

cauliflower with brown butter & crispy crumbs

4 servings

1 medium head cauliflower (about 2 pounds), cut into bite-size florets
2 cloves garlic, roughly chopped
6 tablespoons unsalted butter
1¼ teaspoons kosher salt
⅓ cup fresh bread crumbs (see tip, below)
3 tablespoons minced fresh flat-leaf parsley
  Freshly ground black pepper
  Lemon wedges

1. Preheat the oven to 450°F. Put the cauliflower on a baking sheet and scatter the garlic on top. Melt the butter in a medium skillet and toss 2 tablespoons with the cauliflower and garlic; set the rest aside in the skillet. Toss the cauliflower with 1 teaspoon of the salt. Roast until the cauliflower is quite tender and the edges are starting to brown, 20 to 25 minutes. Transfer the cauliflower to a serving bowl.

2. Reheat the remaining butter over medium-high heat until brown. Add the bread crumbs and cook, swirling the pan and tossing, until they are brown and crisp—this should take less than 1 minute. Pull the pan from the heat and toss the crumbs with the parsley and the remaining ¼ teaspoon salt. Spoon crumbs over the cauliflower and season with pepper. Serve warm or room temperature with lemon wedges on the side.

FROM THE KITCHENS

Sometimes it's the little things that can make the difference in a dish being spectacular or so-so—like using homemade bread crumbs versus store-bought. Crumbs made from quality bread are easy to make. Simply tear up bread, with or without the crusts, and grind it in a food processor—one 2-ounce slice makes about ½ cup of crumbs. If you want moist crumbs—as you do for this crispy topping—start with fresh, not stale, bread. Stale dry bread is better for crumbs used in stuffings or as a binder because the crumbs absorb more liquid.

A perfect accompaniment for antipasti or a roast, this tasty side takes radicchio off those salady sidelines and puts it in the spotlight. It's about time.

roasted pancetta-wrapped radicchio | 4 servings

RADICCHIO

3   heads radicchio
      (about 5 ounces each)
3   tablespoons kosher salt
      Extra-virgin olive oil
12 to 18 slices pancetta (about
      6 ounces) (see tip, below)

VINAIGRETTE

1   tablespoon balsamic vinegar
1   tablespoon honey
1   teaspoon Dijon mustard
1   teaspoon chopped fresh thyme
1   teaspoon kosher salt
      Freshly ground black pepper
¼   cup extra-virgin olive oil

1. For the radicchio: Position a rack in the center of the oven and preheat to 450°F. Trim the base of each radicchio head, leaving the core intact, and remove any damaged or brown outer leaves. Quarter each head lengthwise through the core (if the heads are large, cut them into 6 wedges). Stir the salt into a bowl of cold water until dissolved, add the radicchio wedges, and weight them with a small plate to keep them submerged. Soak for 10 minutes; drain and pat dry with paper towels. (This tempers the radicchio's assertive bitterness.)

2. Lightly brush a roasting pan with olive oil. Drape a slice of pancetta over the peak of each radicchio wedge and secure it with a toothpick. Place the radicchio in the pan and roast without turning until the pancetta is crisp and the radicchio soft, about 25 minutes.

3. Meanwhile, for the vinaigrette: Whisk the vinegar, honey, mustard, thyme, salt, and pepper to taste in a bowl. Gradually whisk in the oil, starting with a few drops, then adding the rest in a steady stream to make a smooth, slightly thick vinaigrette.

4. Arrange the radicchio on a serving platter; remove the toothpicks. If serving immediately, drizzle some of the vinaigrette over and pass the remainder. The radicchio may also be served at room temperature; in that case, dress it just before serving.

FROM THE KITCHENS

Pancetta is an Italian-style bacon that is cured but not smoked. Recognizable by its rolled shape, it can be sliced or diced and often is the foundation for many Italian sauces or stews. When wrapped around vegetables, fish, or roasts, thin discs of pinwheel-patterned pancetta look as distinctive as they taste. Buy it thinly sliced or in a chunk and store it in the refrigerator for a week or in the freezer for up to 2 months.

braised fennel | 4 servings

2   medium bulbs fennel, tops trimmed
¼   cup extra-virgin olive oil
¼   cup dry white vermouth
½   teaspoon kosher salt
½   teaspoon fennel or anise
      seeds (optional)
    Freshly ground black pepper
½   cup water

1. Cut each fennel bulb through the core into 6 even wedges. Put the wedges in a large skillet with the olive oil, vermouth, salt, fennel seeds (if using), and the pepper to taste. Add enough water to come about halfway up the sides of the fennel. Bring the mixture to a boil over medium-high heat.

2. Cut a circle of parchment paper the size of the pan and lay it over the fennel. Reduce the heat to maintain a gentle simmer and cook the fennel, turning once about halfway through cooking, until tender, about 25 minutes.

3. Serve immediately or remove the parchment, increase the heat to high, and cook until all of the liquid evaporates and the fennel browns, about 8 minutes more.

FROM THE KITCHENS

The more the fennel cooks, the more it will caramelize, so feel free to take it beyond our suggested cooking time. This technique also works for onions, carrots, and parsnips.

We love this rustic Italian-style side alongside our Peppered Beef Tenderloin with Merlot and Blue-Cheese Smashed Potatoes.

confetti coleslaw | 6 servings

SALAD

- 1 small head red cabbage (about 1¾ pounds)
- 1 bunch medium carrots, peeled (about 5)
- 2 tablespoons kosher salt
- 2 Granny Smith apples
- 6 scallions (white and green parts), sliced
- 1 bunch watercress

DRESSING

- 3 tablespoons cider vinegar
- 3 tablespoons honey
- 2 tablespoons Dijon mustard
- 1 tablespoon celery seeds or 2 teaspoons caraway seeds
- 1 tablespoon plus 1 teaspoon kosher salt
  Freshly ground black pepper
- ⅓ cup extra-virgin olive oil

1. For the salad: Quarter and core the cabbage. Set up a food processor with the slicing blade. Slice the cabbage and then transfer it to a colander. Switch to the grating blade and shred the carrots; add to cabbage. Toss the cabbage and carrots with the salt and set colander in the sink until the vegetables wilt, 1 to 4 hours. Rinse cabbage mixture thoroughly in cold water and spin it dry in a salad spinner.

2. Meanwhile, make the dressing: Whisk the vinegar with the honey, mustard, celery seeds, salt, and black pepper to taste in a small bowl. Gradually whisk in the olive oil, starting with a few drops and then adding the rest in a steady stream to make a smooth, slightly thick dressing.

3. Quarter, core, and shred the apples. Toss the cabbage mixture with the apples, scallions, and about ½ cup of the dressing. Refrigerate until chilled and the flavors come together, about 1 hour. When ready to serve, toss the watercress with the remaining dressing. Make a ring on a platter with the watercress, and mound the coleslaw in the middle of the ring.

FROM THE KITCHENS

Salting the cabbage gives the slaw its characteristic tender bite, as well as expressing excess liquid. If you skip this step, your salad will be soggy and bland.

red, white & blue potato salad

4 to 6 servings

POTATOES

4	sprigs fresh thyme
3	sprigs fresh flat-leaf parsley
1	sprig fresh rosemary
1	bay leaf
1	cup dry white wine
2	cloves garlic, smashed
8	ounces small red-skinned waxy potatoes, scrubbed
8	ounces small white-skinned waxy potatoes, scrubbed
8	ounces small blue-skinned waxy potatoes, scrubbed
1	tablespoon kosher salt
2	ribs celery, thinly sliced
2	scallions (white and green parts), thinly sliced
2	tablespoons minced fresh flat-leaf parsley

DRESSING

¼	cup white wine vinegar
1	tablespoon whole-grain mustard
2	teaspoons kosher salt
	Freshly ground black pepper
½	cup extra-virgin olive oil

1. For the potatoes: Tie the thyme, parsley, rosemary, and bay leaf together with a piece of kitchen twine and put the bundle in a medium saucepan with the wine and garlic. Slice the potatoes into ¼-inch-thick rounds and add to the saucepan. Add cold water to cover by about an inch and add the salt. Bring to a boil over medium-high heat and simmer, uncovered, until the potatoes are tender but not mushy, about 5 minutes. Drain; discard the herb bundle.

2. While the potatoes cook, make the dressing: Whisk the vinegar, mustard, salt, and some pepper in a large bowl. Gradually whisk in the oil, starting with a few drops and then adding the rest in a steady stream, to make a smooth, slightly thick dressing.

3. Using a rubber spatula, gently fold the warm potatoes into the dressing, taking care not to break them up. Add the celery and set aside to cool. Just before serving, carefully fold in the scallions and parsley.

FROM THE KITCHENS

Smooth-skinned waxy potatoes hold their shape when cooked, making them the spud of choice for salads, crispy pan-fries, potato pancakes, or roasting. If you want to show off a potato's colorful skin—a healthier and most stylish choice—cut them before cooking, since the skins slip off if cooked whole and then cut.

This three-bean salad is a four-star recipe that will add colorful crunch to any spread anywhere—from picnic blanket to kitchen table.

picnic three-bean salad | 4 to 6 servings

½   small red onion, finely chopped
1   15¼-ounce can kidney beans, rinsed
     and drained
8   ounces green beans
8   ounces wax beans
⅓   cup cider vinegar
¼   cup sugar
¼   cup vegetable oil
½   teaspoon kosher salt, plus additional
     for seasoning
    Freshly ground black pepper
2   tablespoons minced fresh
     flat-leaf parsley

1. To mellow the bite of the raw onion, soak it in cold water for 10 minutes, then drain it well, pat dry, and put it in a serving bowl. Stir in the kidney beans.

2. Fill a bowl with ice water. Bring a saucepan of water to a boil and salt it generously. Add the green and wax beans and cook until crisp-tender, 4 to 5 minutes. Drain the beans and plunge them into the ice water to stop the cooking and set their color. Drain the beans well, pat dry, and toss them with the kidney beans and onion.

3. Bring the vinegar, sugar, oil, and the ½ teaspoon salt to a boil in a small saucepan and immediately pour over the beans. Marinate the beans at room temperature for 1 hour, tossing several times.

4. Just before serving, taste the beans, season with salt and pepper to taste, and stir in the parsley.

FROM THE KITCHENS
Pack your picnic foods—such as slices of cake, cups of chilled soups, or salads—in individual portions. It makes serving the food effortless and gives company the freedom to eat at whatever pace they choose.

It just doesn't get more summery or seasonal than fresh, vine-ripened tomatoes.

heirloom tomato & mint salad

4 servings

2   pounds vine-ripened heirloom
    tomatoes, assorted varieties
    preferred
1   shallot, thinly sliced
1   teaspoon coarse sea salt
    Freshly ground black pepper
¼   cup fresh spearmint leaves,
    torn into pieces
¼   cup fruity extra-virgin olive oil
2   tablespoons champagne vinegar
    or white wine vinegar

Cut the tomatoes into a variety of sizes and shapes, some thick slabs, wedges, halves, or chunks. Arrange them on a large platter and scatter the shallot over the tomatoes. Season with the salt and black pepper to taste. Set aside until juicy, about 5 minutes. Sprinkle mint over the top and drizzle with the olive oil and vinegar.

FROM THE KITCHENS
▪ When a tomato is ripe, juicy, and ready to go, a good hit of coarse salt and freshly ground black pepper is really all it needs. Salting brings out all the flavor notes—the sweetness of the fruit along with its natural acidity. It also draws out the juices, making its own sauce.
▪ Heirloom tomatoes—found in farmers' markets and in your backyard garden—come in many different shapes, sizes, and colors and often with whimsical names to match, such as Brandywine, Green Zebra, Hillbilly, and Moonglow. Choose by taste and aroma—and never store a tomato in the refrigerator.

spicy carrot & garlic salad | 4 to 6 servings

1   lemon
1   ½-inch piece fresh ginger, peeled and
       finely grated (about 2 teaspoons)
1   tablespoon honey
1   teaspoon kosher salt
¼   teaspoon crushed red pepper flakes
       Pinch ground cinnamon
       Pinch ground cumin
3   tablespoons extra-virgin olive oil
1   pound medium carrots, peeled
       and thinly sliced
1   clove garlic, chopped
¼   cup water
       Handful cilantro leaves, chopped

1. Juice the lemon into a medium bowl. Add ginger to the lemon juice. Whisk in the honey, salt, red pepper flakes, cinnamon, and cumin. Gradually whisk in the olive oil, starting with a few drops and then adding the rest in a steady stream to make a smooth dressing.

2. Toss the carrots, garlic, and water in a medium microwave-safe bowl, cover tightly with plastic wrap, and microwave on HIGH for 3 minutes. Drain off any excess water.

3. Pour the dressing over the hot carrots, toss, and let cool to room temperature. Stir the cilantro into the salad and serve.

little tomato salad
with fresh herbs | 4 servings

1   pint (2 cups) ripe cherry or
       grape tomatoes, halved
       or quartered
       Kosher salt and freshly ground
       black pepper
       Extra-virgin olive oil
       Small handful of fresh herbs,
       such as basil, flat-leaf parsley,
       mint, dill, or tarragon, chopped

Put tomatoes in a medium bowl and season with some salt and black pepper. Drizzle with a couple tablespoons of olive oil, depending on the juiciness of the tomatoes. Stir herbs into the tomatoes. Serve immediately or set aside at room temperature for up to 2 hours. This salad can also serve as a juicy topping for chicken, fish, and burgers, or as an addition to greens.

FROM THE KITCHENS
• Choose vibrant green bunches of fresh basil, parsley, cilantro, and mint, with no yellowing or black leaves. Tarragon should have long, aromatic leaves with no black spots, and dill should have silky bright green fronds.
• Take off any rubber band holding the bunch together before you put away the herbs.
• If you've got roots attached to your herbs, put the roots into a shallow glass of water, then top the whole thing with a plastic bag to create a mini greenhouse in your fridge.
• Wrap rootless herbs loosely in damp paper towels, put them into resealable plastic bags, and wash right before you use them.

celery & soppressata salad with lemon

¼   medium red onion, very thinly sliced
1   pound celery (about half a bunch), with leaves
3   ounces soppressata salami, in a chunk or sliced (see tip, below)
6   fresh basil leaves, torn into small pieces
2   teaspoons finely grated lemon zest
2   tablespoons freshly squeezed lemon juice
½   teaspoon kosher salt
    Freshly ground black pepper
⅓   cup extra-virgin olive oil
1- to 2-ounce wedge Parmigiano-Reggiano cheese

1. To mellow the raw bite of the onion, soak the slices in cold water for 10 minutes, then drain, pat dry, and put them in a serving bowl.

2. Peel the tough, stringy fibers from the celery ribs. Slice the celery and some of the inner leaves very thinly on an angle. If you have a chunk of soppressata, dice it; if slices, cut them into thin strips. Toss the celery, soppressata, basil, lemon zest, and lemon juice with the onion. Season with salt and a generous grinding of pepper. Toss the salad with the olive oil.

3. Divide the salad among 4 serving plates. Use a vegetable peeler to shave large, thin pieces of Parmigiana-Reggiano over each portion and serve immediately.

FROM THE KITCHENS

There is a whole world of Italian cured meats and salamis to choose from, and soppressata—a dry-cured pork salami—is one of our favorites. If you can't find it, feel free to subsitute another hard slicing salami. Not sure what to buy? Don't be shy about asking for tastes at the deli counter. It's one of the rewards of shopping.

watermelon &
baby arugula salad | 4 to 6 servings

SALAD
½   red onion, thinly sliced
4   pounds watermelon, preferably
    seedless, rind removed, cut into
    ¾-inch cubes (about 8 cups)
2   teaspoons chopped fresh
    oregano leaves
8   cups baby arugula (about 4 ounces)
¾   cup crumbled ricotta salata or feta
    cheese (about 4 ounces)
½   cup pitted niçoise olives (optional)
    Freshly ground black pepper

DRESSING
2   tablespoons white wine vinegar
1¼ teaspoons kosher salt
    Freshly ground black pepper
⅓   cup extra-virgin olive oil

1. For the salad: To mellow the onion, soak it in cold water for 10 minutes, then drain well, pat dry, and put in a serving bowl.

2. Meanwhile, make the dressing: Whisk the vinegar, salt, and black pepper to taste in a bowl. Gradually whisk in the olive oil, starting with a few drops and then adding the rest of the oil in a steady stream to make a smooth dressing.

3. Toss the watermelon and oregano with the onions and the dressing, taking care not to break up the watermelon chunks. (The salad can be made to this point up to 30 minutes in advance.)

4. When ready to serve, toss the arugula with the dressed watermelon. Scatter the cheese, olives (if desired), and a generous grinding of black pepper over the top.

FROM THE KITCHENS
• To pit the olives you can use a special tool if you are into gadgets. But really all you need is a broad knife. Place the olive under the flat side of the knife and give it a good whack. It cracks the olive and frees the fruit from the pit.
• Even though we don't eat the melon skin or rinds, it's a good idea to wash the watermelon before cutting it. If bacteria are present on the outside of the melon, the knife—in the process of cutting—can transport them to the flesh, which can cause food-borne illnesses.

Get fresh.
Lovely greens
catch your eye
at the farmer's
market? Take
them home
and dress them
in something
delicious.

vinaigrette

extra-virgin olive oil

radicchio

balsamic
vinegar

Dijon mustard

freshly
ground
black pepper

fresh lemon

mixed greens

shallot

kosher salt

garlic

FROM THE KITCHENS

A simple green salad can be a triumph. Salads can be easily improvised and have endless variations. Combine lettuces to balance their qualities, pairing mild, crisp lettuces, for instance, with peppery, textured greens. Simple vinaigrettes start with salt and pepper blended with 1 part vinegar or freshly squeezed citrus juice. Then 3 or 4 parts of a tasty extra-virgin olive oil are slowly whisked in to make a smooth dressing. Adding mustard before whisking in oil gives the dressing a kick while keeping it creamy. For riffs on the same basic theme, add flavorings such as minced garlic, shallots, herbs, and spices—or use nut oils such as walnut or hazelnut oil instead of olive oil.

greek rice & herb salad | 4 to 6 servings

RICE

2	teaspoons extra-virgin olive oil
1½	cups long-grain rice, not converted
2¼	cups water
1	teaspoon kosher salt

SALAD

⅓	cup extra-virgin olive oil
5	tablespoons freshly squeezed lemon juice
2	teaspoons kosher salt
¼	teaspoon ground allspice
2	ripe medium tomatoes
1	Kirby cucumber with peel, seeded and finely diced (see tip, page 75)
2	scallions (white and green parts), thinly sliced
¼	cup minced fresh flat-leaf parsley
¼	cup minced fresh dill
¼	cup minced fresh mint
½	teaspoon finely grated lemon zest
	Freshly ground black pepper
	Hot pepper sauce
1½	cups coarsely crumbled feta cheese (about 6 ounces)
	Lemon wedges

1. For the rice: Heat the oil in a medium saucepan over medium heat. Add the rice and cook, stirring, until slightly toasted and golden, about 1½ minutes. Stir in the water and salt, bring to a boil, cover, reduce the heat, and simmer for 18 minutes. Then let the rice rest off the heat for 5 minutes—please don't lift the lid to give a peek or stir or the rice will not cook evenly. Put the rice in a large serving bowl, fluff and separate the grains with a fork, and cool to room temperature. (Don't refrigerate the rice or it will get grainy.)

2. For the salad: Whisk the oil, lemon juice, salt, and allspice in a small bowl. Toss the dressing with the cooled rice. Halve the tomatoes crosswise to expose their seeds. Use your fingertip to pop the seeds out of the flesh and discard. Cut the tomatoes into fine dice. Add the tomatoes, cucumber, scallions, parsley, dill, mint, and lemon zest to the rice mixture and toss again. Season with pepper and hot pepper sauce to taste. Scatter the feta cheese across the top and serve, passing the lemon wedges.

scalloped potatoes with gruyère

4 to 6 servings

1 large clove garlic, smashed
2 tablespoons unsalted butter
2¼ pounds Yellow Finn or other waxy
 potatoes (about 6), peeled
2 cups half-and-half
2 teaspoons chopped fresh thyme
2½ teaspoons kosher salt
 Freshly ground black pepper
 Pinch freshly grated nutmeg
1 cup grated Gruyère cheese
 (about 2 ounces)

1. Preheat the oven to 350°F. Rub the garlic all over the inside of an 8x8x2-inch casserole dish. Mince what is left of the garlic clove. Smear some of the butter all over the inside of the dish.

2. Using a mandoline or vegetable slicer, slice the potatoes about ⅛ inch thick and put them in a large saucepan with the minced garlic, remaining butter, the half-and-half, thyme, salt, pepper to taste, and nutmeg. Bring to a boil over medium-high heat and cook, stirring, until the mixture has thickened slightly, 1 to 2 minutes. Transfer the mixture to the prepared baking dish and shake the pan to distribute the potatoes evenly. Bake, uncovered, occasionally spooning some of the liquid over the top, until the potatoes are fork-tender, about 50 minutes. Sprinkle the cheese over the top and bake until brown and bubbly, about 15 minutes more. Remove from the oven and let casserole cool 10 minutes before serving.

FROM THE KITCHENS

Boiling the potatoes in the cooking liquid before layering them in the baking dish is the key to superior scalloped potatoes. As the half-and-half heats, it draws the starch from the potatoes and turns into a satiny sauce. To lighten up this classic, use the same technique with chicken broth.

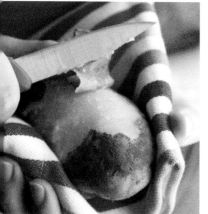

Play with
your food.
Smashed
potatoes are
the perfect
vehicle
for boldly
flavored
add-ins.
These are a
few of our
favorites, but
feel free to
experiment
with the
condiments
you like best.

smashed potatoes | 4 servings

2 pounds medium red-skinned potatoes, scrubbed
2 whole garlic cloves (optional)
1 sprig fresh thyme or rosemary (optional)
½ cup chicken broth or ¾ cup milk
2 tablespoons extra-virgin olive oil or unsalted butter
2 teaspoons kosher salt, plus additional for salting water
Freshly grated nutmeg
Freshly ground black pepper

FOR BROTH-BASED POTATOES

1 tablespoon chipotle chiles en adobo
⅓ to ½ cup baba ghanoush or hummus
⅓ to ½ cup onion jam
¼ to ⅓ cup truffle or other flavored oil (omit olive oil)
2 to 4 scallions, finely chopped

FOR THESE, OMIT OLIVE OIL AND ADD A COUPLE MORE TABLESPOONS BROTH

½ cup pesto
½ cup sun-dried tomato tapenade
⅓ cup artichoke tapenade

FOR MILK-BASED POTATOES

Crumbled bacon
2 to 3 teaspoons chopped fresh rosemary or thyme
2 tablespoons horseradish mixed with 2 tablespoons sour cream
½ to ⅔ cup crumbled blue cheese
⅔ cup freshly grated Parmesan cheese

1. Put the potatoes, garlic, and herbs, if using, in a medium saucepan, cover with cold water, and season liberally with salt. Bring to a simmer over medium heat and cook until the potatoes are very tender, about 20 minutes. Drain and discard the herb sprig, if using.

2. Heat the chicken broth or milk in a microwave-safe bowl in the microwave until hot, about 1 minute. With a potato masher or large fork, smash the potatoes into a chunky puree, adding the hot liquid as you do. Stir in the olive oil or butter and season with the 2 teaspoons salt, nutmeg, and pepper to taste.

FROM THE KITCHENS

If you like your potatoes smashed with olive oil, then use chicken broth as the liquid. If you prefer the taste of butter, then opt for milk. If you want to amp up the flavor of your smashed potatoes, consider one of the add-ins at left.

cheesy grits | 4 servings

2 cups chicken broth
2 cups milk
¾ cup old-fashioned grits
1 sprig fresh thyme
1 tablespoon unsalted butter
½ teaspoon kosher salt
Pinch cayenne pepper
1 cup grated cheddar cheese or
   ½ cup grated pecorino cheese

Stir the chicken broth, milk, grits, thyme, butter, salt, and cayenne pepper in a large microwave-safe bowl or glass measuring cup. Microwave on HIGH, uncovered, for 12 minutes and then stir. Grits should be fairly thick but still moist—they will thicken more once you add the cheese. If they still seem too loose, microwave up to another 3 minutes. Remove the thyme sprig from the grits, stir in the cheese, and serve hot.

FROM THE KITCHENS
Flavor and texture always outrank speed. That's why we choose old-fashioned grits over the quick-cooking variety.

polenta | 4 to 6 servings

2 cups chicken broth
2 cups whole milk
¾ cup quick-cooking polenta
¼ to ½ cup freshly grated
   Parmesan cheese
2 tablespoons unsalted
   butter, cut into bits
½ teaspoon kosher salt
Freshly ground black pepper

1. Put the broth and milk in a medium saucepan and bring to a boil over high heat. Slowly whisk in the polenta, reduce the heat to low, and cook, whisking occasionally, until the polenta is thick and creamy, about 15 minutes.

2. Pull the saucepan from the heat and whisk in the cheese, butter, salt, and pepper to taste. Serve immediately.

FROM THE KITCHENS
To make polenta cakes to use as a side dish or as a base for hors d'oeuvres, spread the warm polenta in a 13x9-inch baking dish, chill, cut, then grill in a grill pan or on an outdoor grill.

American grits and Italian polenta provide delicious comfort for both cook and company.

breads & other baked things

Fresh-from-the-oven bread is a welcome addition to any meal—breakfast, lunch, or dinner (or any time in-between).

chile cornbread | 6 to 8 servings

Unsalted butter, at room
temperature, for buttering pan
2   cups yellow cornmeal, preferably
stone-ground
1   cup all-purpose flour
¼   cup sugar
4   teaspoons baking powder
1¼ teaspoons fine salt
1   large ear fresh corn, shucked
1   cup milk
½   cup buttermilk
2   large eggs at room temperature
1   to 2 chopped roasted green chiles,
such as Anaheim or poblano
(fresh or canned), seeded
6   tablespoons unsalted butter, melted

1. Preheat the oven to 400°F. Butter a 9-inch cast-iron skillet or cake pan.

2. Whisk the cornmeal, flour, sugar, baking powder, and salt in a large bowl. Cut the corn kernels from the cob with a knife. Working over a medium bowl, run a knife along the cob to press out the milky liquid. Whisk in the milk, buttermilk, eggs, corn, and chiles.

3. Fold the milk mixture into the cornmeal mixture until almost completely incorporated, then fold in the melted butter. Take care not to overwork the batter or the bread will be tough. Transfer the batter into the prepared skillet or pan and bake until lightly browned and a toothpick inserted in the center comes out clean, about 30 to 35 minutes. Set aside to cool slightly before serving.

FROM THE KITCHENS
• Stone-ground cornmeal has a better texture and a "cornier" taste than most commercially available cornmeal. It's worth searching out, but once you buy it, keep it refrigerated as it will go rancid faster than other types.
• Loosen the cornbread and serve it in wedges straight from the skillet. It'll add a "down-home" touch to your table.

double-chocolate zucchini bread

2 loaves (about 16 servings)

2½ cups all-purpose flour
¼   cup unsweetened natural cocoa
        (not Dutch-process)
        (see tip, below)
1   teaspoon baking soda
½   teaspoon ground cinnamon
        Pinch ground cloves
1   cup unsalted butter,
        softened (2 sticks)
1½ cups sugar
¼   cup vegetable oil
2   large eggs, at room temperature
1   teaspoon pure vanilla extract
½   cup buttermilk, at room temperature
2   cups shredded unpeeled zucchini
        (about 8 ounces)
4   ounces bittersweet chocolate,
        finely chopped

1. Position a rack in the center of the oven and preheat to 350°F. Butter and flour two 9x5x3-inch loaf pans. Whisk the flour with the cocoa, baking soda, cinnamon, and cloves in a medium bowl.

2. Beat the butter and sugar in a medium bowl with an electric mixer on medium-high speed until light and fluffy, about 4 minutes. While mixing, drizzle in the oil and beat until incorporated. Beat in the eggs, one at a time, beating well after each addition.

3. Add the vanilla to the buttermilk. Slowly mix the flour mixture into the beaten butter mixture in 3 additions, alternating with the buttermilk in 2 parts, beginning and ending with the flour. (Scrape the sides of the bowl between additions, if needed.) Fold the zucchini and chocolate into the batter. Divide batter between prepared pans and bake until a toothpick inserted in the center comes out clean, about 55 minutes. Cool in pans on a rack before unmolding and slicing.

FROM THE KITCHENS

▪ This quick bread can do more than double-duty rounding out a variety of occasions. Serve it toasted for breakfast, wrapped up in a lunch box, alongside a pot of afternoon tea, or with a dollop of ice cream for dessert.

▪ Unsweetened cocoa powder comes in two forms. Dutch-process cocoa is treated with alkali, which softens the cocoa's acidity and mellows the intensity of the cocoa flavor. The natural form of cocoa gives sweets a more intense chocolate flavor. They both have their place, depending on the effect you're after in the finished product.

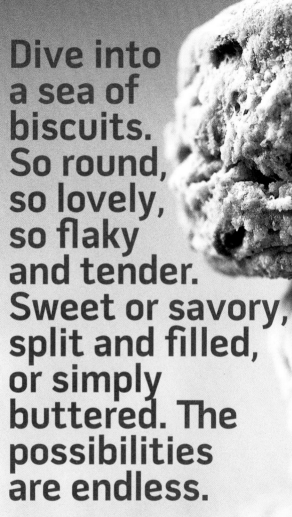

Dive into a sea of biscuits. So round, so lovely, so flaky and tender. Sweet or savory, split and filled, or simply buttered. The possibilities are endless.

FROM THE KITCHENS

Making fabulous biscuits has much to do with how you work the butter into the flour mixture. First, the butter must be very cold. The first bit is worked in thoroughly to help hold the dough together and make the biscuit tender throughout. The second bit is left in pea-size pieces so that when the biscuits bake, the small chunks of butter form flaky layers. As with any quick bread, the less you have to work the dough, the more tender the end result will be.

cornmeal–buttermilk biscuits | 8 biscuits

1⅓ cups all-purpose flour
⅔ cup yellow cornmeal
2½ teaspoons baking powder
1 heaping teaspoon sugar
1 teaspoon fine salt
¼ teaspoon baking soda
6 tablespoons cold unsalted butter, sliced into tablespoon-size pieces
¾ cup buttermilk

1. Position a rack in the center of the oven and preheat to 450°F. Line a baking sheet with parchment paper.

2. Whisk flour, cornmeal, baking powder, sugar, salt, and baking soda in a medium bowl. Rub in 2 tablespoons of the butter with your fingertips until no visible pieces remain. Rub in the remaining 4 tablespoons butter just until it is in even, pea-size pieces. Very gently stir in buttermilk to make a shaggy, loose dough.

3. Turn dough onto a lightly floured work surface and pat into a rectangle about ½ inch thick (don't worry if dough doesn't all come together). Fold dough in thirds, like a business letter, and pat lightly into an 8x5-inch rectangle—about ¾ inch thick. Using a 2- to 3-inch round biscuit cutter, cut 6 biscuits and place on baking sheet. Press dough scraps together and cut 2 more biscuits. Bake until tops are lightly browned, about 15 minutes. Cool slightly on a rack; serve warm.

parmesan, pepper & lemon biscuits

8 biscuits

2 cups all-purpose flour
1 tablespoon sugar
1 tablespoon baking powder
1 tablespoon finely grated lemon zest
1 teaspoon cracked black pepper
½ teaspoon fine salt
6 tablespoons cold unsalted butter
½ cup diced plus ¼ cup finely grated
   Parmigiana-Reggiano cheese
¾ cup milk

1. Position a rack in the center of the oven and preheat to 450°F. Line a baking sheet with parchment paper.

2. Whisk the flour with the sugar, baking powder, lemon zest, pepper, and salt in a large bowl. Cut butter into tablespoon-size pieces. Work the butter in as directed for Cornmeal-Buttermilk Biscuits (see recipe, page 332). Scatter grated and diced cheese over the top and toss with a rubber spatula. Using a wooden spoon, stir the milk in to make a loose dough. Fold, cut, and bake as for Cornmeal-Buttermilk Biscuits.

sweet potato biscuits

8 biscuits

1½ cups all-purpose flour,
   plus additional for dusting
1 tablespoon baking powder
1 tablespoon light brown sugar
½ teaspoon fine salt
¼ teaspoon ground cinnamon
⅛ teaspoon ground allspice
5 tablespoons cold unsalted
   butter, sliced
¾ cup mashed whole canned
   sweet potatoes
½ cup milk

1. Position a rack in the center of the oven and preheat to 425°F. Line a baking sheet with a double layer of parchment paper.

2. Whisk the 1½ cups flour, baking powder, brown sugar, salt, cinnamon, and allspice in a medium bowl. Work the butter in as directed for Cornmeal-Buttermilk Biscuits (see recipe, page 332). Combine the sweet potatoes and milk and stir into the flour mixture to make a moist dough.

3. Fold and cut the dough as directed for Cornmeal-Buttermilk Biscuits. Bake until lightly browned, about 12 minutes. Cool briefly before serving.

butternut squash, apple & onion galette with stilton | 6 servings

DOUGH

1¼ cups all-purpose flour
Pinch salt
8 tablespoons cold unsalted
butter, diced (1 stick)
1 large egg, lightly beaten

FILLING

1 large baking apple, such as Rome
Beauty or Cortland
1 small or ½ medium butternut squash
(about ¾ pound), halved, seeded,
and skin on
1 small yellow onion, peeled, root end
trimmed but intact
3 tablespoons unsalted butter, melted
2 teaspoons chopped fresh rosemary
2 teaspoons chopped fresh thyme
Kosher salt and freshly ground
black pepper
2 tablespoons whole-grain mustard
⅓ cup crumbled Stilton or other blue
cheese (about 1½ ounces)

1. For the dough: Pulse the flour and salt together in a food processor. Add the butter and pulse about 10 times until the mixture resembles coarse cornmeal with a few bean-size bits of butter in it. Add the egg and pulse 1 to 2 times more; don't let the dough form a mass around the blade. If the dough seems very dry, add up to 1 tablespoon of cold water, 1 teaspoon at a time, pulsing briefly. Remove the blade and bring the dough together by hand. Shape the dough into a disk, wrap it in plastic wrap, and refrigerate at least 1 hour.

2. For the filling: Halve and core the apple. Cut each half into 8 wedges and put them in a large bowl. Slice the squash and cut the onion into wedges so that both are as thick as the apple wedges and add them to the apples. Add the butter, rosemary, and thyme and toss gently to combine. Season with salt and pepper and toss again.

3. Preheat the oven to 400°F. Roll the dough on a lightly floured surface into a 12-inch disk. Transfer the dough to a baking sheet and brush with mustard. Starting 2 inches from the edge, casually alternate pieces of apple, squash, and onion in overlapping circles—if you have extra pieces of one or another, tuck them in where you can or double them up to use all the filling. Fold and pleat the dough over the edge of the filling. Bake until the crust is brown and the apple, squash, and onion are tender and caramelized, about 55 minutes. Scatter the cheese over the filling and bake until melted, about 5 minutes more. Cool the galette briefly on a wire rack. Cut into wedges and serve.

FROM THE KITCHENS

Don't be afraid to cook this galette—or any of your pies or tarts, for that matter—until the crust is a rich golden brown. A pastry's buttery taste and flaky crispness really come through when it is fully cooked.

dinner rolls | 12 rolls

7   tablespoons unsalted butter
2   cups milk, plus 2 tablespoons
3   tablespoons sugar
1   package active dry yeast (¼ ounce)
5   cups unbleached all-purpose flour,
        plus additional for kneading
1   tablespoon fine salt
    Vegetable oil

1. Melt 3 tablespoons of the butter in a small saucepan over medium-low heat. Add the milk and sugar and heat, stirring, until lukewarm (about 110°F). Sprinkle the yeast over the surface and set aside until foamy, about 10 minutes.

2. Whisk the flour and salt in a large bowl. Stir the yeast mixture into the flour mixture to make a soft, shaggy dough. Turn the dough onto a floured work surface and knead until it is soft and elastic, about 10 minutes. Lightly oil a large bowl. Shape the dough into a ball and place it in the bowl. Cover with a clean kitchen towel and let rise at room temperature until doubled in size, about 2 hours. (At this point you can also cover the bowl with plastic wrap and refrigerate it overnight. Bring it to room temperature before proceeding.)

3. Butter a 13x9x2-inch baking dish. Turn the dough out of the bowl and gently deflate it. Divide the dough into 12 equal pieces and roll each piece into a ball. Arrange the balls seam side down, in 3 rows of 4, across the length of the prepared baking dish. Cover the dish with a clean kitchen towel and set aside at room temperature until the rolls rise almost to the rim of the baking dish, 2 to 2½ hours.

4. Position a rack in the center of the oven and preheat to 400°F. Melt the remaining 4 tablespoons butter and brush it liberally over the rolls. Bake until golden brown, about 25 minutes. Cool the rolls in the pan briefly before transferring them to a rack to cool completely.

FROM THE KITCHENS
If you're a novice bread baker, use a thermometer to judge the temperature of the milk in Step 1. If it's too hot, it kills the yeast.

rosemary & sea salt focaccia

one 11x17x1-inch focaccia (8 to 10 servings)

1¾ cups warm water (about 110°F)
4½ cups bread flour, plus additional
     for kneading
1 package active dry yeast (¼ ounce)
2 teaspoons fine salt
½ cup extra-virgin olive oil
2 tablespoons coarsely chopped
     fresh rosemary
½ teaspoon coarse sea salt

1. Put the water in a medium bowl; whisk in 2 tablespoons of the flour, then sprinkle the yeast over the surface. Set aside until foamy, about 10 minutes.

2. Whisk the remaining flour and the fine salt in a large bowl. Make a well in the center and pour in the yeast mixture and ¼ cup of the olive oil. Gradually stir the liquid into the flour with a wooden spoon to make a shaggy, loose dough. Turn the dough out of the bowl onto a lightly floured work surface. Knead the dough until smooth and elastic, about 10 minutes. (Add just enough flour so the dough is workable but still moist.) Form dough into a ball.

3. Lightly oil a large bowl and place the dough in the bowl; turn the dough around the bowl to coat. Cover bowl with a slightly moist clean kitchen towel and set aside to rise at room temperature for 45 minutes. Turn dough onto a lightly floured work surface, punch it down, and knead briefly before reshaping into a ball. Return to the bowl and set aside to rise for another 45 minutes to 1 hour.

4. Pour remaining ¼ cup olive oil into an 11x17-inch jelly-roll pan. Turn dough onto pan and flatten by hand. Set aside for 10 minutes until dough spreads easily on the pan. Turn dough over so both sides are well coated with oil. Stretch and press dough from center to the edges of the pan. Make indentations in dough with your fingertips and sprinkle with rosemary. Cover with a towel and let rise until puffy, about 1 hour.

5. Preheat the oven to 425°F. Sprinkle the dough with the sea salt. Bake until golden brown, about 20 minutes. Slip the focaccia from the pan and cool on a rack.

FROM THE KITCHENS
Experienced bread bakers know that the slower a bread rises, the better its taste and texture. (That's why this bread rises twice before forming.) Set breads aside in a warm-but-not-too-hot spot to let them proof gently.

honey challah | one 2-pound loaf (24 servings)

1 cup warm water, about 110°F
1 teaspoon sugar
2 teaspoons active dry yeast
4 cups all-purpose flour, plus about
     1 cup for kneading
⅓ cup honey
2 whole large eggs
3 large egg yolks
3 tablespoons extra-virgin olive oil
1 tablespoon kosher salt
1 tablespoon poppy seeds

1. Combine water and sugar in a small bowl. Sprinkle the yeast over the top. Set aside until foamy, about 8 minutes.

2. Put 1 cup of the flour in a large bowl and make a well in the center. Whisk honey with 1 of the whole eggs, the yolks, olive oil, and salt in a small bowl and pour into the well. Stir to combine. Add yeast mixture and remaining 3 cups flour and stir to make a soft, shaggy dough. Knead dough on a lightly floured surface until soft and supple, about 10 minutes.

3. Shape dough into a ball and place in lightly oiled large bowl. Cover with a clean kitchen towel and let rise until doubled in size, about 1 hour. Turn dough onto a lightly floured surface; knead for just a minute, shape into a ball and return to bowl. Cover and let rise again until doubled in size, about 1 hour.

4. Line a baking sheet with parchment paper. Form loaf according to instructions, below. Cover with a clean, dry kitchen towel and set aside to rise until doubled, about 1 hour.

5. Place a rack in the center of the oven and preheat to 375°F. Beat remaining egg. Brush loaf with egg and sprinkle with poppy seeds. Bake until golden brown, about 35 minutes.

FROM THE KITCHENS
Worried about how to tell when this bread is baked? Insert an instant-read thermometer into the middle of the loaf after about 35 minutes in the oven. When it registers 190°F, it's ready to come out.

1. Turn dough onto a clean work surface and divide into 3 equal pieces. Roll and stretch each piece into a rope 12 to 15 inches long. Arrange ropes side by side on the work surface. 2. Starting at the far end, braid the ropes. 3. When the braid is finished, tuck both ends under and pinch to seal. Place loaf on prepared baking sheet.

grissini | 20 breadsticks

¾ cup warm water (about 110°F)
  Pinch sugar
1 teaspoon active dry yeast
2 cups all-purpose flour
1 teaspoon fine salt
3 tablespoons extra-virgin olive oil,
    plus additional for brushing
  Coarse sea salt, cumin, caraway,
    and/or fennel seeds, or cornmeal
    (optional)

1. Whisk the water and sugar in a small bowl, then sprinkle the yeast over the surface. Set aside until creamy, about 5 minutes.

2. Whisk flour and fine salt in a medium bowl. Make a well in the center and pour the yeast mixture and the 3 tablespoons oil in the center. Gradually mix the liquid into the flour to make a soft, shaggy dough. Turn the dough out onto a floured work surface and knead until smooth and elastic, about 10 minutes. Brush a large bowl with oil. Shape dough into a ball and put it in the bowl, cover with a clean kitchen towel, and set aside at room temperature until tripled in size, 2 to 3 hours.

3. Preheat the oven to 400°F. Line 2 baking sheets with parchment paper. Turn the dough onto a clean work surface and press into a rectangle about 4x14 inches. Use a pizza wheel to cut a plus sign through the dough, dividing it into quarters. Form breadsticks according to instructions below. (If dough snaps back to its original length when rolling, let it rest, covered, for 10 minutes.)

4. Bake grissini until golden brown, rotating the baking sheets once during baking, about 22 minutes. Cool on a rack.

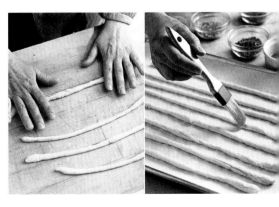

1. Cut each quarter of dough lengthwise into 5 long strips. 2. Roll and stretch each piece with the palms of your hands into very thin strips about 14 inches long. 3. Transfer grissini to 2 parchment-lined baking sheets. Brush each with olive oil and sprinkle with sea salt, seeds, or cornmeal, if desired.

sweets

Whether it's a luscious brownie with afternoon tea or an elegant slice of torte at midnight, dessert is our favorite time of the day.

coconut brownies | 24 brownies

BROWNIES

- 10 ounces semisweet chocolate, finely chopped
- 2 ounces unsweetened chocolate, finely chopped
- 8 tablespoons unsalted butter, cut into pieces (1 stick)
- 1½ cups all-purpose flour
- 1½ teaspoons baking powder
- ¼ teaspoon fine salt
- 2 cups sugar
- 4 large eggs
- 1 teaspoon pure vanilla extract

GLAZE

- 6 ounces semisweet chocolate, finely chopped
- ½ cup canned unsweetened coconut milk
- 1 cup unsweetened coconut chips (see tip, below), toasted

1. For the brownies: Position a rack in the middle of the oven and preheat to 350°F. Line a 13x9x2-inch baking pan with parchment or waxed paper so the edges of the paper come up the sides all around the pan. Press paper into the corners, but don't worry if it isn't absolutely smooth. Lightly butter paper.

2. Put the semisweet and unsweetened chocolates and the butter in a heatproof bowl. Bring a saucepan filled with an inch or so of water to a very slow simmer; set the bowl on the pan (without touching the water). Stir occasionally until melted and smooth.

3. Whisk flour, baking powder, and salt in a medium bowl. Whisk sugar, eggs, and vanilla in a large bowl. Gradually stir the chocolate mixture into the egg mixture until blended. Add the flour mixture to the chocolate mixture and stir again until just blended. Scrape the batter into the prepared pan. Bake until a wooden toothpick inserted into the center of the brownies comes out coated with fudgy crumbs, about 35 minutes. Cool on a rack.

4. For the glaze: Put chocolate in a medium bowl. Bring coconut milk to a boil, stirring constantly, and pour it over the chocolate. Let the mixture stand for 10 minutes, then stir until smooth. Spread the warm glaze evenly over the brownies, then scatter the coconut over the top. Refrigerate, loosely covered, until glaze sets, about 2 hours. Lift the paper to remove brownies from the pan, fold back the sides, and use a warm knife to cut the brownies into 24 squares.

FROM THE KITCHENS
Coconut chips are large-flake, slightly crisp, unsweetened coconut. We find them in Middle Eastern stores and in specialty and natural-food stores. If you can't find them, use unsweetened shredded or flaked coconut.

strawberry shortcut cake

8 servings

CAKE

- 1 cup all-purpose flour
- ¾ cup granulated sugar
- 1 teaspoon baking powder
- ½ teaspoon fine salt
- 4 tablespoons unsalted butter, melted
- 1 large egg, beaten
- ½ cup whole milk
- 1 teaspoon pure vanilla extract

STRAWBERRIES AND CREAM

- 2 pints strawberries
- 1 tablespoon granulated sugar
- 1 cup heavy cream
- 1 tablespoon confectioners' sugar
- ½ teaspoon pure vanilla extract

1. For the cake: Preheat the oven to 375°F. Butter an 8-inch round cake pan, line it with parchment paper, butter the paper, and dust the pan lightly with flour.

2. Whisk the flour with the granulated sugar, baking powder, and salt in a medium bowl. Lightly whisk in the butter, egg, milk, and vanilla, just until smooth. Pour the batter into the prepared cake pan and bake until a toothpick inserted in the center comes out clean, about 25 minutes. Cool on a rack for 10 minutes, then turn it out of the pan, flip upright, and cool completely on the rack.

3. For the strawberries and cream: Set aside 1 pint of the best-looking whole berries for topping the cake. Hull and thinly slice the rest of the berries and toss with the granulated sugar. Set aside. Whip the cream with the confectioners' sugar and vanilla to soft peaks. Refrigerate until ready to use.

4. To assemble the cake: Cut the cake in half horizontally with a serrated knife. Place the bottom layer cut side up on a cake stand or serving plate. Drizzle the juices from the sliced berries over the cut sides of both halves. Fold a couple tablespoons of the whipped cream into the sliced berries and spread over the bottom layer. Top with the other piece of cake, cut side down. Spread the remaining whipped cream on the top of the cake and top the cake with the whole berries.

FROM THE KITCHENS

Cutting a cake into layers is easy as saw-spin-separate: Begin to saw the cake in half horizontally. Just before you reach the middle of the cake, give it a quarter turn. Continue to saw almost to the center, then give it another quarter turn and saw again until you reach your original point of entry. Saw completely through the cake's center and separate the layers.

Simple, creamy, rich, and dreamy— how can you not love a strawberry shortcake? Make it for a birthday or any day, then watch it quickly disappear.

birthday cake with chocolate frosting | one 8-inch layer cake (8 servings)

CAKE

	Oil for brushing the pans
2	cups cake flour or 1 $\frac{2}{3}$ cups all-purpose flour plus $\frac{1}{3}$ cup corn starch
2	teaspoons baking powder
$\frac{1}{2}$	teaspoon fine salt
1$\frac{1}{2}$	cups plus 2 tablespoons sugar
$\frac{1}{2}$	teaspoon finely grated orange zest
1	cup unsalted butter, room temperature
$\frac{1}{2}$	cup milk, at room temperature
3	large eggs, at room temperature
2	teaspoons vanilla extract

FROSTING
Makes about 4 cups

1$\frac{1}{4}$	pounds milk chocolate
12	ounces semisweet chocolate
2	cups sour cream (16-ounce container)
1	tablespoon coffee
1	tablespoon pure vanilla extract

1. For the cake: Position a rack in the center of the oven and preheat to 350°F. Brush two 8-inch round cake pans with oil, line the bottoms with circles of parchment paper, lightly brush the paper and pan with oil, and dust with flour.

2. Put the flour, baking powder, and salt into the bowl of a food processor. Add the sugar and orange zest and pulse a few times to combine evenly. Cut the butter into small pieces and add to dry ingredients. Pulse until the mixture looks like coarse sand, with some pea-size bits of butter, about 5 times.

3. Whisk the milk, eggs, and vanilla together in a liquid measuring cup. With the processor running, pour in the wet ingredients and process to make a smooth batter (this takes less than a minute). Divide the batter between the prepared pans and bake until a toothpick inserted in the center comes out clean, about 25 minutes.

4. Cool the cakes on a rack for 15 minutes. Run a knife around the edges of the pans, turn the cakes out onto a plate, and peel off the paper. Flip the cakes upright and cool completely on the rack, about 45 minutes.

5. Meanwhile, make the frosting: Break or chop the chocolates into small pieces and put in a microwave-safe bowl. Microwave on medium for a minute, stir, and repeat until chocolate melts, about 3 minutes in all. Or put chocolates in a heatproof bowl set over an inch or so of water at a very slow simmer; set the bowl on the pan; don't let the bowl touch the water. Stir occasionally until smooth.

6. Let chocolate cool slightly, about 3 minutes. Stir the sour cream, coffee, and vanilla together. Add to the chocolates. Beat with a handheld mixer until frosting is silky and fluffy. (Spread frosting soon after making it; it firms up at room temperature.)

7. Set a large flat plate on a large inverted bowl or bottom of a salad spinner (if you have a cake stand, use that), dabbing a little frosting on the bottom of the plate to secure it. Place a cake layer top side up on the plate. With an offset or rubber spatula, scoop about one-third of the frosting onto the cake and spread it evenly to the edge of the cake. Place the other layer on top and press down lightly. Spread another third of the frosting around the sides with a knife or offset spatula. Spread the remaining frosting on top of the cake. Lightly touch the frosting with the back of a spoon to make swirly peaks. Serve immediately or set aside at room temperature for up to 2 hours before serving. If refrigerating the cake, bring to room temperature 30 minutes before serving.

quick & easy chocolate cake | 6 servings

8 tablespoons unsalted butter
½ cup freshly brewed coffee
¼ cup unsweetened Dutch-process cocoa (see tip, page 329)
1 cup all-purpose flour
1 cup granulated sugar
¼ teaspoon baking powder
¼ teaspoon fine salt
⅛ teaspoon baking soda
¼ cup sour cream
1 large egg, room temperature
½ teaspoon pure vanilla extract
Confectioners' sugar for dusting
Ice cream or sweetened whipped cream, for serving (optional)

1. Preheat the oven to 350°F. Butter a 9-inch round cake pan, line bottom with a round of parchment paper, then lightly butter the paper.

2. Put the butter, coffee, and cocoa in a microwave-safe bowl, cover with plastic wrap, and microwave on HIGH until the butter melts, about 2 minutes. Whisk to combine.

3. Meanwhile, whisk the flour, granulated sugar, baking powder, salt, and baking soda in a large bowl. Beat the sour cream with the egg and vanilla in a small bowl. Whisk the hot cocoa mixture into dry ingredients. Stir in the sour cream mixture just to combine; don't overmix. Scrape the batter into the prepared pan and bake until a toothpick inserted in the center of the cake comes out clean, about 35 minutes.

4. Cool the cake on a rack for 15 minutes, then unmold, turn it upright, and cool completely on the rack. Dust with confectioners' sugar and serve with ice cream or whipped cream, if desired.

FROM THE KITCHENS
We prefer Dutch-process cocoa here over natural cocoa for its mellower flavor.

Italian pine nut torte

one 10-inch cake (10 to 12 servings)

2 cups pine nuts
6 tablespoons unsalted butter
1½ cups granulated sugar
1 cup all-purpose flour
1 teaspoon finely grated orange zest
9 large egg whites, at room temperature
⅛ teaspoon fine salt
⅛ teaspoon cream of tartar
Confectioners' sugar for dusting

1. Position a rack in the middle of the oven and preheat to 350°F. Butter a 10-inch round cake pan and line bottom with parchment paper. Set aside ¾ cup of the pine nuts; spread remaining nuts on a baking sheet and oven-toast, stirring once, until light brown, about 10 minutes. Cool completely.

2. Meanwhile, melt the butter in a small saucepan over medium heat and cook, swirling the pan frequently, until butter is light brown and fragrant, about 6 minutes. Cool. Pulse cooled toasted nuts with ¾ cup of the granulated sugar, the flour, and the orange zest in a food processor until sandy.

3. Whip the egg whites, salt, and cream of tartar in a large bowl with an electric mixer at medium-high speed until foamy. Increase the speed to high, gradually pour in the remaining ¾ cup sugar, and whip until the whites form soft peaks. Stop beating. Sprinkle the flour mixture over the whites; fold the batter together with a rubber spatula until just a few streaks remain. Drizzle in the browned butter, including any toasted bits on the bottom of the pan, and finish folding the batter. Pour batter into the prepared pan and scatter the reserved (untoasted) nuts over the top.

4. Bake the cake until a wooden toothpick inserted into the center comes out clean, about 45 minutes. Rotate the pan halfway through baking so the nuts brown evenly. Cool on a rack for 10 minutes. Run a knife along the inside of the pan to loosen the cake from the edges and invert the cake onto a piece of parchment paper on the rack. Leave the cake nutside down until it is completely cool. When cool, turn the cake nut side up, dust with confectioners' sugar, and serve.

FROM THE KITCHENS
Most ovens have hot spots. Ensure that your cakes, breads, pastries, and cookies bake evenly by rotating the pans once during baking time.

This authentic Sicilian dessert looks great from all angles and tastes even better with a strong cup of piping-hot espresso.

blueberry buttermilk bundt cake

8 servings

BLUEBERRIES

- 4 tablespoons unsalted butter, plus additional for pan
- ½ cup light brown sugar
  Juice of ½ lemon
- 1 teaspoon vanilla extract
- 1½ cups blueberries

CAKE

- 2¼ cups all-purpose flour
- 2 cups granulated sugar
- 1½ teaspoons baking powder
- ½ teaspoon baking soda
- 12 tablespoons unsalted butter, at room temperature
- ¾ cup buttermilk
- 2 teaspoons vanilla extract
  Finely grated zest of 2 lemons
- 5 large eggs

1. Preheat the oven to 350°F. Butter a 12-cup bundt cake pan.

2. For the blueberries: Heat the 4 tablespoons butter, brown sugar, and lemon juice in a small saucepan over medium heat, stirring occasionally, until the sugar dissolves. Remove from the heat and stir in the vanilla and berries. Spread evenly in the bottom of the prepared pan.

3. To make the cake: Sift the flour, granulated sugar, baking powder, and baking soda into the bowl of a stand mixer. Add the butter and beat slowly with the paddle attachment until a fine crumb forms.

4. Whisk the buttermilk, vanilla, and lemon zest in a liquid measuring cup. Stop the mixer and change from the paddle to the whisk attachment. While beating at a medium speed, gradually pour all the liquid into the flour mixture. Add the eggs one at a time (scraping the sides of the bowl as needed), beating until the mixture is very light, about 3 minutes. Pour batter over berries in the prepared pan.

5. Bake until a toothpick inserted into the cake comes out clean, 45 to 50 minutes. Cool on a rack for 20 minutes before inverting onto the rack to cool completely.

FROM THE KITCHENS

- Don't flour the pan or the blueberries will stick.
- Most bundt cakes are best if allowed to ripen for a day before serving. If you make the cake ahead, wrap it tightly. The cake will keep at room temperature, tightly wrapped, for 4 days.

little devil's food cakes

12 cupcakes

CUPCAKES

1	cup all-purpose flour
6	tablespoons natural unsweetened cocoa (not Dutch-process) (see tip, page 329)
½	teaspoon baking soda
¼	teaspoon baking powder
¼	teaspoon salt
8	tablespoons unsalted butter, softened (1 stick)
1	cup sugar
2	large whole eggs, at room temperature
1	large egg yolk, at room temperature
1	teaspoon pure vanilla extract
½	cup water

FROSTING

8	ounces semisweet chocolate, finely chopped
¾	cup heavy cream
	Optional flavorings for 1 batch frosting: 2 tablespoons coffee liqueur, eau de vie (fruit brandy—such as framboise, a raspberry-flavored brandy), or dark rum; or ½ teaspoon mint extract or orange extract
	Fresh raspberries, colorful candies, or chopped pistachios (optional)

1. For the cupcakes: Position a rack in the middle of the oven and preheat to 350°F. Line twelve ½-cup muffin cups with paper liners. Whisk the flour with the cocoa powder, baking soda, baking powder, and salt.

2. Beat the butter with an electric mixer at medium speed until smooth, about 2 minutes. Increase the speed to medium-high and gradually add the sugar. Beat until light and smooth, about 5 minutes. Reduce the speed to medium-low and beat in the whole eggs and yolk one at a time, incorporating each fully before adding the next. Beat in the vanilla. Scrape down the sides of the bowl.

3. Bring water just to a boil in a small saucepan and remove from the heat. With the mixer at low speed, beat the flour mixture into the butter mixture in 4 additions. Drizzle in the hot water, about 2 tablespoons at a time, and mix briefly to make a smooth batter. Divide the batter among the muffin cups, filling them ⅔ full. Bake until the centers of the cupcakes spring back when pressed gently, about 20 minutes. Cool cupcakes in the tin on a rack for 10 minutes, then remove from the tin and cool completely before frosting.

4. For the frosting: Put chocolate in a medium heatproof bowl. In a small saucepan, bring cream to a boil. Pour cream over chocolate and shake bowl gently so cream settles around the chocolate. Set mixture aside until the chocolate is soft, about 5 minutes. Whisk gently until smooth, taking care not to incorporate too many air bubbles. Stir in one of the flavorings, if desired. Dip the tops of the cooled cupcakes into the frosting. (Frosting can also be chilled and whipped, then piped or spread onto the cupcakes.) Set them upright and let stand a minute or two, until frosting is slightly set, then decorate with fresh berries, candies, or chopped pistachios, if desired. Let cakes stand on rack until frosting is completely set.

A cake with a built-in sauce—how could you go wrong? Have the ingredients ready to go in your pantry to satisfy your sweet tooth any time.

coconut-lime pudding cake

4 servings

2 tablespoons unsalted butter, softened, plus a bit for the pan
¾ cup granulated sugar
¼ cup all-purpose flour
3 large eggs at room temperature, separated
½ cup limeade concentrate, thawed
¾ cup canned unsweetened coconut milk
¼ teaspoon fine salt
Toasted coconut, for garnish (optional)

1. Position a rack in the center of the oven and preheat to 325°F. Lightly butter a 1-quart gratin dish or 8-inch round cake pan and set it in a roasting pan.

2. Beat the 2 tablespoons butter with ½ cup sugar in a large bowl until creamy, using a handheld electric mixer. Beat in the flour, then the egg yolks, limeade concentrate, coconut milk, and salt. (For the airiest egg whites, clean the beaters thoroughly so none of this mixture is left on them.) In another medium bowl whip the egg whites until they form soft peaks. While whipping, slowly pour in the remaining ¼ cup granulated sugar and continue beating until the whites hold stiff, glossy peaks. Fold a quarter of the whites into the coconut-lime mixture, then fold in the remaining whites.

3. Pour the batter into the prepared baking dish and add enough boiling water to the roasting pan to come halfway up the side of the dish. Bake about 35 minutes or until the top of the pudding cake is slightly puffed and golden. Remove from the water bath and cool on a wire rack for 10 minutes; serve warm. Garnish each serving with toasted coconut, if desired.

FROM THE KITCHENS
Baking the cake in a water bath ensures that it will bake evenly and retain its luscious, saucy bottom.

Individual cheesecakes are more than just cute—they're quick. Faster baking than a big cheesecake, these little guys are also good for those who never learned how to share.

little cheesecakes with strawberry sauce | 6 servings

CHEESECAKES
- 10 chocolate graham crackers, broken
- ¼ cup semisweet chocolate chips
- 3 tablespoons unsalted butter, melted
- 1 pound cream cheese, softened
- ¾ cup sugar
- 2 large eggs, room temperature
- 2 teaspoons pure vanilla extract
- 1 teaspoon grated orange zest

SAUCE
- 1 cup frozen strawberries, thawed
- 2 tablespoons sugar

1. For the cheesecakes: Preheat the oven to 325°F. Process the graham crackers and chocolate chips in a food processor until finely ground. Add the butter and pulse until the mixture is sandy and moist. Divide mixture evenly among 6 jumbo muffin cups, then press it evenly over the bottoms and about two-thirds of the way up the sides. Bake just until crusts are set, about 8 minutes.

2. In a clean food processor bowl pulse the cream cheese, sugar, eggs, vanilla, and orange zest until smooth. Divide the filling evenly among the muffin cups and bake until the rims are slightly puffed and the centers are almost set, about 30 minutes. Cool the cheesecakes in the cups on a rack, then refrigerate, uncovered, for at least 2 hours.

3. Meanwhile, for the sauce: In a food processor or a blender puree the strawberries with the sugar.

4. When you are ready to serve, run a small knife around the outside of the cheesecakes, then use the knife to gently lift them from their molds. Transfer cheesecakes to dessert plates. Spoon some sauce over each and serve.

FROM THE KITCHENS
- To test for doneness, shake the pan a little. When the cheesecakes are mostly set but still shimmy slightly in the center, they're done. If they crack, don't worry—dress with strawberry sauce and no one will be the wiser.
- If you need to get the cream cheese and eggs up to room temperature quickly, microwave the cream cheese on HIGH for 15 seconds; place the eggs in a bowl of warm (not hot) water.

apple & nut crumb pie

one 9-inch pie (8 servings)

DOUGH

1¼ cups all-purpose flour
2 teaspoons sugar
½ teaspoon fine salt
8 tablespoons cold unsalted butter
1 large egg, lightly beaten
1 teaspoon pure vanilla extract

FILLING

1 cup sugar
1 teaspoon ground cinnamon
½ teaspoon ground allspice
¼ teaspoon ground nutmeg
½ teaspoon kosher salt
3½ pounds baking apples
8 tablespoons unsalted butter
2 teaspoons pure vanilla extract
1 tablespoon all-purpose flour

TOPPING

1¾ cups all-purpose flour
¾ cup sugar
½ cup pecan pieces
1½ teaspoons ground cinnamon
¾ teaspoon ground allspice
    Pinch nutmeg
¼ teaspoon fine salt
10 tablespoons unsalted butter, melted
1½ teaspoons pure vanilla extract

1. For the dough: Pulse flour, sugar, and salt in a food processor briefly. Cut butter into dice. Sprinkle butter over and pulse until mixture resembles coarse cornmeal but a few bean-size bits of butter remain. Drizzle egg and vanilla over and pulse once or twice; don't let dough form a mass around blade. Remove blade and bring dough together by hand. Shape dough into a disk, wrap in plastic wrap, and refrigerate 1 hour.

2. Dust work surface with flour. Roll dough into a 12-inch circle; center in pie plate. Trim overhang to 1 inch and fold it under to create a double-thick rim for crust; flute. Pierce bottom of dough 5 or 6 times with a fork and freeze for 20 minutes.

3. Position a rack in the lower third of the oven and preheat to 425°F. Line crust with parchment paper and fill with dried beans. Bake until firm and just set, about 18 minutes. Reduce temperature to 375°F. Remove paper with beans. Return crust to oven and bake until golden and dry, about 10 minutes.

4. For the filling: Whisk sugar, spices, and salt in a large bowl. Peel, core, and cut apples into ½-inch chunks; toss with sugar mixture. In a large skillet, melt half the butter over medium-high heat. Add half the apples, tossing to coat. Cover and cook until apples are tender, 6 to 8 minutes. Transfer to a colander set over a bowl. Repeat with remaining butter and apples.

5. Pour juices into skillet and simmer until thick and beginning to caramelize, about 4 minutes. Put apples in large bowl and fold in thickened juices; sprinkle vanilla and flour over and toss. Pour filling into pie shell, mounding slightly in the center.

6. For topping: Whisk flour with sugar, pecans, spices, and salt. Drizzle butter and vanilla over and toss. Squeeze mixture to make crumbs. Some should be large, some small. Sprinkle over filling and bake until juices are bubbling and crust is golden brown, about 35 minutes. Cool until warm and serve.

individual deep-dish berry pies

4 small pies

4   cups mixed berries, such as
    raspberries, blueberries,
    blackberries, or stemmed and
    halved strawberries
⅓   cup sugar, plus additional for
    sprinkling
2   tablespoons instant tapioca
1   teaspoon pure vanilla extract
2   tablespoons unsalted butter
1   sheet frozen puff pastry
    (8 ounces), thawed
    Whipped cream or vanilla ice cream,
    for serving

1. Position a rack in the center of the oven and preheat to 400°F. Toss the berries with the ⅓ cup sugar, tapioca, and vanilla extract in a large bowl. Divide the fruit among four 6-ounce ramekins and dot each with some butter.

2. Using a pizza wheel or very sharp knife, divide the puff pastry sheet into 4 squares. Brush the outsides and rims of the ramekins with water. Lay a puff pastry square over the top of each ramekin and gently press the points that drape over the sides against the ramekins to seal. Lightly brush the tops with water and sprinkle with sugar.

3. Bake the pies on a baking sheet until the pastry is puffed and golden brown, 25 to 30 minutes. Cool at least 20 minutes before serving with a dollop of whipped cream or a scoop of vanilla ice cream.

FROM THE KITCHENS
These little pies are best if served the day they're made. If you're not serving them right away, keep them at room temperature before reheating—don't refrigerate them or the crust will get soggy.

strawberry–rhubarb tart

one 13x5-inch tart (4 to 6 servings)

TART

1 sheet frozen puff pastry
(8 ounces), thawed
1 tablespoon milk
2 cups strawberries, stemmed
1 cup sliced rhubarb (1 large rib,
trimmed but not peeled)
¼ cup sugar
1 teaspoon pure vanilla extract
2 tablespoons unsalted butter

GLAZE

1 tablespoon currant jelly
1 tablespoon very hot water
Confectioners' sugar, for dusting
Lightly sweetened whipped cream,
for serving

1. Position a rack in the center of the oven and preheat to 375°F. Line a baking sheet with parchment paper. Roll the pastry into a rectangle about ⅛ inch thick. Cut two ¾-inch-wide strips from a long side. Cut remaining pastry into a 13x5-inch rectangle and place on the prepared baking sheet. Brush a ¾-inch border down one long side with water and lay one narrow strip on top, pressing gently. Repeat on the other side. (The filling should be thick enough so you don't need pastry strips on the short sides of the tart to keep the filling from spilling out when the tart is assembled.) Trim any overhang, if necessary. Very lightly roll a pizza wheel along the inside of the strips to score halfway through the base. Brush the top of the strips with milk, taking care not to drip down the sides. Pierce the base all over with a fork, line it with a piece of aluminum foil that extends along the sides of the strips but not over, and weigh foil down with pie weights or dried beans. Use a paring knife to flute the outer edges of the tart by making small cuts an inch apart. Bake until set, about 15 minutes. Remove the foil and weights and bake until light golden brown, about 15 minutes more. Cool on a rack.

2. Trim the strawberries' broad tops and put the trimmings in a small saucepan with the rhubarb, sugar, and vanilla extract. Simmer over medium heat, stirring frequently, until fruit is thick and jamlike, about 15 minutes. Add butter and puree with an immersion blender or in a food processor until smooth. Cool. Halve the remainder of the strawberries lengthwise.

3. To assemble the tart: Spread cooked mixture in the shell. Arrange strawberries in shingled rows down length of the tart.

4. For the glaze: Stir together jelly and hot water. Brush warm glaze over strawberries. Dust the sides lightly with confectioners' sugar, slice, and serve with whipped cream.

FROM THE KITCHENS
Buy strawberries of roughly the same size so that when they're "shingled" on the tart, they fit together nicely.

summer berry tapioca trifle

4 servings

2 cups fresh raspberries, blueberries, blackberries, sliced strawberries, or a mix
½ cup plus 1 tablespoon granulated sugar
¾ cup milk
1 large egg
¼ cup quick-cooking tapioca
¼ teaspoon fine salt
1 cup buttermilk
1 teaspoon pure vanilla extract
8 ladyfingers
¾ cup heavy cream
2 tablespoons confectioners' sugar
2 teaspoons light rum

1. Toss the berries with the 1 tablespoon of granulated sugar and set aside. Whisk the ½ cup granulated sugar, the milk, egg, tapioca, and salt in a medium saucepan and set aside to plump the tapioca, about 5 minutes. Cook over medium heat, stirring occasionally, until the mixture boils, about 6 minutes. Pull saucepan from the heat and stir in buttermilk and vanilla.

2. Quarter the ladyfingers crosswise and set aside 12 rounded end pieces. Put 5 pieces in the bottom of each of 4 wine or parfait glasses; top with about ⅓ cup of berries and then a quarter of the tapioca mixture. Press 3 of the reserved ladyfinger pieces, rounded tip up, around the inside of each glass and into the tapioca. Cover loosely with plastic wrap and chill until set and quite cold, about 1 hour in the refrigerator or 30 minutes in the freezer. While the trifle chills, whip the cream to soft peaks; add the confectioners' sugar and rum and whip until the cream holds a slightly firm peak. Keep the cream and reserved berries refrigerated until ready to serve.

3. To serve, top each trifle with a dollop of whipped cream, then spoon on some of the reserved berries.

FROM THE KITCHENS
A trifle of ladyfingers simply layered in a goblet or flute with berries, tapioca, and whipped cream is one of the easiest desserts to pull off.

brown sugar– glazed pears

4 servings

PEARS

- 2 tablespoons unsalted butter
- ⅓ cup firmly packed dark brown sugar
- 4 Bartlett pears, peeled, cored, and halved lengthwise
- 1 tablespoon freshly squeezed lemon juice
- ½ teaspoon pure vanilla extract
- ⅛ teaspoon almond extract (optional)
  Gingery Mascarpone (see recipe, below) or whipped cream cheese
  Toasted slivered almonds

MASCARPONE

Makes 1 cup

- ½ cup mascarpone cheese
- ¼ cup confectioners' sugar
- ⅓ cup chilled heavy cream
- 1 teaspoon freshly grated ginger
- ½ teaspoon pure vanilla extract
  Few drops mint extract

1. Position an oven rack about 6 inches from the broiler and preheat to high. Melt the butter in an ovenproof skillet just large enough to hold the pears in one layer. Crumble the brown sugar into the skillet and add the pears cut side down. Cook until the sugar begins to melt and the pears get juicy. Turn the pears with a wooden spoon or heatproof spatula to coat evenly with the melted sugar, then position them cut side down in the pan and transfer the skillet to the oven. Broil the pears, swirling the pan occasionally and turning the pears once, until they are brown on both sides and the sugar begins to caramelize, about 10 minutes in all.

2. Using a slotted spoon, transfer 2 pear halves to each of 4 small plates. Whisk the lemon juice, vanilla, and almond extract, if using, into the skillet until smooth. Spoon this sauce around and on top of the pears. Spoon a dollop of Gingery Mascarpone or whipped cream cheese next to the pears and scatter some nuts over the tops.

GINGERY MASCARPONE

Lightly blend the mascarpone and sugar in a bowl. Beat the cream to soft peaks in another bowl with the grated ginger, vanilla extract, and mint extract. Gently fold the mixture into the mascarpone.

FROM THE KITCHENS

When buying pears, remember your ABCs—Anjou, Bartlett, and Comice. For baking, they're the tastiest and juiciest.

baked apples
with maple-cream sauce | 6 servings

APPLES

2	tablespoons unsalted butter, softened
1	tablespoon maple syrup
2	teaspoons finely grated lemon zest
2	nut biscotti, crumbled (not chocolate)
3	tablespoons dried currants
6	large red baking apples, like Rome Beauty
¼	cup lemon juice
6	cinnamon sticks
2	cups apple cider or juice

SAUCE

7	tablespoons maple syrup
6	tablespoons bourbon
1	cinnamon stick
1	cup heavy cream

1. For the apples: Preheat the oven to 375°F. Using a fork, blend the butter, maple syrup, and lemon zest in a small bowl. Work in the crumbled biscotti and the currants.

2. Slice about ¼ inch from the top of each apple. Use a melon baller to scoop out the seeds and cores, but don't cut through to the bottom of the apples. Remove a ½-inch band of peel from around the holes with a vegetable peeler. Stand the apples in a baking dish just large enough to hold them. Brush the peeled flesh and the insides of the apples with some of the lemon juice. Spoon some of the butter mixture into each apple and place a cinnamon stick in the center to make a "stem." Pour the cider around the apples and bake until tender, basting occasionally with the cider, 35 to 40 minutes.

3. While the apples bake, make the sauce: Put the maple syrup, bourbon, and the cinnamon stick in a small saucepan. Bring to a boil, reduce the heat, and simmer, uncovered, until the sauce is thick and syrupy. Whisk in the heavy cream, bring to a boil, and cook until just thickened, about 3 minutes. Serve the apples in small bowls with the warm sauce spooned over and around them.

FROM THE KITCHENS

Some apples are best for baking, others for eating out of hand. For cooking apples, look for Rome Beauty, Braeburn, and York Imperial. If you want the best of both worlds, look for Granny Smith, Newtown pippin, and Winesap, all good all-purpose apples. For pies, use a mix of apples to get the benefit of the fruits' different qualities.

fruit oatmeal crumble | 6 servings

CRUMBLE TOPPING

½ cup all-purpose flour
1 cup quick-cooking oats
¾ cup packed light brown sugar
   Pinch fine salt
6 tablespoons unsalted butter
¾ cup chopped nuts, such as
     walnuts, almonds, or pecans

FRUIT

2 pounds baking pears, apples,
     or stone fruit such as peaches,
     apricots, or plums
2 to 4 tablespoons light brown or
     white sugar
2 tablespoons all-purpose flour
½ teaspoon pure vanilla extract
   Freshly grated nutmeg
   Pinch ground cinnamon
   Pinch fine salt

FOR SERVING

Ice cream or sweetened
whipped cream

1. Preheat the oven to 375°F.

2. For the crumble: Whisk the flour, oats, brown sugar, and salt in a medium bowl. Melt the butter, covered, in the microwave, or in a small saucepan on the stove. Add the melted butter to the flour mixture and toss together with a fork until evenly moistened; stir in the nuts. Squeeze handfuls of the crumble mixture together and drop them onto a cookie sheet to get a good proportion of large and small crumbs. Freeze for 10 minutes while you prepare the fruit.

3. For the fruit: Halve, core, and slice the fruit and put in a large bowl. Toss the fruit with the sugar (use more or less depending on the sweetness of the fruit), flour, vanilla, nutmeg, cinnamon, and salt. Transfer to an 8x8-inch glass baking dish.

4. Evenly sprinkle the crumble mixture over the fruit and pack down lightly. Bake the crumble until the topping is golden brown and the fruit is juicy and bubbly, 40 to 45 minutes. Let sit for 5 to 10 minutes before serving. Serve warm with ice cream or whipped cream.

FROM THE KITCHENS

• Why add salt to desserts? Salt intensifies the flavors that are already there; your dessert won't taste salty if you add salt—it'll just taste more like itself.
• Upgrade this homey dessert by adding 1/4 cup dried cranberries to the sliced apples or pears.

poached peaches
with sabayon

4 servings

PEACHES

½	vanilla bean
6	cups water
3	cups sugar
3	sprigs fresh mint or lemon verbena
3	coin-size slices fresh ginger, unpeeled
2	long strips lemon peel, without white pith
6	firm ripe peaches, halved and pitted
1	cup raspberries

SABAYON

4	large egg yolks
⅓	cup sugar
1	teaspoon finely grated lemon zest
⅔	cup Prosecco (a dry Italian sparkling wine)

1. For the peaches: Split the vanilla bean and scrape the seeds into a medium saucepan. Add the scraped pod, water, sugar, mint, ginger, and lemon peel and stir. Add the peaches skin side down. Bring to a boil. Place a circle of parchment directly on top of the fruit and adjust the heat to maintain a very gentle simmer. Cook until the peaches are easily pierced with a knife without resistance, about 5 minutes. Add raspberries and pull the pan from heat; cool. With your fingertips, pinch the skins from the peaches and discard. If they don't come off easily, don't fret. Refrigerate the fruit in the liquid, covered, until ready to serve, up to 3 days.

2. To assemble: Divide fruit among 4 bowls, with a splash of poaching liquid in each.

3. Put about 1 inch of water in a saucepan and bring to a simmer over medium heat. In a heatproof bowl that can rest in the saucepan without touching the water, use an electric mixer or whisk to beat the egg yolks, sugar, lemon zest, and Prosecco until light and foamy, about 30 seconds. Set the bowl over the simmering water and beat until the eggs thicken, about 4 minutes. Spoon the sabayon over the fruit and serve.

FROM THE KITCHENS

The poaching liquid is too good to throw away. Use any leftover liquid for poaching more peaches, flavoring iced tea, or in your favorite peach cocktail. Or reduce about 2 cups of the poaching liquid until thick and syrupy; serve with the fruit and sabayon.

orange semifreddo | 4 servings

3   oranges, peeled and segmented
       (see tip, below)
¼   cup orange liqueur
       Finely grated zest from 2 oranges
2   large eggs
½   cup sugar
½   cup vodka
½   teaspoon pure vanilla extract
2   cups heavy cream, chilled
24   vanilla wafers

1. Dampen the inside of a 10-cup stainless steel bowl (it will be 8 inches diameter at the top), line with plastic wrap, and set aside. Put the orange segments in the orange liqueur.

2. Put about 1 inch of water in a saucepan and bring to a simmer over medium heat. In a heatproof medium bowl that can rest in the saucepan without touching the water, beat the zest, eggs, yolks, sugar, vodka, and vanilla with a whisk until foamy and light, about 30 seconds. Set the bowl over the water and whip with an electric mixer or whisk, moving in a circular motion around the bowl, until the mixture turns a pale yellow and an instant-read thermometer inserted into the mixture registers 170°F. Set the bowl in a bowl of ice and whisk the mixture until cooled.

3. Strain the liqueur from orange segments into the heavy cream. Line the prepared bowl with 8 to 10 orange segments in a pinwheel pattern. Roughly chop the remaining orange segments. Whip the heavy cream to soft peaks. Gradually fold the egg mixture and chopped oranges into the cream. Pour the cream mixture into the prepared bowl. Coarsely crumble the vanilla wafers and lightly press them onto the surface of the semifreddo to cover. Wrap in plastic and freeze until set, about 4 hours.

4. About 1 hour before serving, unmold the semifreddo onto a platter. Refrigerate until creamy and very cold but not frozen.

FROM THE KITCHENS
To section an orange or grapefruit, cut off the ends of the fruit. Remove the remaining peel by cutting down the fruit from one end to the other. Working over a bowl to catch any juices, cut between the sides of each section and the membrane to the center of the fruit. Turn the knife and slide it alongside the membrane up the other side of the section. Repeat with the remaining sections.

ice cream sandwiches | 6 servings

¼ cup all-purpose flour
¼ cup Dutch-process cocoa
¼ teaspoon fine salt
⅛ teaspoon baking powder
3 tablespoons unsalted butter, softened
1 tablespoon shortening
½ cup sugar
1 large egg, beaten
½ teaspoon pure vanilla extract
2 pints any flavor ice cream

1. Preheat the oven to 350°F. Line two baking sheets with parchment paper.

2. Whisk the flour with the cocoa, salt, and baking powder in a small bowl. In another bowl beat the butter, shortening, and sugar with a handheld electric mixer until fluffy. Add the egg and vanilla and beat until smooth. Stir in the flour mixture by hand to make a smooth dough.

3. Using 1 heaping tablespoon per cookie, drop 6 mounds of dough on each baking sheet, leaving a couple inches between each cookie. Bake for 15 minutes. (For even baking, rotate the pans from top to bottom and back to front about halfway through baking.) Using a spatula, transfer the cookies to a wire rack and cool completely.

4. Meanwhile, turn the ice cream pints on their sides and use a serrated knife to slice each through the container into 3 even rounds. Freeze the ice cream disks until ready to assemble the sandwiches.

5. To assemble: Peel the cardboard from the ice cream disks and sandwich each between two cookies. Serve immediately, or wrap individually in plastic wrap and freeze for up to 1 week.

FROM THE KITCHENS
The bottoms of some ice cream containers have a little lip to them, so take that into consideration when you are cutting the disks.

1. While the cookies bake, turn ice cream pints on their sides and slice each container into three even rounds. 2. Freeze ice cream disks on a baking sheet until

Your favorite ice cream + two incredibly decadent cookies = an ice cream sandwich worth screaming for.

chocolate– cherry jubilee | 8 servings

1¼ pounds sweet cherries, pitted
     and halved
¾ cup dark rum
½ cup granulated sugar
1 teaspoon finely grated orange zest
1 teaspoon vanilla extract
6 ounces semisweet chocolate,
     finely chopped
¾ cup heavy cream
2 tablespoons light corn syrup
½ gallon boxed vanilla ice cream
8 or 9 chocolate wafer cookies,
     coarsely crushed (2 ounces)
½ gallon boxed chocolate ice cream

1. The day before assembling: Put the cherries, rum, granulated sugar, orange zest, and vanilla in a small saucepan and bring to a simmer. Cook, stirring occasionally, until the cherries soften, about 5 minutes. Transfer to a medium bowl, cover, and refrigerate overnight.

2. Put the chocolate in a medium bowl. Bring the cream and corn syrup to a simmer in a small saucepan and immediately pour over the chocolate, shaking the bowl slightly to settle the cream. Let the mixture stand a few minutes, then stir until the chocolate is melted. Cover and refrigerate overnight.

3. Line a 9x5x3-inch loaf pan with a piece of parchment paper that hangs over the side by a couple inches. About 15 minutes before using, bring the chocolate to room temperature and stir until it is easily spooned.

4. Drain the cherries and reserve the liquid. Turn the vanilla ice cream out of the carton onto a cutting board (run the box under warm water, if necessary). Save the box. Cut a ¾-inch-thick slab with a warm knife from the long side of the ice cream and press it into the pan. Patch, if needed, with more ice cream to cover the bottom. Spread half the cherries on top and cover with another ¾-inch-thick slab of vanilla ice cream, pressing to make a snug fit. Return the remaining vanilla ice cream to the box and save for other desserts.

5. Scatter the chocolate cookies over the ice cream. Remove the chocolate ice cream from the carton onto a cutting board (run the box under warm water, if necessary). Save the box. Cut a ¾-inch-thick slab from the long side of the ice cream and press it into the pan. Scatter the remaining cherries over the chocolate ice cream and spoon about half of the chocolate mixture on top. Reserve the rest of the chocolate for sauce. Finish the terrine with another ¾-inch-thick slab of chocolate ice cream. Return remaining ice cream to the box. Fold the parchment over the top of the terrine and freeze 4 hours or overnight.

6. Simmer the reserved cherry liquid until syrupy. Remove from heat and whisk in the remaining chocolate mixture until smooth.

7. When ready to serve, lift the terrine out of the pan by the paper and invert it onto a cutting board. (Run warm water on the loaf pan, if necessary, to release it.) Slice into 1-inch-thick pieces and serve with the chocolate-cherry sauce.

This classic dolce has graced every trattoria menu since the '80s. This new rapido version made us fall for it all over again.

tiramisù rapido | 4 servings

¼ cup coffee liqueur
¼ cup water
2 tablespoons espresso powder
6 tablespoons confectioners' sugar
8 ladyfingers (see tip, below)
8 ounces mascarpone cheese
½ cup heavy cream
2 teaspoons ground chocolate or
    sweetened cocoa

1. Whisk the coffee liqueur, water, espresso powder, and 2 tablespoons of the confectioners' sugar in a glass measuring cup until smooth. Pour about ⅓ cup of the mixture over the ladyfingers in a shallow bowl, then toss and set aside.

2. Gently beat with a handheld mixer the remaining espresso mixture and the remaining 4 tablespoons confectioners' sugar into the mascarpone until smooth. Take care not to overbeat it or the mascarpone will be grainy. Using the same beaters (no need to clean them), beat the whipped cream to soft peaks and fold it into the mascarpone mixture.

3. To assemble the tiramisù: Crumble half the soaked ladyfingers into four 8-ounce parfait or wine glasses. Spoon ¼ cup of the mascarpone mixture over the ladyfingers and press and spread gently with the back of the spoon to fill the spaces between the ladyfinger pieces. Repeat with remaining ladyfingers and mascarpone mixture. Sprinkle ½ teaspoon ground chocolate over each tiramisù, cover with plastic wrap, and refrigerate for at least 1 hour or overnight before serving.

FROM THE KITCHENS
Ladyfingers are little oblong sponge cakes that look like wide fingers. We prefer the crisp Italian savoyardi variety of ladyfingers to the soft sponge-cake type.

flan | 8 servings

1¼   cups sugar
2   tablespoons water
1   teaspoon freshly squeezed
     lemon juice
4   cups milk
6   large eggs
2   teaspoons pure vanilla extract

1. Position a rack in the middle of the oven and preheat to 350°F. Set an 8x8x2-inch glass baking dish next to the stove. Stir ¾ cup of the sugar, the water, and lemon juice in a small saucepan. Bring to a boil over medium-high heat and cook, swirling the pan but not stirring, until the sugar is amber-colored caramel. Pull pan from the heat and pour the caramel into baking dish. Working quickly so caramel doesn't harden, tilt and rotate the dish to coat the bottom and sides. Set aside.

2. Put milk in a medium saucepan and bring to a simmer over medium heat, stirring occasionally. Whisk eggs with the remaining ½ cup sugar. Gradually whisk milk into egg mixture. Add vanilla. (Don't beat mixture too much or flan will have air bubbles.) Strain mixture into a large degreasing or glass measuring cup or heatproof pitcher. Pour mixture into caramel-lined dish. Skim foam or bubbles from the surface.

3. Put a roasting pan in the oven and set flan in the center. Pour enough hot water into the pan to reach halfway up the sides of the baking dish. Tent loosely with aluminum foil and bake about 1 hour and 10 minutes, until flan is set around the edges but still wobbles a bit in the center when you give the dish a gentle shake. Cool flan in the water bath on a rack until water is room temperature. Remove the flan from the water and cool. Stretch and seal plastic wrap across the top of the dish but not on the surface of the flan and refrigerate until thoroughly chilled, at least 4 hours or up to 2 days.

4. Gently pull the edges of the flan away from dish with your fingertips. Invert a large, deep serving platter over the baking dish and flip; the flan should fall gently onto the platter and caramel will flow over it. Cut into squares and serve with a spoonful of caramel drizzled around each piece.

crepes

4 to 6 servings (12 crepes)

1 cup all-purpose flour
2 tablespoons sugar
⅛ teaspoon fine salt
1 cup milk
¼ cup water
3 large eggs
1 teaspoon pure vanilla extract
4 tablespoons unsalted butter
About ¾ cup chocolate-hazelnut
   spread (such as Nutella)

FOR SERVING
Ice cream or sweetened
whipped cream

1. Whisk the flour, sugar, and salt together in a bowl or pulse in a food processor or blender. Gradually whisk in the milk, water, eggs, and vanilla extract or process or blend until smooth. Set aside for at least 30 minutes. (The batter can be made to this point a day ahead and refrigerated. Bring to room temperature before adding butter.)

2. Melt the butter in a small saucepan or in the microwave; whisk it into the batter. Pour the batter into a measuring cup with a pouring spout or a small pitcher. Have plates ready for serving.

3. Heat a medium nonstick skillet over medium heat until a drop of water bounces and sizzles in the pan before evaporating. Pour a little less than ¼ cup of crepe batter into the skillet and quickly swirl it to coat the pan evenly. Cook until the batter sets, about 1 to 1½ minutes. The crepe will blister in the middle and the edges will get a little crispy. Using your fingers or a spatula, carefully pick the crepe up by its edges and flip it to cook the other side, 15 to 30 seconds. Repeat with remaining batter, serving or stacking the crepes as they cook.

4. To serve, spread about 1 tablespoon of the chocolate-hazelnut spread in the center of a warm crepe. Fold the top of the crepe over to make a half circle, then fold the right side over to make a triangle. Repeat with the remaining crepes. Serve 2 or 3 crepes per person, topped with a scoop of ice cream or a dollop of whipped cream.

FROM THE KITCHENS

• Stack the crepes as they cook to keep them warm. Crepes can be made a day ahead, wrapped in plastic, and refrigerated. Bring to room temperature at least 1 hour before serving.
• Embellish these chocolate-hazelnut-filled crepes by peeling and slicing your favorite citrus fruit into small pieces. Sprinkle sugar on the warm crepe, then dot with the pieces of citrus.

bread pudding
with whiskey sauce | 4 servings

BREAD PUDDING

- 2 tablespoons unsalted butter, plus more for the baking dish
- ½ cup sugar, plus 1 tablespoon
- ¼ teaspoon ground cinnamon
- 3 large eggs
- 1 large egg yolk
- 2 cups half-and-half
- 2 tablespoons whiskey, bourbon, or rum
- 2 teaspoons pure vanilla extract
- ¼ teaspoon fine salt
  Pinch freshly grated nutmeg
- 10 slices white sandwich bread or 4 (1-inch-thick) slices challah, cut into 1-inch cubes

BROWN SUGAR WHISKEY SAUCE

- ½ cup packed dark brown sugar
- 2 tablespoons white sugar
- ½ cup heavy cream
  Pinch fine salt
- 1 to 2 tablespoons unsalted butter
- 2 to 3 tablespoons whiskey

1. Position an oven rack in the center of the oven and preheat oven to 325°F. Brush an 8x8-inch glass baking dish with some butter. Pour ½ cup sugar into the pan, turning to dust the bottom and sides with sugar. Pour the excess sugar into a large bowl. Stir the 1 tablespoon sugar and the cinnamon together in a small bowl.

2. Whisk the eggs, egg yolk, half-and-half, whiskey, vanilla, salt, and nutmeg with the sugar in the large bowl. Add about ¾ of the bread to the egg mixture and soak for 20 minutes.

3. Pour the bread mixture into the prepared baking dish. Scatter the remaining cup of bread cubes on top of the pudding and gently press them into the egg-soaked bread (if they don't get completely wet, don't worry about it).

4. Melt the 2 tablespoons butter in a small saucepan or in a bowl or cup covered with plastic wrap in the microwave, then brush the top of the bread pudding with butter. Sprinkle the cinnamon sugar on top and bake until golden brown on top and just set, 30 to 35 minutes. Serve with the Brown Sugar Whiskey Sauce.

BROWN SUGAR WHISKEY SAUCE

Put the sugars, cream, and salt in a medium saucepan. Bring to a boil, stirring until melted and smooth. Adjust the heat to maintain a simmer and cook, without stirring, until thicker, about 5 minutes. Pull the pan off the heat and whisk in the butter and whiskey to taste. Serve warm or at room temperature.

FROM THE KITCHENS

Any whiskey is fine here; feel free to use bourbon, Tennessee whiskey, Irish whiskey, or Scotch, depending on your preference. (It's spelled "whiskey" if it's from Ireland or the U.S.A. and "whisky" from Canada or Scotland.)

raspberry & fig gratin | 4 servings

Unsalted butter, softened
8 to 12 fresh black Mission or green figs, stemmed and halved
1 cup raspberries
4 large egg yolks
⅓ cup sugar
1 teaspoon finely grated orange zest
½ cup freshly squeezed orange juice
2 tablespoons Chambord (raspberry-flavored liqueur)

1. Position a rack in the top of the oven and preheat the broiler to high. Lightly brush a 4-cup gratin dish with butter. Spread the figs and raspberries evenly in the dish.

2. Put about 1 inch of water in a saucepan and bring to a simmer over medium heat. In a heatproof bowl that can rest in the saucepan without touching the water, beat the egg yolks, sugar, orange zest, orange juice, and Chambord until foamy and light, about 30 seconds. Set the bowl over the water and whip with an electric mixer or whisk, moving in a circular motion around the bowl, until the eggs thicken, about 2 minutes.

3. Pour the egg mixture over the fruit, place under the broiler, and cook until nicely browned, about 3 minutes. Serve warm.

FROM THE KITCHENS

If the eggs start to thicken up too quickly, simply lift the bowl off the pot and continue beating off the heat for a bit. The eggs are cooked and foamy enough if, when you lift the whisk over the mixture, they slowly fall back into the bowl in a thick, round stream.

What goes around may come around. But it's never out of style to gather around the table.

mexican-style chocolate fondue

4 servings

1 cup heavy cream
4 cinnamon sticks, preferably Mexican canela (see tip, below)
6 ounces chopped semisweet chocolate
Generous pinch ancho chile powder (see tip, page 201)

SUGGESTED DIPPERS
Cubed pound cake
Dried apricots
Mini bananas
Fresh or dried orange slices
Fresh or dried pear slices
Almond cookies
Coconut strips
Strawberries
Sliced mango

1. Heat the cream and cinnamon in a small saucepan over medium heat just until it begins to boil. Pull off the heat, cover, and steep for 15 minutes. Remove and discard the cinnamon.

2. Put the chocolate and ancho powder in a medium bowl. Return the cream to a simmer, pour it over the chocolate, and let stand for 5 minutes. Stir the chocolate mixture until melted and smooth. Transfer the chocolate mixture to a fondue pot and keep warm over a low Sterno flame. Serve with a selection of the dippers.

FROM THE KITCHENS

Mexican cinnamon, or canela, isn't called so because it's grown there, but rather because it's preferred there. The type of cinnamon most commonly sold in the United States is cassia cinnamon. Mexican cinnamon, or Ceylon cinnamon, is considered to be the "true" cinnamon. It has a softer, slightly sweeter taste than cassia. Look for it in Mexican markets and specialty food stores.

Thanks go to the entire Food Network Kitchens for their energy, passion, and their endless appetite for delicious food!

Very special thanks for the great recipes in this compilation go to our Test Kitchen Director Katherine Alford and Developers Mory Thomas, Suki Hertz, Santos Loo, Sarah Copeland, Allison Ehri, Robert Hoebee, and Jay Brooks. Writers Miriam Garron and Rupa Bhattacharya kept our recipes clear and content smart. And final thanks to Food Stylists Mory Thomas, Bob Hoebee, Sarah Copeland, Krista Ruane, Jay Brooks, and Santos Loo.

index

Looking for the answer to the question of what's for dinner? (Or just looking for the answer to a food-related question?) Find it right here.

index

Note: **Boldfaced** page numbers indicate photographs.

A

Want to cook like a star chef?

Food Network Favorites will take you backstage and show you how it's done!

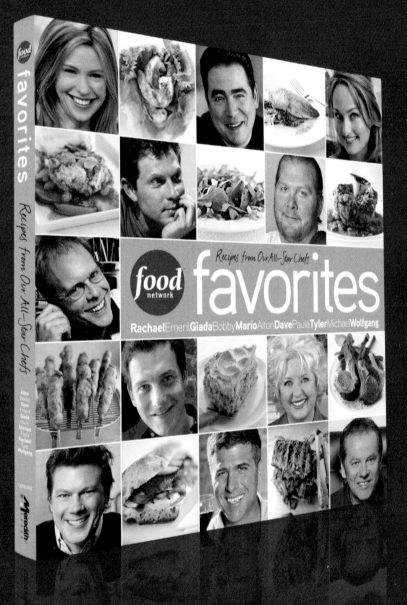

The Food Network has been the meeting place for some of the best and most-beloved chefs, cookbook authors, and a culinary team that tastes, cooks, and styles all the beautiful food you see on the air. Now you can have a little bit of Food Network in your own kitchen with more than 110 favorite hand-picked recipes from 11 of our most popular chefs. Plus, tips, tricks, and behind-the-scenes insights will turn you into the star chef of your own kitchen.

AltonBobby**Dave**Emeril**Giada**Mario**Michael**Paula**Rachael**Tyler**Wolfgang**